D1757657

The Price of
Victory

The Price of Victory

The Red Army's Casualties
in the Great Patriotic War

Lev Lopukhovsky and
Boris Kavalerchik

Translated by Harold Orenstein

Pen & Sword
MILITARY

First published in Great Britain in 2017 by
PEN & SWORD MILITARY
An imprint of
Pen & Sword Books Ltd
47 Church Street
Barnsley
South Yorkshire
S70 2AS

ISBN 978-1-47389-964-3

Typeset by Concept, Huddersfield, West Yorkshire, HD4 5JL.
Printed and bound in Malta by Gutenberg Press Ltd.

Pen & Sword Books Ltd incorporates the imprints of Pen & Sword Archaeology, Atlas, A   y, History, Maritime,
Military, ℓ   Transport, True Crime,
and   Praetorian Press,
                                                          Wharncliffe.

                                                    ase contact
                                                    ED
                                                    0 2AS, England
).uk
                                                    ık

Contents

List of Plates

A German soldier and a dead Soviet tanker with a burning BT-5 tank in the background. Army Group South, June 1941.

A crew member of a Soviet T-26 light tank surrenders to the Germans. Army Group Centre, August 1941.

Soviet POWs captured by the Germans near Stalingrad. Army Group South, summer 1942.

A Soviet POW quenches his thirst from a muddy puddle. Army Group South, July 1942.

A column of Soviet POWs captured during the Battle of Kursk. Summer 1943.

Soviet POWs transported in open freight cars. Army Group Centre, Vitebsk, 21 September 1941.

Soviet POWs in the Mauthausen concentration camp, Austria. October 1941.

A German firing squad executing a group of Soviet partisans. Army Group North, September 1941.

Colonel Nikolai Ilyich Lopukhovsky, commander of the 120th Howitzer Artillery Regiment of the Supreme Command Reserve. The father of one of the authors of this book, he was killed in action on 13 October 1941 while attempting to break out of the encirclement near Viaz'ma.

Soviet POWs captured in the Viaz'ma encirclement. October 1941.

A column of Soviet POWs in the Viaz'ma region. October 1941.

Soviet POWs captured in the Viaz'ma and Bryansk encirclements. October 1941.

Soviet POWs help their wounded comrades. 1941.

A German guard hastens Soviet POWs with a stick. 1941.

Local women bring bread to starving Soviet POWs. 1942.

The infamous 'Uman' pit'. Here, in a clay quarry of a local brick factory, Germans kept 60,000–70,000 Soviet POWs surrounded near Uman', Ukraine. Army Group South, August 1941.

German POWs being marched through the streets of Moscow, 17 July 1944.

German POWs captured near Stalingrad. December 1942.

A German military cemetery in Russia. 1943.

The registration card of a Soviet POW, Sergeant F.A. Anisov. He served in 120th Howitzer Artillery Regiment of the Supreme Command Reserve and was captured on 7 September 1941 near Yelnya. He died on 26 April 1943 in Stalag X-B, located near Sandbostel, Germany.

A Soviet soldier's plastic capsule which contained a paper insert with the soldier's personal information. It belonged to Private N.T. Prilepsky, killed in action on 13 October 1941 while attempting to break out of the encirclement near Viaz'ma.

List of Tables

Foreword

One of the most controversial subjects in Soviet and Russian military history is the cost in terms of soldiers' lives that the Red Army paid for victory over the German Wehrmacht in the Second World War. For almost fifty years after the Soviet Union's so-called Great Patriotic War ended, this human cost was also one of the Soviet Union's best kept secrets. This slim volume is important, first and foremost, because it answers this question as definitively as humanly possible.

Shortly after the war's end, in a March 1946 interview with the newspaper *Pravda*, Iosef Stalin, the Generalissimo of the Soviet State in wartime, declared, 'As a result of the German invasion, the Soviet Union irrecoverably lost around seven million people in fighting against the Germans, as well as because of the German occupation and penal servitude of Soviet people in German forced-labour camps.' This short statement, as obscure as it was, remained the official 'truth of the matter' concerning the Red Army's irrevocable losses in the war until well after the dissolution of the Soviet Union in 1991.

As this book points out, although Soviet written histories of the war remained silent on the subject of combat deaths in the war for about half a century after the war's end, within the Soviet government special commissions spent many years wrestling with this problem. While most families and citizens of the Soviet Union appreciated and experienced the immense scope of these losses, the subject was too embarrassing for the authorities to address openly. For example, a special commission formed near the war's end concluded that more than 9 million soldiers, including prisoners-of-war, were lost in the war. Yet, because these figures exceeded those announced by Stalin, the entire matter remained dormant and opaque until 1988.

Finally, fed by a wave of *glasnost'* (openness) that swept across the country in the late 1980s, Soviet President Mikhail Gorbachev organized a special commission to examine this question. Months later, this commission concluded that roughly 8.6 million servicemen and women perished in the war. The historical candour unleashed by Gorbachev's government culminated in 1993, two years after the fall of the Soviet Union, when a book edited under the auspices of General-Colonel G.F. Krivosheev revealed what it considered to be the last word on the subject. Entitled *Grif seketnosti sniat; poteri vooruzhennykh sil SSSR v voinakh, boevykh deistviiakh i voennykh konfliktakh* (The seal of secrecy has been removed. USSR armed forces casualties in wars, combat operations, and military conflicts), this book concluded that 8,668,400 Soviet servicemen and women had perished in the struggle.

However, as numerous other studies have indicated, Krivosheev's study was clearly not the last word. Although the 1993 book has gone through several new editions, was translated into English by Greenhill Books in 1997, and was expanded, revised, and republished in 2001, many believe that it is still fatally flawed. This is the case because it not only 'low-balls' the Red Army's losses in the conflict but also overlooks the Red Army's losses in numerous so-called 'forgotten battles', engagements that were erased from history to prevent embarrassment to the Red Army and its leaders.

As early as 1999, a Russian archivist asserted that rather than 8.9 million dead in the war, the Red Army likely suffered as many as 14.6 million dead. Now, based on careful research in the Russian archives, Lev Lopukhovsky and Boris Kavalerchik have determined that the chief flaw in Krivosheev's analysis was his reliance on *front* and army casualty reports at a time when many of the Red Army's casualties were occurring in march battalions and companies of personnel replacements either while they were en route to the *front* or immediately after they arrived at the *front*. As a result, when this new category of losses is added to the previous casualty figures, the authors conclude that the price of Soviet victory in the war reached roughly 14.6 million men. Without belabouring this point and 'stealing the thunder of their analysis', I believe that their methodology is sound and their conclusions are credible. In short, this book is characterized by its sound methodology, acute accuracy, and cogent conclusions. As a result, it promises to become an instant 'hit', at least in an historical sense.

David M. Glantz
Carlisle, PA

Preface

The official data on the irrecoverable losses suffered by the armed forces of the USSR in the Great Patriotic War, published in *Russia and the USSR in Wars of the 20th Century*, are subject to great doubt. The difference between them and the data of independent researchers who worked directly with primary archive documents is too great. Because of this discrepancy, issues concerning the calculation of losses have not lost their immediacy even in our day, and have become the object of an intense ideological argument. The fact is that arguments about the scale of human casualties are inseparably associated with the measure of responsibility before the nation of the USSR's military and political leadership at that time. Without a calculation of the colossal human losses and clarification of their reasons, it is impossible to fully assess the results of the war and the significance of the victory that was achieved.

Under the conditions of severe ideological control and all-encompassing censorship in the Soviet Union, silence about and downright distortion of the actual events of the war were common. Right up to 1987, it was not possible to talk directly in the open press about the war's disastrous beginning, the lack of success and the reasons for defeats suffered in the war's first and second periods. If mention was made, it was only in general terms. Moreover, censorship did not allow the publication of concrete information regarding the casualties of Soviet troops in battles and operations. Nevertheless, the determination of the number of human casualties suffered by the armed forces (as well as the size of losses in weapons and war materiel) is an integral part of research into the history of the war as a whole. This lack of data has continuously worried both professional military historians and many ordinary Soviet citizens. The powers that be could not completely ignore it, and so from time to time they have released some information favourable to their own views and ideological goals.

Chapter 1

Circumstances governing the publication of loss data in the Great Patriotic War

In response to questions from a *Pravda* correspondent, on 14 March 1946 I.V. Stalin officially announced for the first time the magnitude of USSR losses during the Great Patriotic War: 'As a result of the German invasion, the Soviet Union irrecoverably lost around 7 million people in fighting against the Germans, as well as through the German occupation and the penal servitude of Soviet people in German forced-labour camps.'

With this statement, the Leader charted the course for the falsification of the history of the Great Patriotic War and the underestimation of Soviet casualties in order to cover up his political and strategic mistakes and mis-calculations on the eve and during the first half of the war, which brought the country to the brink of disaster. Back in June 1945 Colonel Podolsky, chief of the Directorate for accounting and control of the numerical strength of the armed forces, had already prepared 'Information on Red Army Personnel Combat Casualties during the Great Patriotic War' (*see* Appendix A). According to this, losses of servicemen alone (without consideration of the 13,960,000 wounded, of whom 2,576,000 remained disabled) comprised 9,675,000 people, including 3,344,000 prisoners and soldiers missing in action (MIA).[1]

By the autumn of that year the Emergency State Commission [Chrezvychainaia Gosudarstvennaia Komissiia, hereafter ChGK], which had been established in November 1942, had already completed its calculations of the country's civilian casualties and generalized them in a document called 'On the Results of the Investigation into the Bloody Crimes of the German-Fascist Occupiers and Their Accomplices'. According to this document, during the occupation of Soviet territory the Nazis exterminated 6,716,660 USSR citizens and 3,912,883 prisoners of war (POW) by shooting, hanging, burning, poisoning in 'gas vans' and gas chambers, burying alive and torturing, as well as by subjecting them to a deliberate, inhuman system of starvation, exhaustion and exposure to infectious diseases in concentration camps. Stalin, however, did not approve these ChGK data and forbade their publication;[2] after all, they in no way corresponded with the numbers he had announced.

It is hard to say for sure why the Leader chose to significantly understate the true military losses of the USSR. Most likely it was his move in the complex political game that was the Cold War with the West. Stalin did not want to let his future adversaries know to what extent the Soviet Union had been weakened in the recently concluded Second World War.

The Leader could act however he wanted, as no one would dare to object. Immediately following the end of the war, statisticians broached the necessity of conducting the next census of the population of the USSR (the previous census had been in 1939) in order to assess the damage that the war had done. After all, in addition to having inflicted very heavy human casualties and enormous material damage, the war had also disrupted civilian record-keeping. Re-establishing the economy and organizing the life of the population under peacetime conditions required adequate demographic information. Therefore, many recommended proceeding with the planned 1949 census. Stalin, however, declined to do so, since the true scale of war casualties for the Soviet people would have come to light. It is telling that all the countries that had fought in the war took a census of their populations beginning in 1945 and ending in 1951, while in the USSR a census was taken only in 1959, twenty years after the previous census rather than the customary ten.

Work on determining civilian and military casualties continued during this period, but it and its results were not advertised. In 1956 the Central Committee of the Communist Party of the Soviet Union [hereafter, CC CPSU] and the Soviet government established a commission to clarify the number of Soviet POWs. The results of its work were reported to the CC CPSU on 4 June 1956, signed by Minister of Defence G.K. Zhukov, Secretary of the CC CPSU E.A. Furtseva, Minister of Justice K.P. Gorshenin, Chief Military Prosecutor R.A. Rudenko, Chairman of the KGB I.A. Serov and head of a CC CPSU section V.V. Zolotukhin. In particular, the report stated that 'Soviet repatriation organs recorded 2,016,480 imprisoned POWs, of whom 1,835,562, including 126,000 officers, had been repatriated to the Motherland. In addition, according to data from captured files, more than 600,000 Soviet POWs perished in German captivity.'[3]

In that same year the USSR Ministry of Foreign Affairs specified that 504,487 Soviet citizens were located in foreign countries as displaced persons, half of whom were former POWs.[4]

All important announcements in the Soviet Union, especially ideologically significant ones, remained the prerogative of Party and state leaders. After coming to power, N.S. Khrushchev, to spite Stalin, increased the casualty numbers to 'more than 20 million'. During the years of Khrushchev's 'thaw', the archives somewhat 'opened' their storerooms to historians. As a result, books and reports, the contents of which did not always correspond to the official version of events of the past war, began to appear in the open press. Much that had been secret was exposed. The authorities became frightened and, as often happened in Russia, the 'thaw' was replaced by 'frost'. On 3 March 1968 L.I. Brezhnev, who replaced Khrushchev in the highest Party position, announced the following to his Politburo co-workers: 'Recently, much memoir literature has appeared here ... They twist the history of the Patriotic War, they take documents somewhere in the archives, distort them and misquote them ... Where do these people take the documents? Why have we dealt so freely with this issue?'[5]

The current Minister of Defence A.A. Grechko eagerly assured the General Secretary that order would be restored regarding this matter. And, of course, it was restored. Microfilms containing crucial top secret documents about the war's major operations, held at the time in higher military schools and scientific institutions, were recalled and destroyed. By 1972 they only remained at the disposal of researchers from the General Staff Academy and the Frunze Military Academy under guarantee that the strictest secrecy would be maintained. Access to documents stored in the archives was restricted once again, made available only to those official historians who knew which way the wind was blowing. All this was necessary to facilitate the glorifying of the deeds of the next leader and commanders who came into his favour, likely as it was to hinder persistent researchers.

Later, during the years of *perestroika* and *glasnost'*, the demands made by researchers and war veterans to the country's leadership for clarification of the costs of victory increased significantly. M.S. Gorbachev, General Secretary of the CC CPSU at that time, responded that 'the process is under way' and already impossible to stop. As usual, this did not occur without conflicts between assessments of casualties for the population of the USSR and the Red Army during the war years. Some authors, in the pursuit of sensationalism, began to recklessly claim unjustifiably high numbers for those who died, far exceeding all reasonable limits. The issue of publishing reliable numbers of army and navy human casualties in the last war finally came to a head. In such important cases the initiative could not be ceded. In April 1988 a commission under the leadership of General-Colonel (now General of the Army) M.A. Gareev, Deputy Chief of the General Staff (now President of the Academy of Military Science of the Russian Federation), was established in the Ministry of Defence system to calculate casualties.

The commission included representatives of appropriate ministry staffs, directorates and institutes. It met at full strength only twice, including representatives of several interested departments. At the first organization session tasks were assigned to departments and institutes. In the second session the commission secretary reported on the results of its work. According to the testimony of several of the sessions' participants, who had come with their own computations and calculations, tables were posted before the astonished members of the commission with results that had already been prepared. Such work could not have been completed in the short time available, which amounted to hardly more than six months. The basis of the calculations that were presented was the results of the work by a group of General Staff officers under the leadership of General-Colonel S.M. Shtemenko conducted in 1966–1968.

On 16 December 1988 Minister of Defence D.T. Yazov addressed the CC CPSU with a request to examine data about the Soviet armed forces' casualties during the Great Patriotic War, having proposed to publish them in the open press after they had been approved. The text of his speech is cited below.

Memorandum from the USSR Minister of Defence to the CC CPSU on the Soviet Armed Forces' Personnel Casualties during the Great Patriotic War, 1941–1945

16 December 1988
CC CPSU
Secret
Decisions of the XIX All-Union Party Conference on *glasnost'* and the interests of Soviet people's reliable information about the results of the Great Patriotic War require the publication of data about our armed forces' casualties. The necessity for this is also occasioned by the fact that in recent years much contradictory and baseless information about the scope of human losses suffered by the Soviet armed forces and by our nation as a whole during the war has been cited in Soviet and foreign print. The lack of official data on our losses also makes it possible for some authors to distort and minimize the importance of the Soviet Union's victory in the Great Patriotic War.

Taking all this into account, document materials (reports on losses, the orders of battle and strength of *fronts*, fleets and armies),[6] statistical collections and reports from the directorates of the General Staff and Central Military Medicine Directorate, official data published in the Federal Republic of Germany [FRG] and the German People's Republic

[GDR], and captured documents that we have were investigated in the USSR Ministry of Defence by a specially established commission. A careful analysis of all these sources is making it possible to conclude that the irrecoverable losses of USSR armed forces personnel during the Great Patriotic War, including border troops and internal troops, amount to 11,444,100 people.

In studying documents from military-mobilization and repatriation organs, it has become clear when mobilization was conducted in 1943–1944 on Soviet territory that had been liberated, 939,700 servicemen, former POWs and men who had been encircled and who had stayed on occupied territory were re-inducted into the Soviet Army, and 1,836,000 former servicemen returned from captivity after the war ended. Therefore, these servicemen (a total of 2,775,700) have been excluded from the number of irrecoverable losses.

Thus, the Soviet armed forces' irrecoverable losses (killed, died of wounds, MIA, not returned from captivity, and noncombat casualties) during the war, taking into account the Far East Campaign, amount to 8,668,400 men: 8,509,300 in the Army and Navy, 61,400 KGB Border Troops, and 97,700 Ministry of the Interior [MVD] Internal Troops. A significant part of these casualties occurred in 1941–1942, due to the extremely unfortunate circumstances that had developed for us during the first period of the war.

As for data about Fascist Germany's casualties, they are clearly understated in the literature printed in the FRG and other Western countries: they do not take into account the casualties of Germany's allies (Italy, Romania, Hungary, Finland), foreign formations fighting for Fascist Germany (Vlasovites, Slovaks, Spaniards, etc.), rear Wehrmacht establishments, and construction organizations in which mainly other nationalities (Poles, Czechs, Slovaks, Serbs, Croatians, etc.) worked. According to calculated data compiled from captured and other document materials, the Fascist bloc's irrecoverable losses amounted to 8,658,000 men (7,413,000 Germans and 1,245,000 people from its satellites), of which there were 7,168,000 casualties on the Soviet-German Front. After the war 1,939,000 German POWs returned from the Soviet Union.

During the period of combat operations in the Far East (August–September 1945), irrecoverable losses for Japan's Kwantung Army amounted to 677,000, including as many as 83,737 killed.

The USSR Ministry of Defence believes that it is possible to **publish** the above-mentioned data on the Soviet armed forces' casualties during the Great Patriotic war, **after they are approved by the CC CPSU, in the open press**.[7]

Recommendations have been expressed more than once in our press that all MIAs (more than 4.5 million) be considered war veterans. It is obvious from the analysis, however, that many of their number fought against us (the Vlasovites alone numbered 800,000–900,000); they cannot be numbered among the Great Patriotic War veterans or those who died for the Motherland.

In published historical works, encyclopedias and periodicals the overall casualties of the Soviet people during the war were determined to be 20 million people, a considerable part of whom were civilians who died in Nazi death camps and as a result of Fascist repression, illness and starvation, and enemy air raids. Inasmuch as the USSR Ministry of Defence does not have at its disposal comprehensive materials on civilian casualties, work on determining the precise number of civilian casualties in the USSR during the war should, in our opinion, be assigned to the USSR State Statistics Committee.

Materials regarding Soviet armed forces casualties and those of the armies of the Fascist bloc, as well as a draft CC CPSU resolution, are attached.[8]

There is a note on the Memorandum:

Department of Administrative Organs of the CC CPSU.
For submission.
Assistant Secretary of the CC CPSU.
I. Mishchenko.
19 December 1988.[9]

The following materials were prepared as addenda to the Memorandum:

Secret: Appendix 1
Information on the Soviet armed forces' irrecoverable personnel losses during the Great Patriotic War, 1941–1945
(in thousands of men)

Losses	Red Army and Navy	KGB Border Troops	MVD Internal Forces	Total
1. Killed or died of wounds during stages of evacuation and in hospitals	6,287.5	18.9	23.2	6,329.6
2. MIA or captured	4,455.6	35.4	68.0	4,559.0

3. Noncombat losses (died from illness, incidents, accidents, etc.)	541.9	7.1	6.5	555.5
Total casualties	**11,285.0**	**61.4**	**97.7**	**11,444.1**
4. Excluded from casualty figures: a. Servicemen remobilized into the field army (had been captured and on occupied territory)	939.7	–	–	939.7
b. Servicemen who returned from captivity after the war	1,836.0	–	–	1,836.0
Total	**2,775.7**	–	–	**2,775.7**
Total irrecoverable losses	**8,509.3**	**61.4**	**97.7**	**8,668.4**

Information on the irrecoverable losses of Nazi Germany and its satellites during the Second World War (1939–1945)[10] (in thousands of men)

Designation	Total	On the Soviet-German Front
1. Wehrmacht and Waffen SS (within the 1937 German borders).	6,439	5,151
Including:		
– killed or died of wounds	3,050	2,240
– MIA or captured	3,176	2,549
– noncombat casualties (died from illness, incidents, accidents, etc.)	213	162
2. Austrians, Sudeten Germans and those born in Alsace and Lorraine who served in the Wehrmacht	600	560
3. Foreign formations of the Wehrmacht and Waffen SS (Spanish and Slovak divisions, Vlasovite, Muslim, Baltic and other formations)	374	335
Total casualties for Nazi Germany	**7,413**	**6,046**
4. Excluded from the casualty figures: German POWs who returned to Germany from the USSR after the war	1,939	1,939
Total irrecoverable losses for German armed forces	**5,474**	**4,107**
5. Casualties for the armies of Germany's satellites.	1,245	1,005
Including:		
– Italy	330	90
– Finland	85	85
– Hungary	350	350
– Romania	480	480
Total casualties for the Fascist bloc	**6,719**	**5,112**

Top Secret: Appendix 2

Draft Resolution of the Central Committee of the CPSU, 'On the Publication of Information on Soviet Armed Forces Personnel Casualties during the Great Patriotic War, 1941–1945'

1. Agree with the recommendation regarding this issue proposed in the 16 December 1988 USSR Ministry of Defence memorandum (attached).
2. The USSR State Statistics Committee is to work on refining the casualties for the civilian population of the USSR during the Great Patriotic War, 1941–1945.[11]

It should be mentioned that the information about irrecoverable losses for Nazi Germany and its satellites during the Second World War was, judging by everything, prepared hastily. The balance of losses cited there for the Wehrmacht, including Waffen SS (within Germany's 1937 borders), on the Soviet-German Front is off by 200,000. Also, the total losses for the armies of Germany and its satellites was 7,051,000 men,[12] which for some reason does not correspond to the number quoted in the text of Yazov's Memorandum (7,168,000). Furthermore, instead of irrecoverable losses of the USSR's enemies, their demographic losses were calculated in the summation, which, after excluding Germans who returned from captivity (1,939,000), amounted to 5,112,000 people.

It is not at all coincidental that the Ministry of Defence report on the USSR armed forces' casualties also mentioned casualties for the countries of the Fascist bloc. Given the uncompromising ideological opposition of the two political systems, the issue of juxtaposing the latter's casualties with those of the Soviet forces inevitably arose. There is no doubt whatsoever that at that time the Central Committee examined preliminary estimations regarding the ratio of human casualties between the USSR armed forces and those of Germany. It is interesting that, according to some information, A.N. Yakovlev and E.A. Shevardnadze opposed releasing the reported data. One can only guess about the motives for Shevardnadze's objections. However, Yakovlev, a well known champion of *glasnost'* who himself had fought near Leningrad and was a fierce critic of the totalitarian system and its apologists, did not agree with the estimation of Soviet casualties; he thought that it was too low. He hardly approved of the military's calculations of the irrecoverable losses for the opposing sides. Nevertheless, the irrecoverable losses of Germany and its satellites on the Soviet-German Front were consequently increased by almost 1.5 million – from 7,168,000 to 8,649,300. As a result, the ratio was lowered from 1.6:1 in Germany's (with its satellites) favour to a more suitable 1.3:1, which was acceptable to the Soviet political and military leadership.

The importance of the issues raised in the Minister of Defence's report is reflected in the fact that in January–February 1989 they were discussed at the highest level. Several members of the Politburo – Shevardnadze, Yakovlev, V.A. Medvedev and N.I. Ryzhkov – wrote their own comments on the draft CC CPSU resolution.

Here, for example, is Yakovlev's opinion: 'I think that this issue is very important and very serious from all viewpoints. Because of this, it deserves additional, careful study; military historians should be involved in this, etc.' Ryzhkov considered it necessary to introduce an additional point into the resolution, with a proposal to simultaneously publish data in the open press about both the Soviet armed forces' personnel casualties and those of the USSR's civilian population.[13]

In accordance with his suggestion, the following was proposed in the next version of the draft CC resolution: 'Upon completion of the work, data on the Soviet armed forces' personnel casualties and those of the USSR's civilian population during the Great Patriotic War, 1941–1945, will be published simultaneously in the open press on behalf of the scientific collective.'[14]

Despite the policy of *glasnost'* that had been proclaimed at this time, the political leadership was afraid of directly publishing the historians' materials in this way. It was decided that the ultimate determination on the advisability of publishing the results of the calculation of casualties would be made only after the CC CPSU had examined them. Moreover, Gorbachev personally edited the resolution on this subject. This is important evidence of the extreme politicization of the casualties suffered during the Great Patriotic War. It could not have been otherwise in these years: the price of achieving victory was too dear for the Soviet people. Following the final analysis, on 20 February 1989 the CC CPSU adopted a top secret resolution, 'On the Publication of the Soviet Armed Forces' Personnel Casualties during the Great Patriotic War, 1941–1945':

> To assign the USSR State Statistics Committee, the USSR Ministry of Defence and the USSR Academy of Sciences, with participation by interested departments and social organizations, to form a research team to clarify the details of casualties for the Soviet armed forces personnel and USSR civilian population during the Great Patriotic War, 1941–1945.
>
> Upon completion of this work, to report to the CC CPSU data on casualties for the Soviet armed forces personnel and USSR civilian

population during the Great Patriotic War, 1941–1945 and proposals regarding the publication of these materials.[15]

The work was in full swing. Researcher-demographers were enlisted from the USSR Academy of Sciences, the USSR State Statistics Committee, Moscow State University and other research establishments with appropriate profiles. The team of highly qualified specialists worked intensively, using formerly classified documents and documents that had been withdrawn from circulation in the research community about the all-union censuses in 1937 and 1939. This made it possible to determine with an adequate degree of reliability the demographic losses for the country's population. The CC CPSU once again discussed the obtained results.

It was only a year later, on 8 May 1990, that President Gorbachev announced the following in his report to a special session of the USSR Supreme Soviet (celebrating the 45th anniversary of the victory of the Soviet people in the Great Patriotic War): 'The war claimed almost 27 million Soviet lives.'[16] The next day, 9 May, the Minister of Defence stated the number of irrecoverable losses for the Red Army, Navy and NKVD Border Troops from a military-operational point of view: 11,444,100 servicemen.[17] The so-called demographic casualties of armed forces servicemen had also been determined: around 8,700,000.[18]

For a long time it was difficult for independent researchers to study the problem of the decline of the population of the USSR during the war, since the main sources of information were classified. Some commentators and demographers are still arguing about this, claiming that the country lost 30 million or even 40 million lives during the war. Here they are considering not only those people who were killed and died of natural causes, but also children who were not born because of the war; in the majority of cases they are not relying on an adequately sound scientific basis.

We do not intend to discuss or refute their calculations. In this work we are interested, first and foremost, in the irrecoverable human losses for the USSR armed forces during the Great Patriotic War. They are usually examined from a military-operational and demographic point of view.

Irrecoverable losses from a military-operational point of view mean the loss (exclusion from the roster) of armed forces personnel during the war. This includes those who were killed in battle; those who died from wounds, illness and accidents; those who were shot by their own people; and MIAs and POWs, regardless of their subsequent fate (whether they returned or did not return to the Motherland after the war).

Demographic losses include all of the above-mentioned instances of irrecoverable human loss after excluding those who returned from captivity, as well as those surviving servicemen who had been considered MIAs. The ultimate summation of these losses was calculated after the end of the war, after the fates of as many of its participants as possible were brought to light.

Losses from a military-operational point of view are one of the principal indicators of the level of development of a country's military art, illustrating the competency of the military command, which is closely associated with a state's political leadership, and the qualitative state of the armed forces, including the training of staffs and armed forces personnel. For this, however, it is completely inadequate to establish only total figures – summation indicators of casualties during the entire period of the war. The enumerated components change noticeably during the war; therefore, it is important to determine armed forces casualties with respect to the war's periods and major campaigns, down to losses in individual operations and decisive engagements. **This enables the crucial comparison of those casualties with casualties of the opposing side**.

Chapter 2

Soviet troop casualties in certain strategic operations

Detailed statistical data on the servicemen casualties during the last war were published for the first time in 1993 in the work *The Seal of Secrecy Has Been Removed*.[1] When conducting research, the authors' team used data from Shtemenko's group, the General Staff's organization and records directorate, the Main Personnel Directorate of the People's Commissariat of Defence [hereafter cited as NKO], and other archival documents based on military unit reports. This was, of course, a real breakthrough: after long years of 'coffee grounds divination', historians were given the opportunity to set forth the events of the last war in much more detail. The German side had not managed, up to this point, to do similarly detailed research on the periods (campaigns) of the war, strategic operations and decisive battles. It should be kept in mind, however, that immediately following the publication some veterans, especially those who had fully internalized the bitterness of the 1941 defeats and withdrawals, strongly expressed their doubts that Red Army casualties were merely 30 per cent greater than those of the Germans.

Subsequently, the work was updated, broadened significantly and published in 2001 under the title *Russia and the USSR in Wars of the 20th Century: Armed Forces Casualties*.[2] Here, the principal tenets and conclusions of the previous work were maintained almost without any changes. Undoubtedly, the authors' team (hereafter, for brevity, we will cite the name of its leader, G.F. Krivosheev) did enormous and useful work. There is still nothing that compares with it on this theme with respect to volume and scope of material, and nothing like it is foreseen for the immediate future.

When the published work was studied, however, perplexing questions began to arise and multiply. Researchers, especially those who worked directly with the primary archival documents, began to expose numerous discrepancies and inconsistencies in the interpretation of those documents about casualties in individual operations. Comparisons of information from Soviet and German archives periodically revealed clear understatements of Soviet troop casualties. Moreover, it turned out that Krivosheev's team had ignored the

'Mars' strategic offensive operation (25 November 1942–20 December 1942). Some historians state that this operation was conducted for demonstrative purposes, so as not to allow the Germans to transfer forces and means to Stalingrad. It was nothing of the sort. Originally the date of the commencement of 'Mars' was indicated as 12 October, when the Stalingrad strategic offensive operation ('Uranus') existed only as an idea. In addition, in the not-so-long-ago declassified *List of the USSR Armed Forces General Staff*, which was compiled after the war, 'Mars' was included among the main strategic operations. It must have been quite the 'demonstration', given that it concluded with the encirclement of large Red Army groupings! The irrecoverable human losses in this operation alone were, according to official data, 70,400 men, i.e., 14 per cent of the troops present at the beginning of the operation.[3] Some other unsuccessful Soviet *front* operations also remained outside the attention of the authors.

We are going to attempt to further demonstrate that both statistical works are still very far from the realities of the last war. As calculations of force numbers and human losses have become more detailed, resulting casualty counts for various operations have changed. To the surprise of historians and researchers, however, the work's casualty totals for quarters, years, periods and campaigns have invariably coincided with the officially proclaimed maximums, which, according to the authors, reflect actual personnel losses during the war. Information about this has appeared in print from time to time, which has led to numerous heated discussions, including at international conferences and symposia.

Unfortunately, the public cannot obtain answers to many perplexing questions that have arisen during these conferences and symposia. A position of condescending silence is not fitting for serious scholars. The authors of the statistical work could have thoroughly disclosed their methodology for determining Soviet losses in personnel and war materiel, using a concrete example of one of the strategic or *front* operations, citing sources that could be confirmed. However, for some reason they have not deigned to do this. Apparently, they did not view clarity as necessary, and did not wish to respond to justified complaints. Moreover, at times several leaders of the Ministry of Defence angrily attacked critics in the mass media, threatening them with all kinds of punishment up to and including criminal prosecution. This matter resulted in the establishment of the Russian Presidential Commission for Countering Attempts to Falsify History to the Detriment of Russia's Interests. Meanwhile, as will be shown below, it was namely Krivosheev's team who in their books repeatedly (and, judging by everything, deliberately) distorted the most important historical facts. Is this becoming of the respected officers of the General Staff and Military-Memorial Centre of the Armed Forces of the Russian Federation? Do the interests of Russia not suffer here?

At one meeting of the Association of Historians of the Second World War, General-Colonel Krivosheev, Professor of the Russian Federation's Academy of Military Sciences, declared, 'We are being criticized from the right and the left, but we are confident because we are relying on General Staff documents.' They were confident because they were still holding back 'useless scraps of paper' that *front* headquarters, under conditions of defeat, encirclement and panicked withdrawal, not knowing where and in what condition their subordinate armies and divisions were, sometimes sent to the General Staff. Krivosheev once again confirmed that the main official sources when determining human losses were reports on casualties received from *fronts*, armies, divisions and separate units, which were analysed monthly by the General Staff, refined, supplemented with additional materials about unrecorded casualties and, finally, reported to the Supreme High Command General Headquarters.[4] It is interesting that, in private, some of the authors of *The Seal of Secrecy Has Been Removed* admitted that they could not be responsible for the numbers that someone, at some time, had reported. Why not, then, declassify these reports and other appropriate documents in order to assess their reliability and remove any doubts on this account?

At the beginning of the war only a few people in the organization and staff department of the General Staff's Operations Directorate were looking into casualties in the field forces. Only on 9 July 1941 was a department of personnel casualties records organized as part of the Main Directorate of Organization and Recruitment of the Red Army. Among its duties were to keep casualty records and compile an alphabetical card file.

Casualties for Soviet units and formations during combat operations were recorded in accordance with the *Instructions on Records and Accounting in the Red Army*, which was put into force by NKO Order no. 450, dated 9 December 1940. In accordance with the 'Table of Reports on Records of Roster Strength and Order of Battle of the Red Army', data about the composition of troops, their numerical strength, and casualty figures from divisions, armies and *fronts* were presented three times per month (every ten days). In accordance with requirements, personnel casualty records assumed a relatively stable combat situation, in which staff would be able to present continuous reports, in the established period of time, to the higher authorities.[5] A calculation method for enumerating casualties under extreme circumstances, taking into account multiple troop reinforcements, was virtually not employed. The instructions in force did not stipulate this.

The conditions under which the Red Army had to repel the surprise attack of the fully mobilized Wehrmacht are well known. Many historians think that the main reason for the Red Army's defeat in June–July 1941 is that the army had not been brought to full combat readiness and therefore was unable to enter the war in an organized fashion and repel the enemy's surprise offensive. In the military sense surprise is a multilevel phenomenon. **Strategically**, the war was not unexpected for the political and military leadership of the USSR. However, the enemy succeeded in achieving complete **tactical surprise**, thereby thwarting the implementation of Soviet plans to cover the border. The enemy, having immediately seized the initiative and begun the invasion with large forces, also achieved **operational surprise**. Taking advantage of the overwhelming superiority they created in forces and means on selected strike axes, and of the dominance they captured in the air, the Germans ensured a high tempo for their offensive. In the first two days they had already advanced 100–150 kilometres on the main (Western Strategic) axis, creating conditions for the encirclement and defeat of the Western Front's main forces.

For a long time the stunning defeat in the initial period of the war negatively affected all subsequent Soviet troop operations. Failures of varied scale followed the Red Army in both the autumn of 1941 and the summer of 1942, periods not defined by a perfidious enemy surprise attack. Nevertheless, the Germans often succeeded in achieving operational surprise and sometimes pushed Soviet troops to the brink of catastrophe. The defeat of the Red Army, numerically large and well armed, was completely unremarkable given the actual condition of its combat and mobilization readiness on 22 June 1941. It was not prepared for the kind of war that Hitler and his generals unleashed on the Soviet Union. In addition, the blatant mistakes of the USSR's political and military leadership made it impossible at the very beginning of the war to realize the great potential of the Red Army. The enormous sacrifices that the Soviet people suffered on the way to victory are, in large part, on their conscience.

The authors' team of the statistical work admitted that the border military districts immediately lost the great bulk of their personnel. During high-manoeuvre combat operations, especially considering the unsuccessful development of the situation and loss of command, control and communications (because of several resubordinations of units and formations, encirclement or disorganized withdrawal, negligence or enemy penetration, bombings, sabotage, etc.), the system of regular record-keeping often did not work. Moreover, reports on the results of combat operations and troop casualties were often not produced because they had fallen into numerous 'pockets'.

What could be reported from the lower levels in a situation of complete breakdown of the front, encirclement and destruction of headquarters and entire units, and wholesale annihilation of records? The poorly organized accounting of casualties and the often total lack of opportunity to report them made it impossible for headquarters to precisely determine the state of affairs of troops at the front. Units and formations that had fallen into encirclement generally did not produce information about their situation, for understandable reasons. This was the overall picture during the first months of the war.

One can obtain some idea of the scale of casualties suffered by the forces of the principal border military districts (which became *fronts*) during the initial period of the Great Patriotic War from the data in Table 1. These are presented for comparison with the casualties of the opposing enemy groupings during that same period.

Thus, during the first 15–18 days of combat operations, the Red Army lost 747,870 men, of which 588,598 were irrecoverable human losses (79 per cent) and 159,272 were medical losses (21 per cent). According to data from the German Archive, by 10 July 1941 the Germans had captured 366,372 Soviet POWs (including 1969 officers).[6]

It should be noted that the table does not include the casualties of Romanian, Hungarian and Slovak troops operating against the Southwestern Front. However, these losses were relatively minor and had little impact on the overall casualty ratio. Thus irrecoverable Soviet troop losses in men during the initial period of the war were almost 32 times greater than those of the Germans, and overall Soviet troop losses exceed those of the Germans more than tenfold.

Soviet and German casualties during this period are incredibly disparate! Here is not the place to enumerate the reasons for the Red Army's defeat in the border battle. The authors of this work have expressed their opinion on that matter in *June 1941. Preprogrammed Defeat.*[7] Taking into account the results the Germans achieved in the initial period and in subsequent battles on the main strategic axes, the casualties calculated by Krivosheev's team do not particularly inspire trust.

How they managed to so precisely calculate *front* losses, even down to a single man, is a real puzzle. In the situation that had developed, the *front* and army commanders and staffs did not always know the location of their formations, let alone their losses in men, weapons and war materiel. Moreover, what can be said about casualties when, as will be shown later, two reputable scholarly collectives cannot even agree on the matter of the initial strength of the districts (*fronts*)? Obviously they had different approaches to determining personnel strength.

Table 1: Red Army and Wehrmacht casualties during the initial period of the Great Patriotic War*

Front	Northwestern Front and Baltic Fleet	Western Front and Pinsk Military Flotilla	Southwestern Front	Totals
Period	22 June– 9 July 1941	22 June– 9 July 1941	22 June– 6 July 1941	
Number of days	18	18	15	15–18
Troop strength**	498,000 (369,702)	627,300 (673,472)	864,600 (907,046)	1,989,900 (1,950,220)
Red Army casualties				
irrecoverable	75,202	341,073	172,323	588,598
medical	13,284	76,717	69,271	159,272
overall	88,486	417,790	241,594	747,870
% of strength	17.8%	66.6%	27.9%	37.6%
average daily	4,916	23,211	16,106	44,233
Wehrmacht casualties				
irrecoverable	4,878	8,049	5,568	18,495
medical	14,976	20,883	17,250	53,109
overall	19,854	28,932	22,818	71,604
Correlation of casualties				
irrecoverable	15.4:1	42.4:1	30.9:1	31.8:1
overall	4.5:1	14.4:1	10.6:1	10.4:1

* *Russia and the USSR in Wars of the 20th Century*, 2001, pp. 267–8; *Velikaia Otechestvennaia voina 1941–1945 gg. Strategicheskie operatsii i srazheniia. Statistichesky analiz* [The Great Patriotic War, 1941–1945. Strategic operations and battles. Statistical analysis, hereafter cited as *Statistical Analysis*, Book 1], Book 1 (Moscow: Institut voennoi istorii, 2004, pp. 39, 66, 73, 90, 97).
** The numbers in parentheses are the lists of *front* forces according to data from *Statistical Analysis* (see above note).

First and foremost, the casualty numbers for the Northwestern Front do not inspire confidence. By 29 June its troops had suffered defeat and been pushed back to the Western Dvina River, and then to the Velikaia River. The 8th Army had been cut off from the *front*'s main forces and had been withdrawing northward. The *front* had lost 2,523 tanks and self-propelled guns.[8] It is not by chance that General-Lieutenant P.S. Klenov, Chief of Staff of the *front*, was relieved of his duties on 1 July 1941.[9] *Front* Commander General-Colonel F.I. Kuznetsov was removed even earlier, on 30 June, and on 10 July 1941 he was demoted and assigned to be commander of 21st Army.[10] Other leading members of the *front* staff were removed from their posts as well. This would hardly have happened if troop casualties in the border battle had been only 17.8 per cent of their numerical strength, which was noticeably less with respect to percentage than that of other *fronts*.

In the situation that had unfolded, subordinate troops were unable to provide reports about their casualties to *front* headquarters. If there are no reports from the troops themselves, then no information can move upward along the chain of command. Therefore, it was necessary to report to Moscow about the 'shortage' of human resources. What can one say regarding the reliability of the Northwestern Front casualty numbers if the first casualty report since the beginning of the war, which was signed by Colonel V. Kashirsky, Chief of the Recruitment Department of this *front*'s staff, stated that from 22 June 1941 to 1 August 1941 (forty days of combat) the *front* lost 57,207 men? This figure is 1.5 times fewer than that for the men lost in eighteen days, according to information from Krivosheev's team.[11]

According to information from researcher I.I. Ivlev,[12] who for many years has studied this *front*'s combat operations during the Great Patriotic War, under the complex conditions of the beginning of the war and poorly organized withdrawal of *front* forces there was no opportunity to present information on the situation and casualties. Despite working in the ELAR Corporation,[13] he has not been able to discover reports in various archives or in the JDB on casualties of 40 of the 78 formations and units that made up the *front*, including 4 of 9 rifle corps (including one airborne), 17 of 26 rifle divisions, 1 of 4 mechanized corps, 4 of 8 tank divisions, 6 of 10 brigades (all types), and 5 of 14 artillery regiments. There were also no reports of casualties from the 8th Army headquarters.

How did Krivosheev's team compute these losses? If they attempted to calculate them, what formation and unit manning did they take as their base? When determining the casualties of *front* formations and units that had not provided reports, Ivlev used such arithmetic. He proceeded from their numerical strength at the beginning of the war (or time of their introduction into the engagement). He determined the overall casualties as the sum of irrecoverable and medical casualties (for comparison, casualties according to Krivosheev's data are given in parentheses). According to Ivlev's data, on 9 July 1941 Northwestern Front's casualties were as follows: irrecoverable, 246,961 (73,924); medical, 13,337[14] (13,284); totals, 260,298 (87,208). In other words, casualties according to Ivlev's calculations are three times greater than those calculated by Krivosheev. According to Ivlev, by 1 August 1941 Northwestern Front troop casualties amounted to 377,469 men,[15] that is, 6.6 times greater than Colonel Kashirsky reported. How could this happen? It turns out that the *front* reported casualties regarding troops subordinated to it on 1 August 1941 for only 40 of the 216 organizational units that were on the lists for the district (*front*). The report 'forgot' the 8th Army, half of the corps, two-thirds of the rifle divisions and half of the tank and motorized divisions.

Ivlev's calculations are confirmed indirectly by the content of the *front*'s application to the General Staff for delivery of reinforcements to compensate for troop casualties (with respect to conditions on 1 August 1941). In all, *front* headquarters, taking into account what the Centre for Field Replacements had promised it (67,622 men), requested 312,070 men in four applications (dated 2, 7, 12 and 20 July 1941).[16] Why is this fewer than the casualties that had been suffered? By this time they already knew about the loss of the 2nd and 5th Tank Divisions, the 24th Latvian Rifle Corps' scattered 184th Rifle Division (which had been manned using local resources), and the departure of the 126th and 179th Rifle Divisions to the Western Front. The authorized strength of these formations that had been taken from the *front*'s combat strength amounted to around 65,000 men. It was not required to replace them, and the applications for replacements were reduced to 312,469 men (377,469–65,000).[17]

The calculation of casualties according to reports from troops, the basis of which was only the change in their lists for a specific period of time without consideration of replacements they had received, often led to results that were far from the actual losses. The arithmetic method of computing human casualties, employed without consideration of frequent replenishment of units and formations, also did not provide a correct result because the instructions concerning their computation that were in force did not foresee this.

Formations that had broken out of encirclement or completed a forced withdrawal under the complex conditions of the situation characteristic of the first months of the war were, in the majority of cases, hastily replenished or re-formed using field replacements and the remnants of units and formations that had disbanded. An analysis of documents from the collections of TsAMO RF of these formations and units shows that time and again the replacements were not taken into account by casualty reports. Moreover, units and subunits frequently lacked the chance to record their men by name, let alone by the addresses of relatives.

In one of his published addresses, Krivosheev, answering questions from the audience, alleged that it was now impossible to take into account the numbers and arrival time of replacements. Therefore, because of the complexity of accounting for the formations and armies that were brought in and taken out during the course of combat operations, the authors specified only the numerical strength of participating formations and armies at the beginning of an operation, not considering troops and field replacements introduced during the fighting. Casualties, then, were calculated for all forces that were taking part in a given operation. The monthly *front* reports, being the most complete and reliable, were taken as the basis (we will speak about the completeness and reliability of troop reports later).[18]

It is difficult to trust this. How could casualties have been calculated, taking into account mid-battle field replacements, without knowing replacement numbers or arrival times? Meanwhile, all necessary data are in the appropriate collections, which for a long time were inaccessible to researchers. Several meticulous researchers, working on their own, succeeded where the 'respected' G.F. Krivosheev, with his enormous authority and large team, 'failed'.

In 2010 and 2011, on the basis of data from collection no. 16 of the Red Army's Central Military Transportation Directorate,[19] Ivlev created an electronic database on the formation and movement of almost 50,000 trains that were used for the operational transport of troops in 1941. Using this database, one can follow the movement of trains from loading stations to unloading stations, with an indication of the numbers and types of units and formations being transported (including replacements), dates of loading and unloading, and junction stations through which the trains passed. In many cases he succeeded in revealing the departure and arrival times, size and assignment of the replacements being transported.

Consideration of replacements provides a more realistic number of personnel losses during combat operations. The results of the calculation of human casualties for all formations and units that comprised the Northwestern Front's three armies in 1941 are of special interest. Analysing information from the manning and military transportation department of Northwestern Front and army headquarters, the Red Army Military Transportation Directorate, the Main Organization and Recruitment Directorate of the Red Army (Glavupraform), and reserve regiments, and reception and transit stations, Ivlev calculated the overall number of replacements that the *front* received over 188 days of war, beginning on 22 June 1941, to be 341,239 men. Of these, 111,917 were sent by orders of the central authorities as field replacements (battalions and companies) starting in July 1941, and taken into account by *front* and Glavupraform documents in the collections of TsAMO RF no. 221 and no. 56 respectively. The *front* obtained the remaining replacements from 'their own' resources. Here, when calculating monthly casualties, Ivlev took into account formations and units that had been removed from Northwestern Front – a total of 189,572 men.[20]

He analysed the casualties of more than 80 military formations and units, including 7 rifle corps, 1 airborne corps, 36 rifle and motorized divisions, 1 people's militia division, 3 cavalry divisions, 4 mechanized corps (with 8 tank divisions in their composition), 2 rifle brigades, 3 airborne brigades, 2 anti-tank artillery brigades, 3 air defence artillery brigades, 11 artillery regiments and other separate *front* units.

In his calculations Ivlev took into account the fact that on 9 June 1941 the border divisions of the Baltic Special Military District, which immediately after the beginning of the war became the Northwestern Front, were already at authorized wartime strength, or even exceeded it. The divisions that had begun to move to the state border in accordance with the 13 June 1941 People's Commissariat of Defence Directive had already been replenished before the beginning of the war with recruits who had been designated for the deployment of units of the 25th, 41st, 42nd, 44th, 45th, 46th and 48th Fortified Regions and brought up to authorized wartime strength during 10–15 June 1941.[21] Each division was to form artillery and machine gun battalions and other subunits to be included in the fortified regions; however, because the fortified regions had not deployed, the recruits remained in the divisions.

According to mobilization plan MP-41, 230,000 men from the Moscow Military District were assigned to the formations and units of the Baltic Special Military District;[22] they began to arrive for training sessions on 20 June 1941 (citizens of local nationalities were not assigned to the troop composition).[23] After the commencement of open mobilization on 23 June, the remaining assigned staff from the Moscow Military District began to arrive in dozens of troop trains.[24]

Through his calculations, Ivlev obtained actual information on North-western Front casualties in 1941. These substantially exceeded the corresponding data that Krivosheev's team computed: irrecoverable losses by 2.8 times (507,703 vs. 182,264), medical casualties by 1.6 times (143,496 vs. 87,823), and total casualties by 2.4 times (651,199 vs. 270,087).[25]

It should be mentioned that combat support (communications, engineer, road, railway and chemical) and rear support (quartermaster, medical, veterinary, construction, etc.) units, whose actions and fate are difficult to follow in view of frequent replacements, re-formation and disbanding, removal of personnel, etc., are not included in Ivlev's calculations. He also did not take into account casualties from units of the eight fortified regions located on the district's territory, from which not a single report was received (130 different subunits – construction, combat engineer and motor vehicle battalions – were used to build them). The general electronic database has only fragmentary data on the casualties of just two of these battalions. If the casualties from these units are considered, then Northwestern Front personnel losses for the first 188 days of the war would be even greater.

The main category of Red Army casualties at the beginning of the war was irrecoverable losses. This is understandable; due to the complex situation and the rapid and not always organized withdrawal, the Red Army was simply not able to evacuate the wounded and sick. Here, the lion's share of irrecoverable losses fell on the Red Army soldiers and officers whom the Germans had taken prisoner as a result of the numerous encirclements. It is very difficult to establish their precise number, and therefore it is necessary to use German data. Table 2 – Soviet POWs captured in the large encirclements of 1941 – has been compiled on this basis.

It is characteristic that, according to computations by Krivosheev's team, irrecoverable losses for Soviet forces in 1941 operations frequently approximate or barely exceed the number of prisoners taken by the Germans in the large encirclements alone. For example, according to German data, by 9 July

Table 2: Number of Soviet POWs and principal regions of their capture by the Wehrmacht in 1941 (according to German information)*

Date	Army Groups			Region of capture
	North	Centre	South	
9 July		323,000		Belostok-Minsk
Early August			103,000	Uman'
5 August		348,000		Smolensk-Roslavl'
20 August		50,000		Gomel'
23 August	18,000			Lake Il'men'
End of August		30,000		Velikie Luki
4 September	11,000			Estonia
Mid-September	35,000			Demiansk
26 September			665,000	Kiev
End of September	20,000			Luga-Leningrad
10 October			100,000	Melitopol'-Berdiansk
14 October		662,000		Viaz'ma-Briansk
16 November			100,000	Kerch'
Total	84,000	1,413,000	968,000	Total = 2,465,000

*K. Streit, *'Oni nam ne tovarishchi ...' Vermakht i sovetskie voennoplennye v 1941–1945 gg.* ['They are not our comrades ...' Wehrmacht and soviet POWs in 1941–1945, hereafter cited as Streit, *They Are Not Our Comrades*] (Moscow: Russkaia panorama, 2009), p. 87.

1941 Army Group Centre forces had captured 323,000 men in the region of Belostok and Minsk. According to Krivosheev's data, the Western Front's irrecoverable losses for this period amounted to 341,073 men. Of course, in addition to MIAs, some Soviet troops were also KIA, so these numbers correspond well with one another. The same can be said for the casualties of other *fronts* in subsequent battles.

The description by Krivosheev's team regarding casualties in the Kiev strategic defensive operation produces a strange impression. According to the team's data, Southwestern Front forces numbering 628,500 men (including the Pinsk Military Flotilla, which numbered 1,500 men) took part in the operation. They did not indicate the strength of Central Front's 21st Army (10–30 August 1941) or Southern Front's 6th and 12th Armies (20 August 1941–26 September 1941), only taking their casualties into account. The overall casualties for these forces from 7 July to 26 September 1941 amounted to 700,544, including 616,304 irrecoverable losses (88 per cent of the total) and 84,240 medical casualties (12 per cent of the total).[26]

It turns out that Southwestern Front casualties were greater than its numerical strength, as indicated by Krivosheev! Only naïve people (those who themselves were never involved in calculations on the basis of archival information) believe the numbers of Soviet casualties during the Great Patriotic War that were computed during the Cold War and the active struggle against the 'bourgeois falsification of history'. At the same time, the indicated discrepancies for some historians and commentators became the cause for disputing the Nazis' 'myths' about their successes. In particular, they questioned the numbers of Soviet prisoners captured in the encirclements, including near Kiev. All these commentators' arguments basically boiled down to the fact that the number of troops that had been encircled exceeded the numerical strength of the corresponding *fronts*. Possibly they did this from a false perception of the prestige of the Red Army or from a desire to whitewash the Soviet military command, which in the first and second periods of the war had made many errors with grave consequences. Moreover, some of them thought, in general, that the casualties of the USSR population and the Red Army that were cited in *Russia and the USSR in Wars of the 20th Century* were greatly exaggerated.

In fact, according to A. Isaev's data, the number of Soviet troops who fell into encirclement east of Kiev on 1 September amounted to 452,720 men. There were 1,510 artillery pieces (including 316 anti-aircraft guns) in the *front*'s artillery units (not including 21st Army). According to his information, 21,000 men were able to break out of encirclement.[27] Later, on the basis of TsAMO RF archival documents, Isaev refined the strength of the encircled forces: 106,831 men in the 21st Army (11 rifle divisions and 3 cavalry divisions); 93,412 in the 5th Army (10 rifle divisions, an airborne brigade, and an anti-tank artillery brigade); 113,718 in the 37th Army (10 rifle divisions); 85,456 in the 26th Army (7 rifle divisions); and 53,303 in units subordinated to the *front*.[28] Were these archival data really not accessible for the authors of the works under discussion?

According to German reports, 665,212 prisoners were captured in the battle at the basin (bend) of the Dnepr and Desna Rivers. Of them, Army Group South directly captured 440,074 in the encirclement near Kiev from 11 to 26 September (this fully agrees with the number of encircled Soviet forces – 452,720), 41,805 at the Kremenchug bridgehead from 31 August to 11 September, and 11,006 at the Gornostaipol' bridgehead from 4 to 10 September. The remaining 172,327 prisoners had been captured by Army Group Centre at Gomel' (formations from Weichs' 2nd Army and Guderian's 2nd Panzer Group, a total of 25 divisions, of which 6 were panzer and motorized divisions) and in the penetration of Guderian's group to Lokhvytsa. In all these battles the Germans destroyed or captured 824 tanks, 3,018 field guns and 418 anti-tank cannon.[29]

Consequently, the number of Soviet prisoners captured by Army Groups South and Centre exceeds the irrecoverable losses that Krivosheev calculated by almost 50,000. In this regard, great doubt arises regarding the 21st Army's casualties as calculated by Krivosheev – 35,585, including 31,792 irrecoverable losses; that is, around one-third of its strength. After all, according to records of the situation on 2 October 1941, only 15,000 men were listed as having broken out of encirclement. The same can be said about the irrecoverable losses of Southern Front's 6th and 12th Armies, which had been encircled in the Uman' region – 52,900 men. According to German data, 103,000 men were captured there. Can this difference of 50,000 men be explained by these facts? Who counted how many were killed during the fierce (according to German testimony) battles? On average, for 1941, the dead in the Red Army's overall casualties amounted to 10.4 per cent.[30] Thus, the number of irrecoverable losses for Southwestern Front in the Kiev operation amounts to a minimum of 719,000–730,000, which should not be considered an overstatement.

Distrust of the numbers of irrecoverable losses for Southwestern Front forces, as calculated by the authors, is intensified by the following circumstance. During 96 days of fighting (15 in the initial period, 81 in the Kiev operation), the *front* irrecoverably lost 696,900 men,[31] and a total of 717,800 in 1941;[32] that is, during the remaining 92 days the *front* lost 20,900 men. This number corresponds precisely to the losses in two strategic operations:

the Donbas-Rostov defensive operation, in which the irrecoverable losses for Southwestern Front's 6th Army from 29 September to 16 November 1941 amounted to 11,200 men, and the Moscow offensive operation from 6 to 31 December, in which the irrecoverable losses for 3rd Army, 13th Army and General Kostenko's operational group, which comprised the Southwestern Front's right flank, were 9,700 men.[33] It turns out that during combat operations for all of 1941, Southwestern Front forces that did not take part in the above-mentioned operations did not, in general, suffer any irrecoverable losses. Did they not fight at all? How, then, could there have been the Sumy-Kharkov front defensive operation, in which Southwestern Front's 21st, 38th and 40th Armies irrecoverably lost 75,720 men from 30 September to 30 November 1941 (more than half of its initial combat strength)?[34] No, something clearly does not mesh in the arithmetic of the authors of the statistical research ... Or, in this case, they simply disregarded the casualties Soviet forces suffered outside the framework of strategic operations.

It should be emphasized that the authors calculated Southwestern Front casualties without considering replacements that the *front* received in August and September. There are only indirect data about the numbers. It is known that in September the three *fronts* of the western strategic axis received more than 193,000 field replacements (39.2 per cent of the overall number of men sent into the active army) to make up for the casualties they had suffered.[35] Taking into consideration the situation that had developed on the southwestern strategic axis, the Southwestern Front could have received as much as 15 per cent of the overall number of field replacements (492,000), that is, 70,000–75,000 men. It was namely because of the introduction of reserves into the battle and the supplying of field replacements that, on the basis of the Kiev Fortified Region, 37th Army was created on 10 August 1941, consisting of six divisions (147th, 171st, 175th, 206th, 284th and 295th Rifle Divisions). By 1 September, in addition to the fortified region units, there were ten divisions in it. Thus, judging by everything, the *front*'s actual casualties in the Kiev operation greatly exceeded those indicated by Krivosheev's information.

A small digression is needed concerning the combining, somewhat strange at first glance, of such varied regions of German operations into a single battle. The numerous encirclements, with hundreds of thousands of captured prisoners in operations during the first and second periods of the war, are an indirect testament to the much higher level of operational training of the Wehrmacht commanders. By seizing the strategic initiative, they chose the time and direction for strikes. We would like to focus the attention of home-grown strategists on the fact that, as a rule, any encirclement begins with the penetration of the enemy's front and the capture of advantageous bridgeheads for the advance along converging axes, during which a two-sided envelopment and encirclement of the enemy is implemented. Then the encircled forces are destroyed while strikes from outside that might free those forces are repelled. Troop actions (local army and army group operations) during this time are linked with respect to goal, task, place and time, and are aimed at resolving the specific operational-strategic mission on whose resolution the further course of military operations depends. They can be carried out sequentially, as in the battle near Kiev, or simultaneously, as in Operation 'Typhoon'. All this may comprise the content of a single strategic operation on a selected axis.

In this case, Army Group South's offensive in the Uman' region on the right bank of the Dnepr seems somewhat unusual. However, the operations of Colonel-General Guderian's 2nd Panzer Group and Colonel-General Weichs' 2nd Army (Army Group Centre), which on 8 August had shifted to the offensive against the Soviet's Central Front in the direction of Mogilev, Gomel' and Roslavl', Starodub (a total of 25 divisions, of which 6 were panzer and motorized divisions), fit completely into the plan for defeating the Southwestern Front. Moreover, it should be taken into consideration that the enemy command itself was entitled to determine the temporal and territorial framework for the battle, which the enemy's data describes. We will have more to say about the reliability of German data.

Von Rundstedt's forces, which during the battle near Kiev captured 492,885 prisoners, lost 92,205 men (including 3,101 officers), of whom 24,002 (869 officers) were irrecoverable.[36] The ratio of irrecoverable losses amounted to a minimum of 20:1 in favour of the Germans.

Army Group Centre forces that participated in this battle captured 172,327 prisoners. From 11 to 31 August Guderian's forces alone lost 13,300, of whom 3,588 were irrecoverable.[37] Inasmuch as attempts at establishing the casualties of the 2nd Army formations there have not been successful, there is no sense in considering the ratio of irrecoverable losses – the clear disproportion is quite obvious.

*   *   *

The Moscow strategic defensive operation is another example of how great the difference in *front* personnel casualties can be between the data of Krivosheev's team and the data of other researchers. The scope of the Red Army's defeat in this operation is muted in every way possible in the official historiography of the Great Patriotic War. It is usually mentioned in passing that, at the beginning of October, Soviet forces suffered a major set-back, and that the encircled units of the 19th, 20th, 24th and 32nd Armies continued to fight heroically, having contained 28 enemy divisions. Here, questions about Soviet casualties, not to mention about specific reasons for the defeat, are avoided in every way. *The Battle of Moscow. Chronicle, Facts, Men*, published in 2001, states, as before, that 19 rifle divisions and 4 tank brigades were encircled west of Viaz'ma, and that some of them were able to break out to their own forces.[38]

In reality, the Germans succeeded during Operation 'Typhoon' in collapsing the Soviet defensive front on the western strategic axis and encircling and defeating the main forces of three *fronts*. The Red Army suffered enormous damage in personnel, weapons and war materiel. There was no way to reconstitute it because the *Stavka*'s main reserves had been used up even earlier to regenerate the front on the southwestern and Orel axes. There was a gaping breach with a width of as much as 500 kilometres in the strategic defence of the Soviet forces, one which ran 800 kilometres; almost the entire way into the heart of the country had been opened. This was a catastrophe that fundamentally changed the situation on the entire Soviet-German Front. Its severe consequences determined all *Stavka* decisions and subsequent Red Army operations for a long time.

Forces of 13 armies, 7 of 15 field army commands, 64 of 95 divisions (67 per cent of those existing at the beginning of the battle), 11 of 13 tank brigades (85 per cent), and 50 of 62 Reserve of the Main Command [hereafter cited as GHQ reserve] artillery regiments (81 per cent) were encircled at Viaz'ma and Briansk.[39]

Remnants of 32 divisions (including 3 of 6 divisions trapped outside the general encirclement) and 13 GHQ reserve artillery regiments were able to break out. 'Remnants', because they were listed as divisions only by name and number. For example, '681 men remained in the 248th Rifle Division. By 18 October the 13th Army, which on 30 September had 8 divisions and 169 tanks, had less than a single division's worth of men, not a single tank, and not enough artillery pieces to equip a single rifle regiment. In the 50th Army there remained around 10 per cent of the men and 2.4 per cent of the artillery pieces and mortars.'[40]

In the course of two to three weeks some 32 divisions, 11 tank brigades and 37 GHQ reserve artillery regiments were lost. Thus, during the first half of October, Soviet forces suffered a devastating defeat, one which G.K. Zhukov called a catastrophe. In scope and consequences this defeat is not comparable to the defeat of the Western Front's main forces in Belorussia or that of the Southwestern Front in September 1941. Western Front and Reserve Front forces withdrew 250–300 kilometres, while the Briansk Front forces were thrown back 360–390 kilometres. The front line was all of 100–110 kilometres from the capital. This was, perhaps, the most difficult and most tragic stage of the war. The entire world expected that Moscow would soon fall.

Here is how the Germans at that time evaluated the results of the first stage of Operation 'Typhoon'. On 19 October von Bock in his order declared the following to the forces of Army Group Centre:

> The battle at Viaz'ma and Bryansk has resulted in the collapse of the Russian front, which was fortified in depth. Eight Russian armies with 73 rifle and cavalry divisions, 13 tank divisions and brigades, and strong artillery were destroyed in the difficult struggle with a numerically far-superior foe.
>
> The total booty: 673,098 prisoners, 1,277 tanks, 4,378 artillery pieces, 1,009 anti-tank and anti-aircraft guns, 87 aircraft and huge amounts of war materiel.[41]

There is no information in the works of Krivosheev's team about human casualties on the Moscow axis during the first two or three weeks of October. Table 3 shows human casualties for Soviet forces (according to Krivosheev's data) in the 67 days of the Moscow strategic defensive operation (30 September–5 December 1941). For illustration, the force strength of the *fronts* at the beginning of the operation and their casualties are shown in percentages.

The tragedy, however, lies in the fact that Soviet casualties as calculated by Krivosheev do not compare with von Bock's data! They disagree not because

Table 3: Personnel casualties for Soviet forces in the Moscow strategic defensive operation (30 September–5 December 1941)*

Fronts	Strength at the beginning of the operation	Human casualties in the operation			
		Irrecoverable	Medical	Total	Average daily
Western	558,000	254,726	55,514	310,240	4,700
Reserve	448,000	127,566	61,195	188,761	15,730
Briansk	244,000	103,378	6,537	109,915	2,617
Kalinin**		28,668	20,695	49,363	1,050
Total	1,250,000	514,338	143,941	658,279	9,825
Percentage of the strength of the three *fronts* at the beginning of the operation		41.1%	11.5%	52.7%	

* Russia and the USSR in Wars of the 20th Century, 2001, p. 273.
** The Kalinin Front was created on 19 October from Western Front forces.

the Red Army's irrecoverable losses – 514,338 soldiers and officers – are fewer than the number of prisoners captured by the Germans (673,098), but because the commander of Army Group Centre is only talking about the first three weeks of Operation 'Typhoon', during which the Germans captured 673,098 men, while Krivosheev is talking about the 67 days of the operation (to 5 December).

Who, then, is being deceitful here? Perhaps von Bock exaggerated the success of his troops? Let us try to sort this out.

As usual, Krivosheev's information is amazing regarding the precision of the cited casualty numbers – to the man! From where could such information appear, given that in October army and *front* headquarters did not even know where their formations were and in what condition?

That the Operations Directorate of the General Staff was inadequately informed about the actual situation regarding losses on the fronts is evidenced by the 'Information on the Numerical Strength of the Red Army, Replacements, and Casualties from the Beginning of the War to 1 March 1942', signed on 1 May 1942 by Colonel Efremov, Chief of the directorate's Organization and Records Department (see Appendix B). He reached the following conclusions: 'With regard to records, especially casualty records, the period from 1 August to 1 December is the most unclear. One can state with complete certainty that the Organization and Staff Directorate's information regarding casualties for October and November does not at all correspond to reality.'[42]

The authors of *Russia and the USSR in Wars of the 20th Century* admit that, in connection with the difficult operational situation during the battles, military headquarters were sometimes unable to account for casualties. This, first and foremost, is related to the units and formations that were encircled, for which it was not possible to report information about their situation. Therefore, they had to calculate the casualties of small and large formations that the enemy destroyed or encircled using 'their latest reports about personnel strength, as well as **archival materials from the German command**'.[43] We will spend some time on how the authors took into account 'archival materials from the German command'.

In two weeks the Germans succeeded in encircling and destroying the main forces of the Western and Reserve Fronts, as well as in operationally encircling the Briansk Front forces, who also suffered heavy losses. The Western Front, headed by Zhukov, who had been called up from Leningrad, had to be reconstituted once again.

The situation was near-catastrophic. The forces of both *fronts*, which could have resisted the enemy on the path to the capital, were trapped. The

19th Army and General I.V. Boldin's operational group (formed from Western Front reserves), as well as numerous front-subordination units, fought northwest of Viaz'ma. Also in the encirclement were formations of the Reserve Front's 32nd Army. The overall strength of these front-subordination forces and units before the beginning of the operation was no fewer than 250,000 men. However, they all suffered heavy casualties even before the encirclement (for example, the 19th Army lost as many as 20,000 of its 52,000 men).

Enough has been written about the 19th Army's battles in encirclement and its unsuccessful attempts to break out. Much less is known about the operations of the 20th and 24th Armies, which were encircled southwest of Viaz'ma. General-Major K.I. Rakutin, Commander of the 24th Army, died in the encirclement; General-Lieutenant F.A. Ershakov, Commander of the 20th Army (whose composition also included formations from the 16th Army), died in captivity; General-Major N.V. Korneev, Ershakov's Chief of Staff, died during the break-out of the encirclement. Only a few reports that Western Front headquarters and the General Staff received have been saved, but not all of them have yet been declassified (especially the encoded ones).

South of the Minsk-Moscow Highway, fully combat-capable formations, numbering around 87,000 men, fought in encirclement, having suffered almost no casualties before the commencement of their withdrawal. In addition to these, formations of the Reserve Front's 24th and 43rd Armies, which in previous fighting had suffered heavy casualties (before the commencement of the operations their combat strength had been 195,000 men), were encircled. Several units subordinate to the Western and Reserve Fronts also fell here. The overall strength of the forces encircled southwest of the town was approximately 230,000–240,000.

It was not by chance that a significant conclusion was reached in a report on 11 October 1941 by the Supreme High Command of the German Army: '(b) Army Group Centre ... Enemy forces encircled west of Viaz'ma continue brutal attempts to break out, **the main strike is being delivered south of Viaz'ma**. The number of prisoners is growing ...'[44]

Based on previously unpublished German documents, it seems they managed to partially restore the situation southwest of Viaz'ma. The encircled forces delivered the main strike at the junction of the 11th Panzer Division and the 252nd Infantry Division at Chakovo in the direction of Blokhino (8 kilometres south of Los'mino). According to German information, several battalions broke out here, cut off the Blokhino-Viaz'ma road, and continued to break out to the south. The 11th Panzer Division's command post was also attacked.

The following is taken from the daily German 4th Army headquarters report, dated 12 October 1941:

> In the course of a day at the front of the encirclement, the enemy has made several attempts to break out of encirclement, advancing in lines to a depth of up to 15 rows. They were all repelled, with heavy casualties for him.
>
> Units of the 5th Panzer Division and the 252nd Infantry Division had to deliver a counterblow against the penetrating enemy and throw him back, with enormous casualties. Communications were re-established with the 11th Panzer Division. Today more than 25,000 men were captured.[45]

The following is taken from a 4th Army war diary on the same day:

> 21.20 ... the 5th Panzer Division advanced to the 11th Panzer Division's right flank. The number of dead Russians is incredibly great, it is becoming downright strange. Because of the bodies one can hardly advance along the roads. The 46th Motorized Corps alone captured 60,000 prisoners.
>
> 23.25. The 46th Motorized Corps reports that last night and this morning the Russians attempted 15 attacks, one after the other, against the 11th Panzer Division. Some servicemen in the division units ran out of ammunition and they died. The corps captured 160,000 men.[46]

On 10 and 11 October the village of Selivanovo (17 kilometres south of Viaz'ma) changed hands several times. According to testimony from local residents, the bodies of dead soldiers lay in three layers on the field.[47]

Later, through prisoner interrogations, the Germans established the reason for such strong pressure: on the narrow sector in front of the 46th Motorized Corps alone, the Soviets' entire 20th Army and units from the 16th Army were operating. Their overall strength amounted to around 30,000 men, and they were concentrated for a breakout. The army commander himself was in charge of them.

On 13 and 14 October the Germans generally combed over the terrain west of Viaz'ma, with the goal of capturing POWs. The following is taken from a report by 4th Army headquarters [south of the highway]:

> 14.10. From 2 to 12 October, 4th Army units captured 328,000 men. The following were destroyed and captured: 310 tanks, 1,400 artillery

pieces, 26 undamaged aircraft, 6,000 motor vehicles, 45 loaded railway trains, 1 food train, 1 column with ammunition, and 2 fuel storage depots.[48]

One can judge the ratio of losses north of the highway from the report by the 9th Army's 8th Army Corps:

> During the fighting from 2 to 13 October, 8th Army Corps, consisting of the 8th, 28th and 87th Infantry Divisions (not counting divisions that in the course of the offensive were temporarily resubordinated to the corps), lost 4,077 soldiers and officers, including 870 KIA and 227 MIA.
>
> During the same period corps formations captured 51,484 men and destroyed and captured 157 tanks, 444 artillery pieces of all types, 484 machine guns, 23 field kitchens, 3,689 motor vehicles, and 528 horses.[49]

Later, in a letter to A.A. Zhdanov in Leningrad, Zhukov would write the following about those days: 'We are now operating in the west, on the outskirts of Moscow. The main thing is that Konev and Budyonny negligently let their armed forces waste away. I inherited just a mere shadow of them: from Budyonny – his headquarters and 98 men; from Konev – his headquarters and two reserve regiments.'[50]

Zhukov was, of course, exaggerating: there were other forces, including those who had managed to avoid encirclement. However, it was necessary to find them, bring them into order, assign them missions corresponding to the situation and finally assist them logistically. During the defensive operation a total of 6 armies (26 rifle divisions, 14 cavalry divisions, 15 rifle brigades, 2 airborne brigades, and 6 separate machine gun battalions) were introduced into the composition of the newly re-established Western Front. Kalinin Front received an additional three rifle and two cavalry divisions,[51] not including the forces of the Southwestern Front's right flank and the Moscow Defensive Zone, which had taken part in the operation.

What proportion of the declared number of irrecoverable losses (514,300 men) over the 67 days of fighting, in the opinion of the authors of the statistical research, did the October casualties represent? There is no answer. The authors avoided any specification of human casualties in the first two operations – Viaz'ma (2–13 October) and Orel-Briansk (30 September– 23 October), in which Soviet forces suffered a shattering defeat.[52]

The majority of researchers who have studied the Battle of Moscow do not agree with the numbers cited in *Russia and the USSR in Wars of the 20th Century*. We are talking about very serious works. For example, in the 1990s, in accordance with the intention of preparing a new edition of the history of the Great Patriotic War, free from the ideological dogmas and outdated myths of Soviet propaganda, the Institute of Military History developed and published four volumes of military-historical essays about the Great Patriotic War. They examined inadequately researched problems and presented opinions on debatable questions, including the very painful issue of casualties in individual operations.

Of particular interest is the first book, *Severe Trials*, which is mostly devoted to the events of 1941. Examining the results of the first stage of the Moscow strategic defensive operations, *Severe Trials* draws the conclusion that 'during the first 2–3 weeks of fighting near Moscow, the Red Army lost as many as 1 million men who were killed in action, died of wounds, went missing in action or were captured.'[53]

The basis of this conclusion was the calculations of B.I. Nevzorov, a well known researcher of the Battle of Moscow who worked in the Institute of Military History. He used information from the collections of TsAMO RF, to which not all researchers had access at that time. Proceeding from there, Nevzorov determined the approximate magnitude of Soviet human casualties. Around 85,000 men (including 6,308 officers, 9,994 noncommissioned officers (NCOs), and 68,419 enlisted men, a total of 84,721) broke out of the Viaz'ma encirclement and around 23,000 broke out of the Briansk encirclement, for a total of 108,000. On 15 and 16 October, in the Naro-Fominsk region alone, 4,000 men were detained, half of them without weapons. From 10 to 15 October, in the regions of Naro-Fominsk and Volokolamsk, a total of 17,000 soldiers and officers were detained.[54] All those who had broken out of encirclement as individual groups or who had been detained by barrier troops joined their own units or composite detachments.

To the number of those who had broken out of encirclement, Nevzorov added 98,000 men – those from the 29th Army, the 33rd Army and Boldin's group who had avoided encirclement, as well as those from the 22nd Army, where only one division (the 126th Rifle Division north of Rzhev) had been encircled. According to his calculations, approximately 200,000 men had avoided encirclement and joined up with their own forces. However, individual groups continued to break out of the encirclement in November as well and even later. Therefore, Nevzorov rounded off the overall number of men who remained in the ranks from the initial strength of the three *fronts* to 250,000. To summarize, he concluded that **the Red Army lost as many as 1 million men (80 per cent of the initial strength of the three fronts), of whom (according to German information) around 688,000 (that is, 70 per cent of the overall casualties) were captured.**[55] In passing, let us mention that in determining Soviet troop losses Nevzorov did not take into account the replacements the *fronts* received during the operation.

It is worth noting that because the treatment of events in the above-mentioned essays in some cases contradicted the official history of the war, publication was halted. As a result, the approach to many issues sharply changed. Thus, in the Institute's 2004 work *Statistical Analysis*, a name that held much promise, the authors agreed with the figures in *Russia and the USSR in Wars of the 20th Century*, and did not provide their own assessment of the reliability of their colleagues' information. However, using the example of Krivosheev, one can determine the casualties of the Moscow strategic defensive operation, albeit approximately, by the arithmetic method.

It was this method that S.N. Mikhalev, a senior researcher at the Institute of Military History and doctor of historical sciences, used when calculating casualties in the Moscow operation. However, the results he obtained were somewhat different from those of Nevzorov. He calculated human casualties as the difference between the initial strength of the Western, Reserve and Briansk Fronts on 1 October 1941 (1,212,600 men) and the strength of the Western (including Reserve Front's surviving troops), Kalinin and Briansk Fronts on 1 November (714,000 men). The losses amounted to 498,600 men. Taking into account replacements that arrived to these *fronts* during that time (304,400 men), human casualties for October numbered 803,000 men. Considering losses for November, the overall *front* casualties in the operation amounted to 959,200 men, of which 855,100 were irrecoverable (and this is not counting the casualties for four days in December).[56] This figure is **1.7 times greater** than Krivosheev's. The *fronts*' medical casualties amounted to 104,100.[57]

Mikhalev reported his calculations at a military-scientific conference, 'The 50th Anniversary of the Victory in the Battle of Moscow', at which representatives of Krivosheev's team were also present. One would expect them to have disputed Mikhalev's method, pointing out the error of his calculations and the correctness of their own, but they did not do this.

Later, Mikhalev refined the figures for the October 1941 casualties for the three *fronts*:

> In October 1941, at the very beginning of the Battle of Moscow, seven Soviet armies (the 19th, 20th, 24th, 32nd, 50th, 3rd and 13th) were encircled near Viaz'ma and Briansk. As a result, only fragmentary information about personnel casualties of these formations arrived at the headquarters of the Western, Reserve and Briansk Fronts, and the information that *front* headquarters reported to the General Staff was

only a summation of what they had received. The assessment of the
October casualties for the three *fronts*, based on this information, was
around 45,000 men, which clearly did not correspond to reality: by the
commencement of the battle the strength of the three *fronts* amounted to
1,212,600 men, while on 20 October, according to information in the
front report, there remained a total of around 544,000. During this time,
as many as 120,000 replacements arrived there. Consequently, personnel
losses reached 788,600 men ... Let us mention that, subsequently, a
certain portion of the MIAs broke out of encirclement, and the actual
front casualties, in sum, were lower than the figure cited here; however,
by the end of October military-operational casualties had reached almost
800,000 men.[58]

With the calculation of casualties for November (156,000), personnel losses
during the operation in this case amounted to 956,000 men (even not
including casualties for the first four days of December), 442,000 greater than
Krivosheev calculated.

In his calculations Mikhalev reduced the initial strength of these three *fronts*
by almost 38,000 men in comparison with the 1,250,000 listed by the Institute
of Military History researchers. In our opinion, however, these figures also
need to be refined: according to information in *The Seal of Secrecy Has Been
Removed*, by 1 October the overall strength of the Western Front was
588,000, that is, 14,000 more men.[59] On 1 October 1941 the Briansk Front's
50th Army numbered 67,413 men, almost 6,000 more than in the information
from the Institute of Military History.[60] Thus, in calculating human casualties in the operation, it is necessary to start from the actual troop strength in
the zone of the three *fronts* on 1 October – this amounts to no fewer than
1,270,000 servicemen, that is, 58,000 more than Mikhalev calculated.

Moreover, all this does not take into account rear area units, formations,
installations of central subordination and other departments located in the
area of responsibility of the three *fronts* (for example, the military construction
workers of the Western Directorate of Defensive Work). In addition, on
25 September 1941 the NKVD units in the Western Front's zone numbered
13,190 men.[61] In the defensive zones of the Reserve and Briansk Fronts,
NKVD units could have numbered approximately 8,000–10,000.

In this case the actual personnel losses of the three *fronts* amounted to
858,000 soldiers and officers. Taking the November casualties of the Red
Army forces operating on the Moscow axis (156,000) into account, a minimum of 1 million Soviet servicemen were lost; irrecoverable losses here
numbered in the order of 900,000. Some discrepancy in the casualty figures

obtained by different researchers into the Moscow strategic defensive operation is explained by the scarcity of reliable information in this most difficult
period of the Great Patriotic War.

In explaining the results of the Moscow strategic defence operation,
authors state that during the fierce fighting 'Soviet forces stopped the advance
of the main German grouping – Army Group Centre – and soundly defeated
it.'[62] In light of the above results of the research by prominent scholars, this
statement seems a mockery. One could call the number of irrecoverable
Soviet troop casualties in the operation (514,300 men) laughable if it did not
concern the serious issue of the loss of defenders of the Motherland.

This is the perfect time to compare the troop casualties of both sides.
According to captured German documents, in Operation 'Typhoon', from
30 September to 5 December 1941, Army Group Centre lost 145,000 men.[63]
Unfortunately, researchers at the Institute of Military History erroneously
calculated the total number of casualties. If we add up their data properly,
Army Group Centre's overall losses amounted not to 145,000 men, but rather
to 136,278 (including 5,695 officers), of whom 37,453 (1,675 officers) were
irrecoverable. We will not judge: it happens that even well established scholarly teams are at odds with the rules of elementary arithmetic, miscalculating
by millions. Let us note, however, that this figure includes casualties
amounting to 50,000 men for the period 1–17 October.[64] The ratio of overall
casualties for both sides in the operation was 7:1 (1,000,000:136,278) against
the Red Army, while the irrecoverable losses for the Soviet forces exceeded
those for the Germans by 24 times (900,000:37,453).

With such a correlation, is it reasonable to speak about a serious defeat of
von Bock's forces? In fact, at that time the German plans for taking Moscow
were thwarted and the German blitzkrieg failed. These events have great
historical importance in and of themselves, and in no way need to be base-
lessly embellished.

The bulk of Soviet casualties consisted of soldiers who were MIA. Not all
of them died: some scattered throughout the local forests or settled in small
villages. Many of them were mobilized in the winter of 1942 by the forces of
Generals Belov and Efremov, who were operating south of Viaz'ma, or later,
when the regions of the Smolensk and Briansk *oblast'* were liberated from the
enemy.

The larger part had, however, been captured. It should be mentioned that
the Germans began to take prisoners and captured materiel from the first day
of Operation 'Typhoon'. Army Group Centre's intelligence and counter-
intelligence department daily and scrupulously recorded the prisoners and
war materiel the army had captured. Up to and including 9 October (that is,

Table 4: Number of prisoners and war materiel captured by Army Group Centre during Operation 'Typhoon' (according to German information)*

Period (from beginning of operation)	Number (accumulating results)					
	Prisoners	Tanks	Artillery pieces	Anti-tank guns	Anti-aircraft guns	Aircraft
To 5 October	60,783	208	436	131	39	10
To 7 October	103,299	361	671	227	96	10
To 8 October	124,184	524	909	260	157	12
To 9 October	151,323	532	1,091	320	216	13

*TsAMO RF, f. 500, op. 12462, d. 623, vol. 2, l. 3 (Army Group Centre's Intelligence reports). Note: information is incomplete in connection with the absence of the greater part of reports from 2nd Panzer Army.

until the encirclement had been successfully liquidated), the Germans captured more than 151,000 prisoners (see Table 4).

The number of prisoners and materials sharply increased with the liquidation of the encirclement near Viaz'ma. The following is from an Army Group Centre report dated 14 October 1941:

The enemy, encircled by the 4th and 9th Armies west of Viaz'ma, has been completely destroyed. Four Soviet armies comprising 40 rifle and 10 tank divisions have either been destroyed or captured. According to preliminary calculations, more than 500,000 were taken prisoner and 3,000 artillery pieces, 800 tanks and other pieces of military equipment were captured …[65]

It must be said that these men were not only Red Army soldiers and their officers. The German command included among the POWs workers from the Party and Soviet organs, as well as draft-age men who had moved back with those forces who had withdrawn and fallen into encirclement. The following spoke to this: '… it is necessary to arrest not only Russian soldiers, but also, in general, all men from 16 to 50, and send them to POW camps. Civilians arrested with weapons in hand or while carrying out sabotage attacks are to be immediately executed.'[66]

During the fighting in encirclement and pursuit, however, Wehrmacht units had no time for the civilians – everything rested on the rapidity of manoeuvre and the need to free up the forces involved as quickly as possible in order to develop the offensive to Moscow. One can follow this in the daily German troop reports. Moreover, at this time the Germans did not have sufficient forces to convoy POWs. One also should not exaggerate the number of draft-age civilians in the encircled regions. To a significant degree this contingent had already been called up during mobilization. Thus, according to information from the Smolensk *Oblast'* Communist Party Committee dated 15 September 1941, 153,000 men from the territory of the *oblast'* had been drafted into the Red Army.[67] In addition, in accordance with Red Army General Staff Directive no. org/2/524678, dated 8 July 1941, under threat of occupation during the first twenty days of July 1941, human resources from the threatened regions were withdrawing to the east, starting with new recruits and including persons born in or after 1891.[68]

By the way, when Soviet forces crossed the border of the Third Reich, a State Defence Committee resolution dated 3 February 1945 instructed the appropriate *fronts* to conduct a regular mobilization of German civilians (that time on German territory). They were to mobilize 'all German men aged 17 to 50, fit for physical labour and able to carry weapons'.[69] More about this, however, will be discussed in the appropriate place.

According to German information, during the first twenty days of October 787,961 prisoners (including 4,253 officers) were captured on the Western Front.[70] The number of prisoners and the amount of captured materiel increased sharply as the enemy cleared out occupied Soviet territory, and by 31 October the number had reached 1,037,779 men (5,184 officers).[71] Of course, one cannot completely exclude the possibility that the Germans over-stated the number of POWs. Just by how much is difficult to say. This could have happened because of instances of dual reporting when formation sub-ordination changed and information was transmitted to higher authorities (the same men being counted several times), as well as because of a kind of 'com-petition' among commanders over who would capture more prisoners. Even taking into account corrections for some German exaggeration, however, the number of Soviet POWs captured at Viaz'ma and Briansk in no way fits with Krivosheev's information. Thus, his claims are refuted from both sides.

However, here also we find many who wish to completely throw out the results of the research of scholars who have specifically studied this operation. A.V. Isaev, a well known specialist on the encirclements, took a somewhat more balanced position. Even he, however, having reported that 'the figure of 310,240 human casualties [of the Western Front] for the entire defensive period, as announced by Krivosheev's team, seems low', expressed doubt with regard to Nevzorov's and Mikhalev's information on the enormous casualties of the three *fronts* in the operation:

> On the other hand, the assessment of Soviet casualties in 1 million of
> men and more is also far-fetched. This figure was obtained by a simple

subtraction of the strength of those who had occupied the fortification
on the Mozhaisk Line (90,000–95,000) from the overall strength of the
two (or even three) *fronts*. It should be remembered that of the three
fronts' 16 large formations, 4 armies (the Western Front's 22nd and
29th Armies, the Reserve Front's 31st and 33rd Armies) and the
Briansk Front operational group were able to avoid encirclement and
complete destruction. They were simply outside the German 'pincers'.
Their numbers amounted to approximately 265,000 men. Some of the
rear area subunits were also able to leave for the east and avoid
destruction. A number of subunits from the 30th, 43rd and 50th
Armies were also cut off from the encirclements by German tank
group breakouts. A number of subunits from the Briansk Front's 3rd
and 13th Armies withdrew into the zone of the neighbouring
Southwestern Front (these armies were also eventually subordinated to
it). A breakout was not such a rare phenomenon. According to
information received on 17 October 1941, 10,000 men from the
13th Army and 5,000 men from the 20th Army broke out of
encirclement.[72]

Where Isaev got the thesis of 'simple subtraction' from is not clear. If he had
subtracted from the numerical size of the three *fronts*, their apparent casualties
would have far exceeded the losses by 1 million men $(1,250,000 - 90,000 =
1,160,000)$. If he had subtracted from the numerical size of the Western and
Reserve Fronts, their calculated casualties would have amounted to fewer
than 916,000 $(1,006,000 - 90,000 = 916,000)$. No one, however, did the calculations in this way.

It was established that by 10 October the Mozhaisk defensive line had been
occupied by the forces of just four rifle divisions (the 316th, 32nd, 312th and
110th), as well as by detachments of cadets from various military schools,
three reserve rifle regiments and five machine gun battalions. According to
incomplete information, they numbered not much more than 62,000 men.
At the most critical moment (during the last ten days of October), there
remained a total of 90,000 men in the four armies at the disposal of the Soviet
command for the defence of Moscow. These men needed to hold a defensive
line stretching from the Moscow Sea to Kaluga (230 kilometres).[73] What,
however, does this have to do with the *front* forces, whose defence had been
penetrated? In addition to the 31st Army's 110th Rifle Division, numbering
6,000 men, these were forces that had been transferred from other axes and
from the interior of the country, as well as composite detachments from
military schools and newly formed units of the Moscow garrison.

According to Krivosheev's information, during the 67 days of fighting the three *fronts* lost slightly more than half of their initial compositions. For the moment, we will agree with him and assume that, for the first two or three weeks of October, they lost no less than two-thirds of the overall casualties during the defensive operation, in the order of 440,000–450,000 men. In that case, no fewer than 800,000 men would have remained in the composition of those troops who had escaped encirclement and death. If the outcome had been thus, then the situation on the Moscow axis would not have had such an ominous character.

Isaev made the following conclusion in the article: 'In a word, even the calculated differences of 800,000 men between the initial strength of the Western, Reserve and Briansk Fronts and the strength of those troops who remained outside the encirclements do not give us an unambiguous casualty figure.'[74]

Of course, they would not give an 'unambiguous figure' because the troops remaining outside the encirclement also suffered casualties during the operation (everything cannot be reduced to only the 'encirclements'). As for the Western Front's 22nd and 29th Armies and the Reserve Front's 31st and 33rd Armies, which had escaped the encirclement and complete defeat, their strength at the beginning of the operation amounted to 242,000, not 256,000 men.[75] In addition, the 22nd Army's 126th Rifle Division fell into encirclement north of Rzhev, and the 31st Army's 247th Rifle Division did so north of Sychevka. These armies' remaining formations also suffered casualties during the withdrawal, especially the Moscow militia divisions. Thus, according to incomplete information, in the seven former militia divisions that had escaped the 'large' encirclements (the remaining five divisions fell into encirclement and, because of their heavy losses, were disbanded), of the 77,255 soldiers and officers, approximately 13,000 (17 per cent) remained in the ranks after two weeks of fighting.[76] For instance, by 12 October 17 officers and 94 soldiers, with a total of 123 rifles, 2 submachine guns and 1 machine gun, reached their troops in the 17th Rifle Division.[77] By 15 October their number, taking into account two replacement companies (286 men), had increased to 558 men, 5 per cent of the division's initial strength.

As an example, let us calculate the 33rd Army's casualties, which Isaev mentioned. Its five divisions numbered 55,800 soldiers and officers; the total, including army and rear area units, was 72,880 men. By 15–25 October only 4,197 men from the 17th, 113th and 173rd Rifle Divisions had reached their troops. By 5 November the 60th Rifle Division numbered 3,962 men. This, however, obviously already took into account replacements. The 18th Rifle Division, without the 1310th Rifle Regiment, had been withdrawn to the

Zvenigorod region for replacements. Information about its composition and about army unit casualties could not be found. Thus, there remained no more than 8,000–10,000 of the 55,800 original men in the ranks of the divisions, meaning that casualties numbered no fewer than 45,000.[78]

That is how the main forces of three *fronts* – formations of 13 out of 14 armies – were encircled near Viaz'ma and Briansk; only subunits broke out of the encirclements. One can understand from the following what those 30th Army subunits looked like, those that in Isaev's words were 'cut off from the encirclements by the penetrations of German panzer groups'.

In order to stop the Germans, who were attempting to roll up the Soviet defence on the Rzhev-Viaz'ma defensive line, General-Major V.N. Dalmatov, Commander of the 31st Army, was gathering his forces bit by bit. The plan was to transfer the remnants of the 30th Army's 250th Rifle Division, numbering around 500 men, to the Sychevka region by rail. These men had reached the Olenino region (50 kilometres west of Rzhev) by 9 October. Another part of this division (400–500 men) and the remnants of the 242nd Rifle Division had reached the Gusevo region. As many as 500 men from the 251st Rifle Division, who had assembled in the Aleksandrovka region, were also to get to the Sychevka region on the night of 10 October. The troops of the 30th Army's 107th Motorized Rifle Division continued to fight in encirclement in the Skorino region (13 kilometres southeast of Belyi), readying themselves to break out to the east. Remnants of the 162nd Rifle Division had concentrated in the Barkov region (20 kilometres northwest of Rzhev). Here, Dalmatov warned that the officers of units that had withdrawn further than the defensive structures along the Sychevka line and who had not reported their situation would be prosecuted by the 31st Army's military tribunal.[79]

Could Dalmatov have carried out his assigned mission to hold the sector of the defensive line with these forces? In the majority of cases, these were not units and not even subunits, but just **remnants** of formations and units that, first and foremost, had to be brought into order. However, there was no time to do so, and the disparate parts were immediately thrown into the fight. On 12 October 1941 this army was disbanded and its formations and units were transferred to the 29th Army. With regard to a petition from the 29th Army's military council, on 9 November the *Stavka* of the Supreme High Command decided to arrest General-Major Dalmatov and turn him over to the military tribunal for prosecution 'for grave negligence in the command and control of troops in the defence of Rzhev'. During the judicial process he was acquitted, since his personal culpability was not established.

Incidentally, the number of servicemen who returned from encirclement and were once again entered into the ranks should not be exaggerated. Thus, according to information from General-Colonel E.A. Shchadenko, Chief of the Main Directorate of Organization and Recruitment of the Red Army, from the beginning of the war until 1 September 1942 these men totalled 114,000 (see Appendix C).[80] Evidently he had in mind soldiers and officers who had escaped encirclement individually or in small groups, as well as those detained by anti-retreat detachments. After screening, they were either sent to the front line or used as replacements for formations and units.

Let us return, however, to Krivosheev's statement that it was impossible to take into account the numbers and arrival times of replacements. Therefore, regarding formations committed into battle during the operations, the authors of the work about casualties do not indicate the numerical strength or even size of field replacements. However, they supposedly calculated casualties for all the troops that participated in a given operation. It is difficult to believe this. For example, how could casualties be calculated taking into account the field replacements without knowing those replacements' numbers and arrival times? Meanwhile, all necessary information is in the appropriate TsAMO RF collections. We have already mentioned above Ivlev's success in solving this problem.

The stubborn resistance of Red Army troops on the Mozhaisk defensive line won the time needed to regroup forces and means on the Moscow axis from other sectors of the Soviet-German Front and from the interior of the country, to form and move reserve formations and units forward, and to supply field replacements to the front. According to information from B.I. Nevzorov, during the Battle of Moscow 6 armies (consisting of 26 rifle divisions, 14 cavalry divisions, 15 rifle brigades, 2 airborne brigades, 6 separate machine gun battalions, 2 motorized rifle divisions, 2 tank divisions, 22 tank brigades and 11 separate tank battalions) were additionally committed into battle as part of the Western Front before 4 December. To this must be added numerous artillery and engineer units and subunits, air defence units and air force formations (6 aviation divisions). According to Nevzorov's information, the strength of the units and formations committed during the battle numbered 645,000 men. In addition, 271,400 field replacements were supplied to the troops. Thus, taking into account the additional 916,400 men, some 2,166,400 men took part on the Soviet side in the operation from 30 September to 4 December 1941.[81]

Having been silent about this, the authors of the statistical work calculated casualties relative to the initial numerical strength of the three *fronts*: irrecoverable – 514,338 men (41.1 per cent); total – 658,279 (52.7 per cent).[82]

According to Nevzorov's calculations, losses of no fewer than 303,000 men must be added to these figures. In this case, irrecoverable losses amounted to 817,000 and overall losses were 961,500 (37.7 and 44.4 per cent respectively of the overall troop strength). These numbers are in complete agreement with Mikhalev's above-mentioned calculations – 956,000 men (not counting casualties for the first four days of December). Thus, losses of as many as 1 million soldiers and officers from the Red Army's battle formations during the Moscow defensive operations are not at all an exaggeration, no matter how tragic. Of course, not all of them died.

There is one more observation about Isaev's statement that casts doubt on German information regarding the number of Soviet tanks that had been destroyed or captured:

> The first thing that strikes the eye is the lack of accord between the number of tanks the three *fronts* had (1,044) and the figure that von Bock claimed in his order (1,277). Theoretically, the number 1,277 could have included tanks that were in *front* repair facilities. Such a disparity, however, undermines the veracity of the figures claimed by the enemy.[83]

In reality, by the beginning of the operation there were a total of 1,044 tanks in the composition of the three *fronts*. Very few of them were able to break out of the encirclement. Meanwhile, the Germans undoubtedly counted all the tanks they destroyed and captured from the beginning of Operation 'Typhoon' **up to 18 October**. This also included tanks that had been damaged and disabled earlier, which had not been evacuated to the rear from collection areas and repair facilities before 30 September, including those that could not be restored and that were gathered to be sent to the smelter. In the Reserve Front, for example, of the 164 tanks evacuated after the fighting near Elnya, 34 were sent for repair, while the remaining 130 could not be restored. In addition to these, on 23 September another 16 disabled tanks were evacuated and 47 were repaired in local shops.[84] By 30 September the Briansk Front had lost 202 tanks. They could hardly have managed to bring all of these to the rear. A similar picture unfolded for the Western Front.

The main thing, however, is that one should not forget that during the operation both reserve and newly formed Soviet tank formations were committed into battle. Four tank brigades – the 17th, 18th, 19th and 20th – fought on the approaches to the Moscow defensive line alone. The 17th Tank Brigade had already entered the fight at Medyn' on 12 October. In the fighting near Gzhatsk (9–11 October) the 18th Tank Brigade irrecoverably lost 35 of 42 tanks. For the entire period of the Moscow defensive operation, the Red

Army lost, according to that same Krivosheev information, 2,785 tanks and self-propelled artillery pieces.[85]

Now let us try to understand how such a great difference appeared between Krivosheev's data and the casualty figures obtained by such meticulous researchers as Nevzorov and Mikhalev.

We have already shown in numerous examples that the computation of personnel losses according to troop reports is characterized by a chronic underestimation of actual casualties. Now is the time to examine the issue of so-called 'unrecorded' casualties. During the first year of the war, in March 1942, a flagrant disagreement was discovered between the contents of current casualty reports and the remaining combat strength of the armed forces, as recorded by the General Staff. In the aforementioned document, 'Information on the Numerical Strength of the Red Army, Replacements, and Casualties from the Beginning of the War to 1 March 1942', signed by Colonel Efremov, on the basis of summary data about mobilization (taking into account the numerical strength of the army at the beginning of the war) and information about casualties and the return to the ranks of the wounded and sick who had been cured (1 million men), the conclusion was drawn that by the end of February the Red Army (not including the Navy) should have numbered 14,197,000 men. In fact, its numerical strength amounted to 9,315,000. The exposed deficit of 4,882,000 men exceeded by 1.5 times the number of irrecoverable losses documented in the General Staff – 3,217,000 men.[86] Thus, actual personnel losses in the Red Army on 1 March 1942 amounted to 8,099,000 men, exceeding the reported losses by 2.5 times.

In a General Staff document about Red Army combat casualties, quickly compiled after the end of the war in the Western Theatre of Operations, the number of POWs and MIAs was stated as 3,344,000 (see Appendix A).[87] It was then that the concept of 'unrecorded human losses that must be related to casualties at the initial period of the war' was introduced. At that time, in June 1945, these losses were estimated to total some 133,000 men. The appearance of the 'unrecorded losses' concept was inevitable because of the chronic undercounting of casualties in troop reports. It was introduced to eliminate the enormous imbalance in the calculation of the overall losses of USSR armed forces personnel. However, the 1,650,000 unrecorded Red Army and Navy casualties (not counting 12,600 border troop casualties) calculated by Krivosheev's team could in no way compensate for the deficit that had been brought to light.

The 'remainder' of 3,232,000 thus continued to hang over all of the authors' subsequent calculations. This could be followed in quarterly information about the personnel casualties of the active *fronts* and remaining armies. Taking into account those who returned to the ranks (1 million men), the army's numerical strength on 1 March 1942 should have been 18,414,000 men. According to the authors' calculations, casualties by 1 March 1942 amounted to approximately 5,502,388 men (4,308,094 + 1,194,294).[88] In that case, 12,911,600 men (18,414,000 − 5,502,400) should have remained in the ranks. However, on 1 March the numerical strength was, in fact, 9,315,000, a deficit of 3,596,600. To reduce this, the authors of the statistical study had to play a trick with 500,000 MIA mobilized reservists, whom they sometimes added to the armed forces casualties,[89] and sometimes to the civilian population losses.[90] However, the remaining 3,096,600 personnel losses still dropped out of the total casualties calculated by Krivosheev. Even taking those into account, the Red Army's and Navy's irrecoverable military-operational casualties should have amounted to 14,540,700 men. This figure will come in handy later.

Let us now turn to the note made by the authors of the publication of Efremov's document, which is sometimes cited to disavow the colonel's calculations:

> The content of the document attests to the inadequate awareness at that time, on the part of the Operations Directorate, of both the actual casualty situation and the use of mobilization resources. Thus, armed forces combat casualties as of 1 March 1942 were as follows: irrecoverable – more than 3.6 million; medical – as many as 2.5 million. In addition, 0.5 million men who had been mobilized during the first days of the war did not reach their units and were irrecoverably lost. Of the wounded and sick, as much as 23 per cent (more than 570,000) were released from the army (removed from the records or on leave for wounds or illness). A considerable portion of the mobilized contingent was sent to work for the national economy and to replenish NKVD troops and formations of other departments. Those convicted of military crimes (not including those sent to penal subunits) and deserters who were never found also comprise a certain portion of the losses. Their overall number for the entire war amounted to around 800,000.[91]

It should be acknowledged that the arrangement of the material in the document was not entirely competent. There were some mistakes and misprints (for example, personnel strength on the fronts on 1 December was 3,207,000, not 3,267,000). Apparently, something prevented Efremov, who was preparing material for the inquiry, from giving a more complete form to the text. Moreover, the army's irrecoverable losses by 1 March were computed incorrectly. According to the document, overall casualties from the beginning of the war numbered 5,682,000 (of which 667,000 were before 1 August, 3,377,000 were from 1 August to 1 December, and 1,638,000 were from 1 December to 1 March). Taking into account medical casualties (1,665,000 men), irrecoverable losses numbered 4,017,000, not 4,217,000. Thus, the deficit of personnel losses increases by 200,000 men.

However, all these flaws did not affect the conclusions Efremov reached. Did the authors who published the document really want to prove that he did not know that a considerable portion of the mobilized contingent did not reach the army, but rather were sent as replacements for the NKVD troops (who, by the way, also suffered losses recorded by Krivosheev) and formations of other departments, as well as for work in the national economy? Of course he knew, and took into account only those that the army received. Perhaps, also, units and field replacements sent to the front were recalled directly from there in order to transfer men into industry or elsewhere? On the contrary, reservists were repeatedly withdrawn from industry and NKVD formations after having their exemptions from military service cancelled. **On 1 September 1942** 280,000 men were sent to staff the NKVD.[92] Of the number of reserve contingents, 250,000 who belonged to nationalities of countries fighting against the USSR (the Volga Germans and Germans from other regions, Romanians, Finns, Hungarians and Italians) were excluded.[93] For the most part, it was from them that labour columns were created. Taking them into account, the size of the deficit of personnel losses, even if its estimation changes somewhat, remains in the order of 3 million men. Therefore, the authors of the work on losses do not even make ends meet.

It should be taken into consideration that the Operations Directorate of the General Staff was interested, first and foremost, in the order of battle and strength of the Red Army. It was on this basis that it planned operations and assigned missions to armies and *fronts*. The directorate calculated actual numerical troop strength, taking into account battle casualties and replacements that had arrived, both in whole formations and field replacements. Officers of the Organization and Personnel Management Directorate oriented themselves on 'documented' casualties. Were casualty reports that reached the General Staff hidden from them? Of course not – **such was the record and such were the reports**. It was namely this that Efremov's document was about.

Let us also mention that the authors of the note increased the army's irrecoverable losses (3.6 million) by including those who had been convicted of military crimes and even deserters who had not been found (for the entire war, for some reason). They also counted the overall personnel losses of the active *fronts* and separate armies not as of 1 March, but rather as of 1 April, when losses had climbed to 6.1 million.[94]

Now let us turn to the work of Krivosheev's team. The concepts of 'unrecorded losses' and 'roster strength', under conditions of inaccessibility for researchers of General Staff documents about casualties, became a magic wand for any manipulations of the casualty figures. According to troop reports and information from repatriation authorities, over the entire war 3,396,400 men were MIAs or had been in enemy captivity.[95] This number, however, was approximately equal to the number of prisoners captured by the Germans in 1941 alone. One could not ignore such an obvious absurdity. In 1990, during the preparation of *The Seal of Secrecy Has Been Removed*, the authors added to the aforementioned number the unrecorded casualties (of troops that had not been in reports) of the first months of the war – 1,162,600,[96] which increased the number of servicemen who had been captured and were MIA by 25 per cent and brought the figure to 4,559,000.[97]

One can get an impression of the methodology and reliability of the authors' calculations by following the changing opinion of the team leader regarding the problem of unrecorded losses when preparing the new work about casualties. In a talk at the meeting of the Association of Historians of the Second World War on 29 December 1998, Krivosheev himself posed the question (undoubtedly in reaction to bewildered questions from the historians):

> They can ask me the question, 'Were there always reports from the formations and separate units?' And what could be done if there were no such reports? However the complex situation developed, reports were presented, with the exception of those cases when the formation or unit had become encircled or had been destroyed, that is, when there was no one to make a report. There were such instances, especially in 1941 and the summer of 1942. In 1941, in September, October and November, 63 divisions had become encircled and were unable to produce reports. According to the last report, their numerical strength amounted to 433,999 men. Let us take, for example, the Southwestern Front's 7th Rifle Division. Its last report arrived on 1 September 1941, stating that its composition was as follows: 1,022 officers, 1,250 noncommissioned officers and 5,435 enlisted men, for a total of 7,707 men. With these personnel, the division became encircled and was unable to break out. We associated these personnel with the irrecoverable casualties and, moreover, with the MIAs. During the war a total of 115 divisions – rifle, cavalry and tank – and 13 tank brigades

were encircled, and, according to the latest reports, they numbered 900,000 men. We associated this information, or, more precisely, these figures, with the unrecorded war casualties. Thus, we reviewed literally all formations and units from which reports did not arrive. This was very painstaking work, which we were involved in for several years.

These unrecorded casualties amounted to 1,162,600 for the entire period of the war. Thus, the 11,444,100 men also include these men.[98]

In *Russia and the USSR in Wars of the 20th Century*, published in 2001, this approach was somewhat transformed, as described in the text:

In July–October 1941 alone, reports on personnel strength and casualties were not received from 35 of the Southwestern Front's rifle divisions, 16 of the Western Front's divisions, 28 of the Southern Front's divisions and 3 of its brigades, 5 of the Briansk Front's divisions, and 1 of the Reserve Front's divisions. The total strength of these troops alone, judging from their last reports, numbered 434,000 men ...

Therefore, when determining the number of casualties of the formations and armies routed by the enemy or in encirclement, their last reports on personnel strength were used ...

Casualties that were unrecorded because of this were associated with the number of MIAs and included in information of the corresponding *fronts* and separate armies that had not sent reports in the third and fourth quarters of 1941.[99]

It is difficult to understand the reasoning of the authors of this statistical research. At first they talk about 900,000 unrecorded casualties during the entire war; then the number 1,162,000, also for the entire war, appears from somewhere. This comprises around 10 per cent of the total servicemen irrecoverable casualties. Finally, it turns out that these casualties are associated with the third and fourth quarters of 1941. Did it happen that after 1941 Soviet troops no longer became encircled or found themselves in a situation in which staffs were no longer able to calculate casualties? Did the Red Army really no longer have unrecorded losses attributable to 'the treacherous invasion of Hitler's multi-million-man Wehrmacht'?

Furthermore, how did the authors calculate these unrecorded casualties? First they claim 63 divisions, comprising 433,999 men (what precision), as the forces that were encircled and did not send reports. However, the book makes mention of 85 divisions and 3 brigades (including 5 Briansk Front divisions and only 1 (!) Reserve Front division) with an overall strength once again of 434,000 men (they added 22 divisions, 3 brigades and one single man!).

Moreover, the number of Western, Reserve and Briansk Front formations and units that were completely lost (32 divisions, 11 tank brigades and 37 GHQ reserve artillery regiments) **in October alone** significantly exceeds the authors' calculated total of 22. This does not even count the large number of tank, cavalry and other formations and separate units of *front* and army subordination.

It is not understood when and how formations and armies 'that were routed by the enemy or encircled' were able, in view of this, to send reports on their roster strength. During the initial period of the war, some armies did not even have stable communications with *front* headquarters, not to mention formations and units. How could casualty reports have reached the General Staff? And what of the rifle and mechanized corps, and the rifle, tank and motorized divisions that were encircled and defeated during the initial period of the war? They were, in general, unable to send the appropriate reports.

Krivosheev's team assures us that:

> Unrecorded losses are associated with **the MIAs** and included in information from the corresponding *fronts* and separate armies that did not send reports in the third and fourth quarters of 1941. Although the information about the casualties for these troops, obtained by calculation, is not absolutely precise, it provides, on the whole, the actual picture of the number of human losses, especially in the initial strategic defensive operations.[100]

Well, there is no point in even talking about the precision of the team's calculations. Moreover, according to Table 120 in the statistical work, servicemen **who died and who were MIA** (such games are played with terminology throughout the entire work) are associated with the number of unrecorded casualties (1,162,000) during the first months of the war.[101]

Later in his talk Krivosheev declared: '... **during the war** a total of 115 divisions – rifle, cavalry and tank – and 13 tank brigades were in encirclement, and, according to the latest reports, they numbered 900,000 men'. (At this point we should recall that 124 divisions were disbanded because of the loss of combat capability during the 1941 campaign alone.[102])

Firstly, 11 tank brigades were encircled near Viaz'ma and Briansk in October 1941 alone. Secondly, what does **the first months of the war** mean: until 4 December (the end of the defensive operation) or up to the end of 1941? After all, Krivosheev was speaking about unrecorded casualties **during the whole war**.

There is yet another issue: if, during four months of the war, unrecorded casualties for five *fronts* amounted to 434,000, then troop casualties for the remaining *fronts* (Karelia, Leningrad and Northwestern) for this same period ought to be more than 1.5 times higher (716,000, taking into account border troop casualties). Knowing the nature of military operations on the main strategic axes of the Soviet-German Front, it is difficult to believe this.

So how, after this, can one trust the calculations of the author team?

A few more questions for the authors: how, and in the information from which specific *fronts*, were these casualties included? Was it really hindsight? What part of the above-mentioned 434,000 figure was included in the Soviet troop casualties in the Moscow strategic defensive operation? After all, enormous losses in personnel, weapons and war materiel in October predetermined, in great part, the nature of subsequent Soviet military operations on the Moscow axis.

Let us try to follow the dynamic of the Western Front's personnel losses. Its total irrecoverable troop losses in three consecutive operations (in Belorussia, the Battle of Smolensk and the Moscow defensive operation) reached 905,697 men. According to Krivosheev's information, this *front*'s irrecoverable losses for all of 1941 amounted to 956,293. The difference of 50,596 men apparently came mainly from the casualties in the Moscow offensive operation (5 December 1941–7 January 1942), in which the *front* irrecoverably lost 101,192 men (the question arises as to how they were divided by month?).[103] Moreover, during the period between these strategic operations on the Western Front, heavy local fighting continued, in which soldiers were still being killed and captured, going MIA, and dying of wounds and diseases. Where, then, are the 'unrecorded losses'?

When determining these casualties by calculation, the period in which combat operations were conducted has great importance. It is one thing to denote the initial period of the war as encompassing only the war's first weeks – from 22 June to 6–9 July 1941 – and something else completely to include the autumn of 1941.

And then, which table of organization (TOE) was the source for the authors' calculations? It is known that in April–May 1941 the People's Commissariat of Defence and the General Staff, with the government's agreement, began to conduct training assemblies for reservists in fourteen military districts. A total of 802,138 men were called up for these assemblies before war was declared; this comprised 17.7 per cent of the army's total peacetime strength (17.4 per cent of the mobilization requirement).[104]

Because of this the army managed to reinforce half of all rifle divisions (99 out of 198), mainly designated for operations in the west. Here, the composition of the rifle divisions of the border districts, whose authorized strength was 14,483 men, was brought up to the following: 21 divisions to

14,000 men; 72 divisions to 12,000 men; and 6 divisions to 11,000 men.[105] Other units were also replenished. Incidentally, in *The Seal of Secrecy Has Been Removed*, the authors stated that, by the commencement of the war, the Red Army and Navy numbered 4,826,907 men, of whom 767,750 were reservists at training assemblies.[106] In the next edition of their work, *Russia and the USSR in Wars of the 20th Century*, they increased this figure to 805,264,[107] that is, by 37,514 men. This is a strange discrepancy. In addition, starting on 22 June 1941, by orders from Moscow, field replacements (battalions and companies) began to arrive in the border districts. How did the authors take this into account?

Meanwhile, by autumn a completely different situation had developed at the beginning of Operation 'Typhoon'. Starting on 19 September, in connection with the great losses in men, weapons and war materiel, Red Army formations were transferred in large masses from the prewar TOE to reduced TOEs, which had already been introduced on 29 July. For example, in accordance with the new TOE no. 04/600, the number of rifle division personnel was reduced to 10,859 men. This was only 75 per cent of the previous TOE for a wartime rifle division, no. 04/400, which had been introduced on 5 April 1941 and which had set the division's strength at 14,483 men.[108] Under conditions of an acute shortage of people and war materiel, the Red Army did not want to reduce the number of divisions, so reduced their strength instead.

V.T. Eliseev, senior researcher at TsAMO RF and PhD in Historical Sciences, cites the next graphic example of an undercount at that time of Red Army formation casualties on the basis of the notorious 'roster strength'. The 43rd Army's 53rd Rifle Division was numbered among the active divisions in the field forces[109] as a single formation from 2 July 1941 to 11 May 1945.[110] In fact, this division had been defeated during the first week of the Moscow defensive operation. The division (essentially formation II), which had been regenerated under the same numerical designation, was in action from 13 October to 23 October. On 23 October K.D. Golubev, Commander of the 43rd Army, reported to Zhukov that 'the 53rd and 17th Rifle Divisions are demoralized and will be subject to disbanding'.[111] On the same day, its commander died and its remnants (1,000 men), together with the remnants of two other formations, were combined into a composite division, which received the numerical designation of 312th Rifle Division on 26 October. On 30 October the 312th Rifle Division was redesignated the 53rd Rifle Division (formation III), which then was in operation until the end of the Battle of Moscow.

Eliseev discovered twenty-seven such rifle divisions, which, during the Battle of Moscow, were operating as the same numbered military organism but were completely independent (in comparison with the General Staff's Register no. 5). One can imagine what kind of reports about these divisions' casualties were sent 'to the top' (if they were sent at all) and how those reports might have been summed up. Eliseev cites the concrete example of a particular worthless piece of paper sent to the General Staff. According to the 'Report on Personnel Casualties for Western Front Units for October 1941', troop casualties amounted to 66,392 men, of whom 32,650 were irrecoverably lost (including 26,750 MIAs and 80 POWs).[112] However, according to Eliseev's estimate, casualties for the *front*'s 17 rifle divisions and 2 motorized rifle divisions that had been encircled near Viaz'ma alone amounted to more than 130,000 men.[113] There were many similar examples during the war; it is impossible to list them all.

One can come to only one conclusion from the above: the number of 'unrecorded casualties' was lowered unjustifiably, and by quite a lot. Even if they had been included in the overall balance of Red Army personnel, they were not included in Soviet troop casualties in the individual strategic and front operations described in the works being critiqued. A striking difference also arises between the information from Krivosheev's team and the results of independent research. Moreover, the casualties in each of them, stated in statistical research, comprise only a part of the actual casualties that Soviet troops suffered. This must definitely be taken into account in each assessment of the results of each operation.

By the way, on 1 September 1942 field replacements amounting to 8,215,570 men had been sent to the front (field forces). On the very same date 177,000 men had died of wounds in hospitals, while the dead, captured and MIA had numbered 4,920,300.[114] Thus, irrecoverable losses by 1 September 1942 amounted to 5,097,300 soldiers and officers. At this point, the future still held two years and eight months of war, Stalingrad, the Caucasus, Kharkov, Kursk, the Dnepr, the liberation of European countries ...

As an aside, let us mention that the authors' uncritical use of troop reports when calculating casualties does not provide an actual picture of the magnitude of losses, either in people or in weapons. This can be seen in the example of losses in weapons in the Battle of Moscow. Let us recall that, according to the information from the authors of *Russia and the USSR in Wars of the 20th Century*, in the Moscow **defensive** operations human casualties during the 67 days of fighting amounted to 658,279 men, including 514,338 irrecoverable losses (in fact, these figures were considerably greater). During this time, according to the authors' calculations, Soviet troops lost only 250,800 small arms of all types. This was under conditions of the heaviest defeat, when the main forces of three *fronts* were encircled! Does it follow that they succeeded in retrieving the remaining weapons? This would have been possible only if von Bock had allowed them to remove from encirclement the weapons of those Red Army soldiers who had died or were missing in action!

In the Moscow strategic **offensive** operation (the counteroffensive) Soviet troops lost roughly half as many – 370,955 men, including 139,586 irrecoverably (3.7 times less) in 34 days (from 5 December 1941 to 7 January 1942). However, small-arms losses were **4.4 times greater** – 1,093,800 pieces of all types. Artillery losses were, respectively, 13,350 guns and mortars versus 3,832.[115]

Can this be explained logically? In fact, yes. This disproportion arose as a result of the fact that the authors calculated casualties only according to troop reports without paying attention to their reliability. They took into account only what had been reported. Since reports were not sent from encirclement, it meant that there were no casualties. Even though the calculation method could have been employed here as well, the authors avoided doing so because this would have resulted in unwanted conclusions about human losses. Moreover, there was no time to compute. On 5 December, with the shift to the counteroffensive, the opportunity arose to calculate weapons losses more accurately. With 1941 coming to an end, it was necessary to determine more precisely what there would be to fight with the following year. This was actually done and yielded results: during the Battle of Moscow a total of 1,344,000 small arms were lost. This number is closer to the actual **irrecoverable human losses** during the two operations (defensive and offensive), taken together, than the losses according to Krivosheev's information – 653,924 men.[116]

In connection with the great losses in weapons and war materiel, the responsibility of Red Army soldiers, officers and commissars for lost weapons was made even more stringent. Many units and separate subunits of the different branches of the army had to be disbanded or shifted to a reduced TOE.

In particular, on the basis of State Defence Committee Resolution no. 966, dated 26 November 1941, on reducing the numerical strength of the Red Army, People's Commissariat of Defence Order no. 00123, dated 24 December 1941, removed 64 artillery regiments from the composition of the GHQ reserve artillery units.[117] Subsequently, the released trained personnel, motor vehicle transports, weapons and other property were directed to reinforce or form other units.

The reader should not be surprised at the phrasing of the order. The war is on and yet we find a resolution 'on reducing the numerical strength of the Red Army'. The authorities would not announce the loss of artillery regiments in numerous encirclements.

In addition, by People's Commissar of Defence Order no. 00131, dated 27 December 1941, 68 rifle divisions were disbanded from the composition of the Red Army. Of them, 27 divisions had taken part in the Battle of Moscow, including 23 divisions that had ceased to exist during the first half of October.[118] Taking into account the number of encircled and defeated Soviet units and formations, only those who have never worked in the Russian archives and who themselves have never made similar calculations would believe the officious casualty figures for the Moscow defensive operation. After all, there were several similar unsuccessful operations during the first and second periods of the war.

During the years of Gorbachev's *glasnost*, *The Great Patriotic War, 1941–1945: Events, Men, Documents* was published. On the basis of an analysis of archive documents, it stated that for the six months of 1941 Soviet troops lost 5.3 million dead, MIA and POW.[119] This very number was later repeated in *VIZh*.[120] After the publication of the statistical works *The Seal of Secrecy Has Been Removed* and *Russia and the USSR in Wars of the 20th Century*, according to whose data irrecoverable casualties for 1941 were 3,137,673 men[121] (that is, almost 2.2 million fewer), the number 5.3 million was happily forgotten. And to no purpose ...

One can cite many examples of lowering reported casualties in operations, and not only with regard to the experience of unsuccessful combat operations in 1941. Sometimes, in order to reduce the enormous disproportion of casualties for the opposing sides, Krivosheev's team of authors manipulated the casualty figures even in operations during the second half of the war, when Soviet troops were achieving undisputed success.

As an example, let us examine the **Kursk strategic defensive operation**, which was conducted from 5 to 23 July 1943 by the Central, Voronezh and Steppe Fronts. *Front* defensive operations on the Orel-Kursk and Belgorod-Kursk axes were conducted within the framework of this operation. The following was said about them in Krivosheev's book:

> During defensive battles, the Central and Voronezh Front troops
> exhausted and then stopped the advance of the German-Fascist Army's
> shock groupings, and created favourable conditions to shift to the
> counteroffensive on the Orel and Belgorod-Kharkov axes. Hitler's plan to
> defeat Soviet forces in the Kursk salient was completely shattered.[122]

Soviet forces succeeded in accomplishing their assigned mission at the price of considerable losses in men, weapons and war materiel that, as we will see later, were incommensurable with enemy losses.

Let us take a look at Krivosheev's data on Red Army troop casualties in this operation (Table 5). From this table it follows that the overall casualties of the Steppe Front were approximately equal to the casualties of the Voronezh Front, and the difference between the irrecoverable losses for both *fronts* was all of 90 men! The impression is that the authors simply divided the casualties for the two *fronts* in half. Even the figures are the same, only arranged in a different order.

Despite the generally accepted order, Krivosheev's team prudently did not point out (for reasons we will discuss below) the Steppe Front's composition and strength when it took part in the operation. They mentioned only that the headquarters of the Steppe Front, the headquarters of 4 combined-arms armies (the 5th Guards and the 27th, 47th and 53rd Armies), the 5th Guards Tank Army, the 5th Air Army, 5 tank corps, 1 mechanized corps, 19 divisions, and 1 brigade were additionally introduced during the combat operations.[123]

Without any grounds whatsoever the authors cited 9 July as the date of the beginning of active operations for this *front*. After all, the rear Steppe Military District (the *Stavka*'s strategic reserve) was renamed the Steppe Front only on 10 July. At that time its troops were hundreds of kilometres from the front line. In fact, this front joined the operation only on 19 July; its forces actually entered the fight on the morning of 20 July.

Officially, the Voronezh Front's defensive operation ended on 23 July. This date is directly associated with the order from the Supreme High Command, dated 24 July 1943, on the results of the defensive period of the Battle of Kursk. In particular, the order said, 'Yesterday, 23 July, the Germans' July offensive from the Orel region and north of Belgorod in the direction of Kursk was finally liquidated ...'.

It turns out that Steppe Front troops participated in combat operations for a total of four days. Here, according to Krivosheev's calculations, they managed to lose as many troops as had the Voronezh Front, which had been fighting fiercely for 19 days, losing 13.8 per cent of its strength. Possibly the authors, with respect to the report, took the date of the commitment of the 5th Guards Tank Army and the 5th Guards Combined-Arms Army forces into battle. Both of these armies were, however, included in the composition of the Voronezh Front. Steppe Front commander I.S. Konev, categorically objecting from the very beginning to 'pulling apart' the Steppe Front, was very dissatisfied that, instead of the two full-blooded Guards armies of General A.S. Zhadov and General P.A. Rotmistrov, he received General M.S.

Table 5: Order of battle, troop strength and human casualties in the Kursk strategic defensive operation*

Name of formations and the period of time of their participation in the operation	Order of battle and troop strength at the beginning of the operation		Human casualties in the operation (number of men)			
	Number of formations	Troop strength	Irrecoverable	Medical	Total	Average daily
Central Front (5–11 July 1943)	41 rifle divisions 1 destroyer division 4 tank corps 5 rifle brigades 3 separate tank brigades 3 fortified regions	738,000	15,336	18,561	33,897	4,842
Voronezh Front (the entire period)	35 rifle divisions 1 mechanized corps 4 tank corps 6 separate tank brigades	534,700	27,542	46,350	73,892	3,889
Steppe Front (9–23 July 1943)	–	–	27,452	42,606	70,058	4,670
Totals	77 divisions 9 tank and mechanized corps 14 brigades 3 fortified regions	1,272,700	70,330	107,517	177,847	9,360

* *Russia and the USSR in Wars of the 20th Century*, 2001, p. 285.

Shumilov's weakened 7th Guards Army and General V.D. Kriuchenkin's weakened 69th Army, which before inclusion into the Steppe Front's composition had lost no fewer than 55,000 men. Moreover, according to testimony by General M.I. Kazakov, Konev's deputy, the latter succeeded in obtaining permission from the *Stavka* to remove part of the personnel from the divisions of the 47th Army, which was being transferred to the Voronezh Front, although they also had a personnel shortage. The 'removal' was done directly on the march, during brief halts. Around ten battalions, extracted in this way, were sent to replenish the 69th Army.

The authors of the statistical work contrived to compute the total number of Soviet forces taking part in the operation without taking this *front* into account. Let us correct their blunder. On 20 July 1943 the Steppe Front's personnel strength was as follows: according to the roll, 451,524 (according to the TOE, 572,683), of whom the 4th Guards Army numbered 83,391 (83,385), the 7th Guards Army 80,367 (118,919), the 47th Army 82,831 (93,807), the 53rd Army 72,035 (85,480), the 69th Army 70,028 (111,562), the 5th Air Army 16,316 (18,220), and units of *front* subordination (not including establishments of the state bank, etc.) 46,556 (61,310).[124] In July the 27th Army and the 47th Army were not conducting combat operations.

From 20 July the 7th Guards Army, the 69th Army and the 53rd Army, with a total strength of 222,400 men, shifted to the offensive in the first echelon of the Steppe Front. The authors of the statistical work calculated *front* casualties for the period to 23 July inclusive. According to the *Stavka*'s insistence, however, troops of both *fronts* (with the exception of the 5th Guards Tank Army) continued to advance even after 23 July. It would have been more logical to include troop casualties for this period in the operation's overall casualties. After all, the divisions, which, on the shoulders of the withdrawing enemy, were trying to capture the line in the Belgorod region that the enemy had occupied earlier, were fighting right up until the end of July. For example, the 93rd Guards Rifle Division kept fighting to the complete exhaustion of the physical and moral strength of its personnel, and shifted to the defence of the line assigned to it only on 30 July, having its total combat strength at only 220 men.[125] After 23 July the 5th Guards Army alone lost almost 8,000 men – one-third of its total casualties for July – while the 69th Army lost in the order of 14,000 men. Where were these casualties included? Were they even included anywhere, in general?

Having 'hung' part of the Voronezh Front's casualties on the Steppe Front, the authors equalized those *fronts*' total and irrecoverable losses. One cannot agree with such an alignment of losses between the *fronts* because this contradicts the general course of the operation, the nature of the combat and, crucially, the 24 July 1943 report by the Voronezh Front's chief of staff to the General Staff. According to him, during the 19 days of the operation *front* forces lost 100,932 men, which is 27,040 men more than in Krivosheev's data. Moreover, from 20 to 31 July Konev's forces, advancing under conditions in which the enemy's main forces were already beginning to withdraw to their initial positions, lost half as much as Krivosheev and his team had calculated – 34,449 soldiers and officers.[126] The different versions that come to light when analysing the archival TsAMO RF documents can be seen in Table 6 (see Steppe Front, Columns 2 and 5)

Table 6: Personnel casualties for the Voronezh and Steppe Fronts in the Kursk strategic defensive operation according to data from various sources

Type of casualty	According to Krivosheev's data, 5–23 July (19 days)*	According to Front Headquarters report**			Front casualties for July***
		Total for operation	Including		
			4–16 July	16–22 July	
1	2	3	4	5	6
Voronezh Front from 4 to 22 July (19 days)					
Irrecoverable, inc.	27,542	46,505	42,977	3,528	61,302
– dead		20,578	18,097	2,481	30,003
– MIA		25,898	24,851	1,047	31,226
Medical	46,350	54,427	47,272	7,155	92,196
Total	73,892	100,932	90,249	10,683	154,352
Steppe Front losses for the period	9–23 July			20–31 July	20–31 July
Irrecoverable, inc.	27,452		–	8,657	8,748
– dead			–	6,167	6,258
– MIA			–	2,490	2,490
Medical	42,606		–	25,683	25,792
Total	70,058	21,000	–	34,340	34,686
Total for the two *fronts*	143,950	122,000	–	45,023	189,038

* *The Seal of Secrecy Has Been Removed*, p. 188.
** TsAMO RF, f. 203, op. 2843, d. 301, l. 255; f. 240, op. 2795, d. 3, l. 204ob.
*** Ibid., f. 203, op. 2870, d. 44, ll. 801, 840, 848, 931; f. 426, op. 10753, d. 8; f. 240, op. 2795, d. 35, l. 123; f. 7th Guards Army, op. 5317, d. 11, l. 376 (calculated by the authors; the table shows only the main types of casualty).

How could such a great discrepancy in the *front* casualty figures have arisen? Let us turn to the casualty reports for July. As experience shows (and Krivosheev confirms this), the monthly reports compiled with consideration of types of casualties and personnel categories are more complete and precise (Column 6 in Table 6). Moreover, both Voronezh and Steppe Front forces did, in fact, conduct active operations until the end of July. By this time headquarters had acquired the ability to calculate casualties more precisely.

According to the monthly report, Voronezh Front forces lost 99,596 soldiers and officers from 1 to 30 July 1943.[127] This number is practically the same as the one given in the report from the *front*'s chief of staff. However, there is another document in the archive in which the Voronezh Front's total casualty figures are given, taking personnel categories into account; they exceed the figures cited in *The Seal of Secrecy Has Been Removed* by 1.5 times (see Table 7).

The difference in the figures is explained by the fact that casualties from the 7th Guards Army (23,390 men) and the 69th Army (26,267 men) for the period 1–15 July (a total of 52,657 men) were excluded from the reports in connection with their transfer into the composition of the Steppe Front. However, in Steppe Front documents these two armies' casualties were, quite logically, taken into account only from the moment of their inclusion into the *front*'s composition. Konev did not want to take upon himself the blame for something that was not his responsibility in the first place (he hardly would have agreed during his lifetime with such a distribution of casualties between the *fronts*). As a result, the 7th Guards Army and the 69th Army casualties for 5–20 July fell out of the total figures for both *fronts*. One cannot in any way agree with this!

Let us try to puzzle out this kaleidoscope of figures. Casualties for both *fronts* are summarized in Table 8 for the clarity and convenience of

Table 7: Voronezh Front personnel casualties, taking into account their categories, for July 1943*

Period	Officers	Noncommissioned Officers	Enlisted	Total
1–15 July	7,648	31,574	70,877	110,099
15 July–1 August	2,911	10,035	25,294	38,240
Total	10,559	41,609	96,171	148,339
Percentage of Total	7.1	28.1	64.8	100.0

*TsAMO RF, f. 203, op. 2843, d. 427, l. 17.

subsequent calculations. Here, troop casualties for the 7th Guards Army and the 69th Army are given in two places: for 1–19 July (and they are greater than for the period 1–15 July) they are included in the composition of the Voronezh Front, and for 20–31 July they are included in the composition of the Steppe Front. This provides a truer picture of the distribution of casualties between the *fronts*, and one which corresponds to the actual course of combat operations (see Table 8).

The Voronezh Front thus lost in the order of 154,600 soldiers and officers, which, taking into account the armies transferred to it from the composition of the Steppe Front, amounts to 24 per cent of its strength. In absolute numbers the *front* lost 4.5 times more than the Steppe Front, whose casualties amounted to 7.7 per cent of its strength.[128] Obviously, therefore, casualties for the 7th Guards Army and the 69th Army for 5–19 July 'fell out' of the totals. The *front*'s average daily casualties for the defensive period from 4 to 16 July, including those of the 7th Guards Army and the 69th Army, numbered no fewer than 12,000 soldiers and officers, that is, three times greater than shown in Table 5.

Thus, without calculating the replacements they received, the Voronezh Front and the Steppe Front lost no fewer than 190,000 soldiers and officers in July. Both *fronts* suffered, in particular, many MIAs, in the order of 33,000 men (20 per cent of the overall casualties). Undoubtedly, a large part of them had been captured. According to German information, 24,000 Soviet soldiers and officers had been captured by 13 July, and an additional 10,000 between 13 and 16 July.[129] These are enormous numbers, considering that Red Army troops exceeded those of the enemy in forces and means.

The 69th Army lost more than everyone in the July fighting – 40,500 men, with 18,800 irrecoverable losses (46 per cent of the overall losses), including 12,400 MIAs (31 per cent). The 7th Guards Army lost 38,300 men in July, including more than 4,000 MIAs. In all, both these armies lost around 79,000 soldiers and officers, including in the order of 55,000 men before being transferred to the composition of the Steppe Front, of whom 14,500 (26 per cent) were MIA.[130]

Proceeding to more precise information for July, we can determine *front* casualties in the defensive operation (to 23 July inclusive). So as not to tire the reader with complex calculations, we will show our results immediately. Voronezh Front casualties for July totalled 154,600 men, and casualties during the operation (not counting the 27th Army and the 47th Army) numbered 144,000 men (approximately 22 per cent of its strength, taking into account the reserves that had been transferred to it); average daily casualties (7,579 men) were twice as high as claimed by official numbers. Steppe Front

Table 8: Summary information about personnel casualties for the Voronezh and Steppe Fronts in July 1943*

Armies (formations)	Total**	Irrecoverable			Medical		POW	Other reasons
		Killed	MIA	Total	Wounded	Sick		
Voronezh Front (July)								
5th Guards Tank Army	10,545	2,780	1,079	3,859	6,465	174	2	45
2nd Guards Tank Corps (from 6 July)	2,314	789	27	816	1,450	46		2
2nd Tank Corps (from 8 July)	2,669	490	1,094	1,584	1,073	9		3
5th Guards Army	23,848	4,881	1,070	5,951	16,981	790		126
6th Guards Army	28,784	5,051	8,041	13,092	14,718	732	36	206
1st Tank Army	12,929	3,517	2,145	5,662	6,847	378		42
40th Army	10,784	1,430	2,565	3,995	5,138	1,530	2	119
38th Army	3,813	460	271	731	1,856	1,171		55
27th Army****	1,362	28		28	56	1,188		90
47th Army****	1,254	34		34	52	1,122		46
2nd Air Army	588	97	352	449	92	39		8
Front units	706	101	20	121	243	328		14
For the *front*, excluding 7th Guards Army and 69th Army	99,596	19,658	16,664	36,322	54,971	7,507	40	756
69th Army (1–19 July)	26,415	4,351	10,587	14,938	11,024	387	27	39
7th Guards Army (1–19 July)	28,578	6,086	3,969	10,055	17,867	591	6	59
Total for the *front*	154,589	30,095	31,220	61,315	83,862	8,485	73	854
Steppe Front (20–31 July)								
69th Army	14,105	2,018	1,807	3,825	9,927	295	43	15
7th Guards Army*****	9,713	2,222	102	2,324	7,066	286	2	35
53rd Army	10,239	1,860	407	2,267	7,345	605		22
5th Army and *front* units	392	66	180	246	57	60		29
Total for the *front*	34,449	6,166	2,496	8,662	24,395	1,246	45	101
Totals	189,038	36,261	33,716	69,977	108,257	9,731	118	955

*TsAMO RF, f. 203, op. 2870, d. 44, ll. 801, 840, 848, 931; f. 426, op. 10753, d. 8; f. 240, op. 2795, d. 35, l. 123; f. 7th Guards Army, op. 5317, d. 11, l. 37.

** All casualty calculations were done without taking replacements into account.

*** According to reports from military units.

**** 27th Army and 47th Army did not conduct active combat operations in July.

***** Casualties for 81st Guards Rifle Division (4,152 men) have been computed in those of 7th Guards Army.

casualties (20–23 July) were in the order of 22,000 (around 5 per cent of over-all strength), with average daily casualties of 5,500. Both *fronts* lost 166,000 soldiers and officers on the southern face of the Kursk salient, that is, 22,000 more than the authors of the statistical study had calculated.

The ratio of personnel casualties for the Voronezh and Steppe Fronts and Army Group South during the defensive operation on the southern face of the Kursk salient was 1:3.8 (44,000:166,000) in the enemy's favour.[131]

*   *   *

Doubts also exist as to the reliability of Krivosheev's information regarding the Central Front's casualties (33,897 men; that is, 4.6 per cent of its initial strength). However, by 12 July (the beginning of the Orel offensive operation) the *front*'s troop strength had dropped by 92,700 men.[132] According to other information, the *front's* troop strength for this intermediate period changed as follows: overall by 70,595 men (711,570 – 640,975), and with regard to the combat strength by 70,600 (510,983 – 440,383).[133] Let us stop at these numbers. For that time the *front*'s order of battle had almost not changed: two rifle brigades had left and one tank brigade had arrived. Because of this, the *front*'s troop strength might have dropped by a maximum of 7,000 men. A loss of 63,000 men (12 per cent of the *front*'s combat strength on 1 July) can in no way be explained other than as combat casualties during the fighting from 5 to 11 July. This is 29,000 men greater than suggested by Krivosheev's numbers.

Thus, three *fronts* (Central, Voronezh and Steppe) lost a total of some 229,000 men during the defensive operation; that is, 85,000 more than the authors of *The Seal of Secrecy Has Been Removed* had calculated.

Casualties for the enemy's Army Groups Centre and South during the offensive on the Kursk salient amounted to approximately 70,000 men. In this case, the ratio of human casualties on both sides was 1:3.3 (70,000:229,000) in the enemy's favour.[134]

There is a strange thing: there is one source for computing Soviet human losses – the Central Archive of the Ministry of Defence – but the difference in total numbers and conclusions is sometimes enormous. This means that Red Army losses need to be verified and corrected, and most probably increased.

At a meeting of the Association of World War II Historians at the end of 2005, Krivosheev negatively responded to the question, 'Will the numbers that have already been published be refined?' Taking advantage of the occasion, one of the authors of this work gave his book about the Battle of Prokhorovka to Krivosheev, asking the latter to turn his attention to the fact that the *front* casualty figures had been manipulated in *The Seal of Secrecy Has Been Removed*. Essentially, the authors of the statistical study had been accused of falsification. Having noted down the giver's address, a staff member of Krivosheev's department promised to respond without fail to the criticism. However, to this day there has still been no response, because in his conclusions the author of the book relied on the same archive documents that Krivosheev had. In fact, in private conversations General Staff officers told that author that he was attacking their chiefs – the heads at that time of the General Staff's archive and military-memorial centre – in vain: because of their official status they were forced to support the official line regarding the issue of Red Army casualties in the Great Patriotic War.

Why were all these contrivances with the casualty figures necessary? Why did the authors of *The Seal of Secrecy Has Been Removed* ignore the summary report of the Steppe Front to the General Staff about casualties for 20–31 July? In the new edition of their work, the authors allotted twice as much space to this operation, including there the subsections, 'Composition of the Forces of the Opposing Sides' and 'Course of the Operation'.[135] As before, however, there was not a word about the Steppe Front, which had suffered the same casualties as the Voronezh Front. In our opinion, the point of the authors' unsubstantiated redistribution of casualties between the two *fronts* was to somehow smooth over the grave impressions of the Voronezh Front's enormous casualties, especially as compared with the enemy's casualties.

During the Kursk defensive operation, Soviet forces suffered huge losses when repelling enemy strikes. In this regard, the idea is sometimes expressed that it would have been better to forestall the enemy by shifting to a strategic offensive and taking advantage of Soviet numerical superiority, and that shifting to a deliberate defence was a mistake. It is much simpler to make an assessment now, when the consequences of some decision or another are known. In our opinion, the mistake was not in their shifting to the defence, but rather in their inability to fully use their advantages.

In 1968 a military-scientific conference was held in dedication to the 25th anniversary of the victory in the Battle of Kursk. During the discussion of the main issues of the battle a conclusion was reached that was bold for its time:

> In researching the events of the Battle of Kursk, as well as of other battles and operations of the past war, **it is extremely desirable to subject to special examination the issue of casualties, after having shown the correspondence of losses to the results that have been**

attained ... [This] **would make it possible to more objectively assess the role of individual armies and officers in the achievement of victory in the Battle of Kursk.**[136]

The preparation of *The Seal of Secrecy Has Been Removed* for publication in 1993 coincided with the 50th anniversary of the Soviet victory in the Battle of Kursk. An unprecedented event was planned for 12 July 1993 in Moscow: a military-historical conference including representatives of the military historians of Germany, the country that had fought against the USSR. In particular, Lieutenant-Colonel Karl-Heinz Frieser, a PhD in History who worked at the Bundeswehr's military history directorate, took part in the conference. Frieser had introduced into scholarly usage a number of previously unknown facts and documents.[137]

It was intended that a similar event, also dedicated to the 50th anniversary of the Battle of Kursk, would be held in West Germany. Undoubtedly, the section of work concerning the Kursk defensive operation was refined, taking into consideration the upcoming debates with the Germans. It is namely for this reason that the authors, when speaking about the results of the operation, left out any mention of the Steppe Front and the losses ascribed to it. In the new military encyclopedia there was also no mention at all of the participation of the Steppe Front in the defensive operation on the southern face of the Kursk salient: 'During the defensive battles, Voronezh and Central Front troops wore down and bled the enemy's shock groups, which had lost around 100,000 men, more than 1,200 tanks and assault guns, around 850 guns and mortars, and more than 1,500 aircraft.[138]

It is difficult to say on what this information about enemy losses is based. However, as a result of this simplistic manipulation of numbers, the ratio of human casualties of the two sides began to look completely decent: the Central and Voronezh Fronts lost (according to Krivosheev's data) a total of 107,800 men, as opposed to 100,000 enemy casualties. One could comfortably go to international symposia with such data.

In his talk in September 1993, one of the Soviet representatives at the symposium in Ingolstadt (West Germany) estimated the human casualty ratio for the opposing sides in the Battle of Kursk as 4.3:1, in favour of the Germans. During Operation 'Citadel' (the German forces' offensive operation), the casualty ratio was 2:1 in the Wehrmacht's favour; during the counteroffensive it was 6:1, once again to the Red Army's disadvantage.[139] [Authors' note: most likely, the unjustifiably increased Steppe Front casualties were shifted here.]

The scale of the reduced human casualties in the Kursk defensive operation of 1943 does not compare in any way with the unsuccessful operations of

1941. In this case, however, the political bias of the authors and their attempts to embellish the picture of the Battle of Kursk, victory in which meant the conclusion of the radical turning point in the Great Patriotic War (which began with the Battle of Stalingrad), are very revealing.

The authors of the statistical study are consistent: they lowered casualties not only for personnel, but also for weapons and materiel. Thus, in his summary, General N.F. Vatutin, Commander of the Voronezh Front, reported that the *front* lost 1,387 tanks and 33 self-propelled guns, while the *front* chief of staff reported (5–23 July) 1,571 tanks and 57 self-propelled guns.[140] However, according to Krivosheev's information, the three *fronts* (Central, Voronezh and Steppe) together lost 1,614 tanks and self-propelled guns;[141] that is, approximately the amount that the Voronezh Front had lost alone according to the reports of its leadership! Meanwhile, according to a 23 July casualty report from the headquarters of the Red Army's armoured and mechanized forces, from 5 to 20 July the Voronezh Front had lost 1,254 tanks out of its available 2,924 (taking into account all newly arrived tank units in its composition). Another document described the loss of 1,223 tanks from 5 to 13 July (if this is true, then during the latter week the *front* lost only 31 tanks, which does not correspond to the information for the 5th Guards Tank Army).

On 17 July Colonel Zaev, Deputy Chief of Staff of Armoured and Mechanized Forces, reported that from 5 to 15 July Voronezh Front had lost 890 tanks (perhaps he meant both tanks and self-propelled guns).[142] Apparently the 5th Guards Tank Army's losses had not been entered into this number under the pretext that the army was associated with the Steppe Front. Comparing this number with the losses of Rotmistrov's army (334 tanks and self-propelled guns), we obtain approximately the same figures: 1,224 or 1,254. Taking into account the latter number, the losses in armour by 20 July for the three *fronts* could have amounted to no fewer than 1,900 tanks and self-propelled guns. If we orient ourselves on the average number of Voronezh Front losses (1,500 tanks and self-propelled guns) and refined information on enemy losses (320), then the ratio of losses of the opposing sides on the southern face of the Kursk salient is approximately 4.7:1 in the enemy's favour.[143]

Colonel I.N. Venkov, a representative of Soviet historians (head of General Staff's archival and military-memorial centre), confirmed this number at the 35th International Symposium on Military History in Ingolstadt in September 1993. Speaking about the Voronezh Front's casualties, he cited the same number of tanks that had been lost: 890. He also estimated Army Group South's losses in Operation 'Citadel' (according to Soviet information) as 2,644 tanks and 35 self-propelled guns, and the Central Front's losses from

5 to 15 July as 651 tanks and self-propelled guns versus 928 for Army Group Centre.[144] As to the reaction of the German participants at the symposium to this 'discovery', one can only guess ...

It is known that a committee was established on Stalin's order, under the chairmanship of G.M. Malenkov, a member of the State Defence Committee and Secretary of the Party Central Committee, to analyse the reasons for the failure of the 5th Guards Tank Army's counterstroke and the large losses in men and tanks during the operation. The materials of this committee on the Voronezh Front (and there are hundreds of pages of documents) have been stored up to now in the Presidential Archive (formerly the archive of the General Secretary of the Central Committee of the CPSU), to which common researchers do not have access. Why were they not declassified? In the end the enemy was defeated in the Battle of Kursk and Soviet forces won an indisputable victory! Evidently, there is something to hide ... There, the losses in men and tanks are not in percentages, as A.M. Vasilevsky reported to Stalin. The reasons for the significant disproportion of troop casualties for the opposing sides are surely made clear and mentioned there. After all, it is thought that the losses for the attackers are usually three times greater than those of the defenders.

The examples examined above attest that the computation of casualties according to troop reports, without taking replacements into account, chronically underestimates the Red Army's actual casualties. To eliminate the enormous hole in the calculation of casualties, the authors had to introduce the notorious 'unrecorded casualties'. Therefore, information about Soviet troop casualties in operations of all scales as described by Krivosheev's team of authors requires verification and correction; as a rule, those casualty numbers should be increased.

The authors of the statistical study state that in their calculations they took into account 'archive materials of the German military command'. They took these into account when they were clearly noted in corresponding captured documents. At least in the description of strategic operations, they usually did not show irrecoverable losses that were fewer than the number of prisoners captured by the Germans. However, in summarizing the results for the year, this approach was not always taken. Thus, according to the authors' information, casualties for 1941 amounted to 3,137,673 men. This is fewer than the Germans captured in that same year: 3,350,639. We have already said that, according to Krivosheev's information, in 1941 there was a total of 2,335,482 MIAs and POWs; that is, a whole million fewer.[145] Therefore, one should not forget about the 5.3 million dead, MIA and POW Soviet troops for the first six months of 1941. These numbers did not come from nowhere.

Chapter 3

Results of the computation of Soviet troop casualties by the authors of *Russia and the USSR in Wars of the 20th Century*

Even using the authors' clearly understated numbers, we notice an overwhelming disproportion in the irrecoverable losses of the opposing sides in those few strategic operations that we have examined. Firstly, we analysed the number of Soviet personnel losses in operations of the first and, in part, second periods of the war, when Soviet forces had to fight severe defensive battles and quickly withdraw into the depths of the country. The main difficulty in computing military-operational losses, including irrecoverable ones, in these operations is that information from formations and armies that had become encircled or had withdrawn to a great depth sometimes failed to reach *front* headquarters and the General Staff.

Poorly organized personnel records in units and formations, along with irregular, unreliable (sometimes simply false) reports from lower headquarters, made the computation of casualties difficult. This particularly characterized operations in which Red Army forces suffered defeat or were unable to achieve their assigned goal. Such losses created incentives for understating the actual number of personnel losses with the aim of reducing or hiding the enormous imbalance of Soviet troop casualties in comparison with enemy casualties.

We have not analysed the offensive operations of 1944 and 1945, in which losses are easier to calculate. Because of the significant reduction in the number of MIAs and POWs, irrecoverable losses were reduced. Beginning in the third quarter of 1942, they dropped below medical casualties.[1] Personnel records somewhat improved within the troop units and at headquarters, and troop reports became more reliable. The operational training of the Soviet command improved immeasurably, and troops acquired great experience in conducting combat actions. The Red Army carried out a series of large-scale operations that ended with the encirclement and defeat of large enemy groupings. Among these was one of the largest: the Stalingrad strategic offensive operation, which marked the beginning of the fundamental turning point in the war. During this operation the enemy lost more than 800,000 men, including more than 91,000 POWs from 10 January to 2 February 1943 alone. Soviet troop casualties were 485,777 men (including 154,885 irrecoverable),[2] a ratio of 1.6:1 in favour of the Red Army. Once again, though, this does not take into account the GHQ reserves and field replacements who had been introduced into the battle.

However, it was not always so. A comparison of two base maps – those of the Battle of Smolensk (10 July–10 September 1941) and the Smolensk offensive operation (7 August–2 October 1943), as referenced in the *Soviet Military Encyclopedia*, Vol. 7, pp. 400–1, illustrates the difference between the Soviet and German planning and conduct of several offensive operations. Even someone who is not versed in military affairs will see the difference. In essence, in this case the Soviet offensive boiled down to frontally squeezing the Germans out of their well fortified positions. Unfortunately, even after Stalingrad, the Red Army did not always have enough military expertise to conduct successful encirclement operations. Time and careful reconnaissance were required to regroup and search for weak points in the enemy's defence. It was simpler to just forge on ahead. However, such a straight-line method of waging war was inevitably accompanied by heavy casualties.

Unfortunately, despite the continual numerical superiority of Soviet forces over the enemy and the latter's complete loss of the initiative after the Battle of Kursk, victory was rarely achieved with little loss of blood. Thus, in the Dnepr-Carpathian strategic offensive operation (24 December 1943–17 April 1944) the Red Army lost more than 1.1 million (1,109,528) soldiers and officers, of which 270,198 were irrecoverable.[3] It must be acknowledged that the Germans often held fast in the face of attack and tended to withdraw in a timely fashion (right up to Berlin!). Therefore, the number of POWs captured by Soviet troops before Germany's capitulation in no way compares with the number of Soviet POWs. This is important since POWs comprised a significant portion of the irrecoverable losses for both sides.

It is well known how disastrously the Great Patriotic War began for the USSR. During the war's initial period, Soviet forces suffered enormous irrecoverable losses. One can see the extent of them in Table 9, where the casualties of the USSR armed forces for the third quarter of 1941, including June, are compared with those of Germany.

It is easy to see that such an unfavourable casualty ratio for the Red Army, especially for irrecoverable losses, is mainly due to the huge number of Soviet MIAs and POWs.

Table 9: Ratio of casualties of the armed forces of the USSR and Germany, 22 June–30 September 1941*

Type of casualty		Red Army	Wehrmacht (including Waffen SS)	Ratio
Irrecoverable	killed and dead	430,578	111,853	3.8:1
	MIA and POW	1,699,099	23,368	72.7:1
	Total	2,129,677	135,221	15.7:1
Medical	wounded, contused, burned	665,961	392,325	1.7:1
	sick	21,665	127,800	1:5.9
	Total	687,626	520,125	1.3:1
Totals		2,817,303	655,346	4.3:1

* *Russia and the USSR in Wars of the 20th Century*, 2001, pp. 250–1, Table 133; *Germany and the Second World War*. Volume V/I. *Wartime Administration, Economy, and Manpower Resources 1939–1941* (New York: Oxford University Press, 2009), p. 1020.

Let us recall that, according to information from Krivosheev's team, irrecoverable losses for Western Front troops were 42.4 times as great as those of the enemy, while irrecoverable losses for the Southwestern Front, despite its superiority over the enemy in forces and means, were 30.9 times greater.[4] In the Kiev strategic defensive operation, irrecoverable losses for Army Group South forces, who captured 492,885 prisoners during the battle, amounted to 24,002, a ratio of 21:1 in favour of the enemy.[5]

Information from independent researchers draws an even more depressing picture. According to Ivlev's computations, the ratio of Northwestern Front's irrecoverable losses was 50:1 (246,961:4,978), and that of its overall losses was 13.1:1 (260,298:19,854) in favour of the enemy.[6] In the Moscow strategic defensive operation the ratio of irrecoverable losses was 23:1.[7]

Thus, the disproportion of irrecoverable losses in 1941 hovers in the range of 15–42, and climbs in some cases to a factor of 50. Suffice to say that in little more than six months of 1941 Soviet troops captured 9,147 prisoners[8] (according to Krivosheev's data: 10,602),[9] while the Germans captured almost 3.4 million. And, of course, there were other battles still ahead that would end with the encirclement and capture of hundreds of thousands of Red Army soldiers and officers. At the same time, before the beginning of the Soviet offensive at Stalingrad on 19 November 1942, there were no masses of Germans surrendering to be taken prisoners. By this time a total of only 19,782 German POWs had been taken to Soviet camps.[10]

Even during the last period of the war, when the situation had fundamentally changed in favour of the USSR, Soviet success was still paid for dearly. In 1944, despite a number of impressive victories, the Red Army's irrecoverable losses equalled those of the Germans. Later, we will illustrate this, as well as the fact that in 1945, Germany, together with Hungary, irrecoverably lost twice as many people as the Soviet Union and its allies. All these impressive achievements, however, in no way fully compensated for the enormous imbalance in irrecoverable losses that distinguished the first half of the war. After all, at that time victory was already near at hand, such that there was simply not enough time to pay the enemy back for the tragedy of the Red Army's first defeats.

Against the background of these facts, the conclusion of the authors of the statistical study – that irrecoverable losses for Germany and its allies on the Soviet-German Front 'turned out to be only 30 per cent fewer than similar losses for Soviet troops (8.6 million men for them, 11.4 million men for us). Thus, the ratio of irrecoverable losses was 1:1.3'[11] – seems strange, to say the least. How and when did they succeed in compensating for such a disproportion in irrecoverable losses?

In his next work Krivosheev repeated this conclusion, with the stipulation that he had in mind casualties **'calculated expeditiously according to monthly troop reports'** – 11,444,100 men (**roster** strength).[12]

This is a very significant stipulation! In any case, he thereby prepares the path for withdrawal: he says that he and his team had nothing to do with any irregularities in the conclusion, and that they were simply working from reports to the General Staff (though at one point one of the authors admitted, in the heat of controversy, that 'we cannot be responsible for the numbers that someone sometime wrote in reports').

What roster strength during the first months of the war could they be talking about? On 16 August 1941 the People's Commissariat of Defence issued Order no. 0296, 'On Putting in Order Records and Reporting the Numerical Strength, Combat Composition and Personnel Losses in Field Armies and in Districts'. The order mentioned that

> ... records of the numerical strength and combat composition, personnel casualties and captured prisoners and materiel in field armies and records of roster strength in military district headquarters are being appallingly kept ... [This] is the result of a criminally neglectful and irresponsible attitude toward records and a lack of understanding of their importance and their absolute necessity for uninterrupted troop supply and personnel replacements.[13]

No less interesting is the authors' concept of 'calculated expeditiously according to monthly troop reports', the value of which we already know. It turns out they introduced this

> ... in order to approximate as closely as possible the calculations and assessments of actual personnel casualties; subsequently, when comparing and analysing the scale of losses with respect to quarters, years, periods and other parameters, the maximum number of irrecoverable losses (11,444,100 men) was taken, as indicated in Table 120, calculated expeditiously during the war. Proceeding from this, all subsequent calculations of the numerical and percentage casualty ratios were produced ...[14]

Essentially, the authors admit that they put the cart before the horse. They used, as the basis for their calculations, the results of the work of the General Staff committee for determining casualties, headed by General of the Army S.M. Shtemenko (1966–1968), and a similar Ministry of Defence committee, headed by General of the Army M.A. Gareev (1988). Let us recall that Gareev's committee was established in April 1988, and on 16 December that same year Minister of Defence D.T. Yazov had already sent a note to the Central Committee of the CPSU in which the number of irrecoverable losses of servicemen was said to be 11,444,100. Could Gareev's committee have verified the reliability of Shtemenko's calculations in just half a year? Had such a task even been assigned?

Then Krivosheev's team engaged in the work; in their words, in 1988–1993 they were involved in comprehensive statistical research of archive documents and other materials containing information about personnel casualties in the army, navy and NKVD border and internal troops. Here the authors discovered many gaps in the casualty statistics in the archive materials for the first period of the Great Patriotic War. No one dared, however, to doubt the authenticity of the number reported to the Central Committee of the CPSU. What was left for the authors to do, other than to adjust their own assessment of actual personnel losses with respect to quarters, years, periods and other parameters to the above-mentioned number? Otherwise their entire calculation concept could have tumbled down overnight.

Thus, according to Krivosheev's calculations, it turns out that, despite the severest defeats in operations during the first and second periods of the war, the Red Army defeated the Wehrmacht with personnel casualties that were only 30 per cent greater than those of the Germans. The unreliability of the casualty reports to the General Staff and a conveniently similar conclusion about casualty ratios arouse legitimate doubt among the majority of independent researchers. Debates about the scale of Soviet troop casualties in the Great Patriotic War and about the ratio of irrecoverable losses for the armed forces of the USSR and Germany have not subsided even to this day.

Let us examine the arguments and calculations of Krivosheev's team. First and foremost, let us analyse their information concerning Soviet MIAs and POWs, who amount to almost 40 per cent of irrecoverable losses for the USSR armed forces, according to the works under examination. Let us try to figure out how many there really were.

First, however, we must unfortunately state that Krivosheev's team was clearly at odds with basic elementary school arithmetic. His people either did not know or were unable to employ in practice the simplest rules of rounding off. Thus, for them, in one table the total irrecoverable human losses of the armed forces of Germany's allies on the Soviet-German Front from 22 June 1941 to 9 May 1945 numbered 1,468,145 men.[15] However, in the following table, located on the next page, this number was for some reason rounded up to 1,468,200.[16] The same also goes for the number of Soviet POWs who returned from captivity at or after the end of the war: 1,836,562 men.[17] After this number is rounded, it for some strange reason turns into 1,836,000.[18] It turns out that the numerous distinguished authors of the statistical study did not know the elementary rules of rounding up and rounding down. Or, perhaps, they did everything they could to play down the Red Army's losses and at the same time to overstate enemy casualties.

This is not, however, the main shortcoming of their book. Others that we are going to spend more time on are much more serious. To start with, let us take their compilation, 'Balance Sheet of the Use of Human Resources Drafted (Mobilized) during the Great Patriotic War, 1941–1945'.[19] There, the army and navy personnel roster strength at the beginning of the war is indicated as 4,826,900 men, while after the end of the war it is listed as 12,839,800. At the same time, such a highly qualified and competent scholarly team as the Russian Federation Ministry of Defence's Institute of Military History published in 1994–1999 the most detailed statistical books on the order of battle and numerical strength of the USSR armed forces in 1941–1945. One can learn from them that, in fact, on the eve of the war the USSR had 4,629,500 men and that immediately after the victory over Germany, at the beginning of June 1945, there were 11,999,100. This includes 10,549,900 in the ranks, 1,046,000 being treated in hospitals, and 403,200 in formations of other departments that were subordinated under the People's Commissariat of Defence.[20]

These numbers were used in the balance sheet of the human resources mobilized during the Great Patriotic War. They were not needlessly introduced; the difference between them is reflected most directly in the magnitude of irrecoverable losses of Soviet servicemen during this period. The greater the difference, the smaller the magnitude of losses as a result of combat operations. If, according to the completely reliable information of the Institute of Military History, this number is 7,369,600 men, then Krivosheev's team changed the count to 8,012,900 without any explanation or citation of other sources.

As we have seen, only due to the use of numbers reflecting the numerical strength of the USSR armed forces before and after the war that did not correspond to reality did Krivosheev, completely without justification, reduce the number of casualties by 643,300 men. At the first appearance of his work in 1993, this still could have been justified by a lack of knowledge of the necessary facts. All subsequent editions (2001 and later), however, continue to be based on this same false information. This is unacceptable and can be explained only by bias on the part of the authors of the statistical study. Apparently, they were content to consciously ignore information that was inconvenient for them, information that by that time had been published by their own Ministry of Defence colleagues.

They did not, however, stop at this. The same balance sheet gives the figure of 3,798,200 servicemen who were released because of wounds and illness. In fact, far from all these men had been released: 1,154,800 of them returned to the ranks from leave after making a complete recovery.[21] Of the 3,614,600 men recorded in this balance sheet who were sent to work in industry, local air defence and interior guard troops, 142,800 were mobilized once again.[22] Krivosheev himself mentioned that another 939,700 were drafted again into the army on liberated territory.[23] For some reason, however, he forgot to add them to the 'receipts' of the above-mentioned balance sheet. This is how the total irrecoverable losses of the USSR armed forces were reduced at once by 2,880,600 men (643,300 + 1,154,800 + 142,800 + 939,700).

Taking into account all these men and, together with them, the 0.5 million MIA mobilized reservists, we see that irrecoverable losses for the USSR armed forces during the Great Patriotic War increase to 14,824,700 men. We will return to this figure, but now let us examine the no less important problem of the number of Soviet POWs.

According to Krivosheev's information, 3,396,400 men became MIAs or POWs during the war (based on reports to the General Staff).[24] Who could believe this number, which is approximately equal to the number of prisoners the Germans captured in 1941 alone? Moreover, the authors of *Russia and the USSR in Wars of the 20th Century* added to this number the so-called 'unrecorded casualties of the first months of the war' – 1,162,600 men,[25] as if in subsequent years Soviet forces were no longer in circumstances preventing headquarters from accounting for casualties. As a result, they obtained the figure of 4,559,000 POWs and MIAs.[26]

We cannot go any further without quoting from the work under examination:

> After a careful analysis of all sources it was preliminarily determined that during the war 5,059,000 Soviet servicemen were MIAs and POWs, of which 500,000 were mobilized reservists whom the Germans captured on their way to their military units. During further investigation it came to light that not all MIAs had been captured. Around 450,000–500,000 of them actually died or, being seriously wounded, remained on the battlefield that had been occupied by the enemy.[27]

We leave explaining the obtainment of these figures to the consciences of the authors. Further: 'As a result of studying various materials, the authors came to the conclusion that there were, in fact, around 4,559,000 servicemen **in German captivity, among whom 500,000 were mobilized reservists.**'[28]

Analysing the various sections of the statistical study, one gets the feeling that, regarding the leader of the team, his right hand did not know what his left hand was doing. Attempting by any means to come up with a ratio of casualties for the opposing sides in the Great Patriotic War that would be as favourable as possible for the USSR, the writers of the individual sections lost sight of the overall picture, and, as a result, began to contradict not only concrete reality but also each other. Having reduced the overall number of MIAs and POWs (to 4,559,000), they painted themselves into a corner. In attempting to cleave to Krivosheev's calculations, one could easily reach the point of absurdity. To illustrate this, let us try to calculate on the basis of his information the number of Soviet servicemen who succeeded in surviving German captivity.

One circumstance on which one cannot fail to pause interferes in these generally rather simple calculations. The authors included 500,000 mobilized reservists in the composition of the POWs, but with a flick of the wrist they numbered them among the ordinary civilian population, refusing them the right to be considered servicemen. These 0.5 million are placed into a separate line in Table 120, in which the computation of irrecoverable losses is presented. It is telling that this number in general affects nothing else there, unlike the other figures presented.[29] It also figures in Table 132, reflecting the balance sheet of the use of human resources who were drafted or mobilized during the Great Patriotic War.[30]

In connection with this, let us return to Krivosheev's talk at the meeting of the Association of Historians of the Second World War on 29 December 1998. Explaining the issue of the 500,000 reservists who had been mobilized but who had not reached their designated units, he claimed the following:

> Those who had been mobilized began to arrive at the military commissariats, and from them began to form teams to be sent to their units. Events, however, developed so swiftly that in the western military districts the teams never arrived at their units. The military commissariats managed to report that they had been conscripted, but the men did not arrive at the units. They were not equipped, had no weapons and had practically never fought. A few people made claims to us: they say that they [the 500,000] had to be associated with civilian casualties. **According to our laws, however, if a man arrived at a military commissariat and his conscription was registered, then he was already considered a serviceman and was part of the total number of those who had been conscripted (34,476,700).** Therefore, we had to consider casualties with and without them. Thus, demographic casualties with these conscripts amounted to 9,168,400 men.[31]

Krivosheev took the correct position during the preparation of *Russia and the USSR in Wars of the 20th Century*. Who, however, were these 'few people' who, despite the law, required that the team leader relegate these 500,000 mobilized men to civilian casualties? Why were their demands carried out? The solution to the puzzle proves quite simple: who could allow anyone to increase the demographic casualties, and therefore irrecoverable casualties, by 500,000 men at one stroke? It was obviously impossible, however, to completely ignore those 500,000. Therefore, the authors calculated the casualties sometimes with them, sometimes without them.

They excluded from the number of MIAs and POWs the 500,000 men who had died on the battlefield, but, at the same time, 'forgot' to add them to the number of dead (for example, a separate column in Table 120). Why all these strange manipulations? Because otherwise in the 'MIA, POW' chart there would have been a total of 4,059,000 Soviet servicemen – a number that is very difficult to justify. Moreover, this would have meant fewer than Germans and their allies in Soviet camps (4,376,300 men).[32]

Let us try to work out how many Soviet servicemen fell into German hands and how many of them survived. Krivosheev's books contain sufficient information to allow us to separate from the total number of MIAs and

POWs those Soviet servicemen who were lucky enough to escape from captivity or who survived the German camps. They can be sorted into the following:

- those released by the Germans before 1 May 1944 – 823,230;[33]
- those who had earlier been in encirclement and were recorded at the beginning of the war as MIA, and who were then conscripted a second time into the army on liberated territory – 939,700;
- those who returned from captivity after the war (according to information from repatriation organs) – 1,836,000;[34] and
- those who immigrated to other countries after the war – more than 180,000.[35]

Here, one must take into consideration an important nuance that somewhat complicates the calculations. Among the 939,700 who were conscripted again there may have also been those whom the Germans had earlier released from captivity. Nowhere does Krivosheev himself mention that these categories of men might overlap, but for the greatest accuracy of results it is necessary to avoid any possibility of double counting. In order to correctly understand this problem it is necessary, to begin with, to break down those whom the Germans released from captivity into separate categories, on the basis of the time of and reasons for their release. This is what we obtain:

1. From 25 July to 13 November 1941 Order no. 11/4590 from the quartermaster-general about the release of Soviet POWs based on nationality was in force. Relegated to this category were the Volga Germans, Balts, Ukrainians and later also the Belorussians. In accordance with this order, a total of 318,770 men had been released, of whom 277,761 were Ukrainians.
2. Subsequently, before 1 May 1944 another 504,460 Soviet POWs were released.[36] They were released only in those cases in which they had entered the ranks of the 'voluntary assistants' (the so-called 'Hiwi'[37]), security guards, *Polizei* or the voluntary Wehrmacht units.[38] In addition to them, the Germans freed only the legless, armless or blind, as well as men whose health was so poor that they were not able to work for the Reich. Some of these POWs were simply executed, while the others were sent back to the Motherland on foot. It is not surprising that in such poor conditions many of them died on the way, and not all those who survived lived until the liberation by the Red Army.[39] Even survivors did not matter for our purposes, as they were in no way fit to be conscripted again.

3. Finally, during the last year of the war the Germans released 200,000 Soviet POWs who had been sent to the 'eastern troops' in desperate attempts to reinforce them.[40] Krivosheev's team simply ignored these men; we, however, are definitely taking them into account.

It is apparent that there were significantly few actual candidates for reconscription among the latter two categories after the liberation of occupied Soviet territory. Indeed, viable candidates could be found only among the former POWs from the very first group. Furthermore, far from all of those could be conscripted, and here is why: their ranks had already begun to thin out in the autumn of 1941, when German *Einsatzgruppen* started a second check of the recently freed POWs. Among them, the Germans discovered 'a considerable percentage of suspicious elements', and, as usual, quickly shot them. When the Germans ultimately acknowledged an acute need for a cheap work force, they began, in March 1942, to once again take into captivity those who had earlier been released, as representatives of 'national minorities'. These acts, by order of the Supreme High Command of the German Army, continued into the future.[41]

Long, hard years of occupation and continuous deprivations, lack of food and illnesses also in no way contributed to the health and numerical strength of the former POWs who had been set free in 1941. Some of them joined the underground fighters and partisans and then perished in the struggle against the invaders. Others were forcefully sent to work in Germany. Among those the Germans had set free from captivity were also those who preferred to join one of the various categories of German minions. As the Red Army approached, these former POWs left for the west, together with their masters. During the Great Patriotic War persons of German nationality were generally not conscripted into the Red Army. Accordingly, those Volga Germans who had already begun their military service before the war and had been set free from captivity could in no way be part of the number of those who had been remobilized.

Today, it is not possible to precisely follow the fates of all Soviet POWs whom the Germans set free in 1941 on account of their nationality. However, information that we have at our disposal makes it possible to assume with a high degree of reliability that of those 318,770 men whom the Germans had set free by 13 November 1941, no more than half (159,000) could have been remobilized. We will use this number in our subsequent calculations. Therefore, the total number of Soviet servicemen who survived the war from the number of MIAs and POWs is 3,819,900 (823,200 + 200,000 − 159,000 + 939,700 + 1,836,000 + 180,000).

We will subtract these men from the overall number of MIAs and POWs (according to Krivosheev's information – 4,559,000, of whom 500,000 died or, being seriously wounded, remained on the battlefield and were captured by the enemy). We obtain a remainder of 239,100 (5.9 per cent of the overall number – 4,059,000) Soviet servicemen who died in German captivity. For comparison: as of 22 April 1956 there were 3,486,200 POWs from the armed forces of Germany and its allies in Soviet camps, of whom 518,500 (14.9 per cent) had died.[42]

An assessment of these numbers shows that the general death rate of Wehrmacht servicemen in Soviet captivity was 2.5 times higher than the same parameter for Red Army soldiers and their officers in German camps! This means that the conditions of existence in German captivity were much better than in Soviet captivity. Then what Nazi villainy can we be speaking of in this case?

Krivosheev's cunning statistics lead to the incredible conclusion that, in fact, there was no premeditated destruction of millions of Soviet POWs by the Germans. On the basis of his numbers, any falsifier of history can easily and simply prove that prisoners did not suffer from hunger, cold, illness or exhausting marches, that they were not shot for the slightest offence, that they were not forced to work to exhaustion for the Reich, that they were not subjected to any special cruelty or devious mockery. Such a thoroughly false summation does, in fact, whitewash one of the most monstrous crimes of the Nazis – the mass extermination of those defenceless Soviet servicemen who had fallen into their clutches.

In their attempt to avoid a similar accusation, the authors performed a trick (it is difficult to choose another word here) by including the 500,000 mobilized reservists in the number of MIAs and POWs, while simultaneously excluding those reservists from the balance sheet of Red Army servicemen casualties. With their inclusion, the number of those who died in captivity increases to 739,100 (16.2 per cent of 4,559,000), and the death rate of Red Army POWs exceeds, albeit by only a little, the corresponding parameter with respect to Germans and their allies in Soviet captivity.

The results of these calculations, both taking into account the MIA conscripted reservists and excluding them, are presented in Table 10.

In any case, the number obtained as a remainder in no way agrees with the number (2.5 million)[43] of Soviet servicemen who died in captivity, as calculated by Krivosheev. It should be noted that in one instance the authors nevertheless relegated the 0.5 million mobilized reservists to the number of irrecoverable casualties, obtaining here an overall loss of 11,944,100 men.[44]

Table 10: Number of Soviet POWs and MIAs according to Krivosheev's information (in thousands of men)

Types of casualties, categories of POWs and MIAs	Number of MIAs and POWs	
	Not including conscripted MIA reservists	Including conscripted MIA reservists
MIA and POW servicemen		
MIAs and POWs (according to troop reports and information from repatriation organs)	3,396.4	3,396.4
Unrecorded casualties from the first months of the war (died and MIAs in troops that did not send reports)	1,162.6	1,162.6
Total	4,559.0	4,559.0
Of whom did, in fact, die or, being seriously wounded, remained on the battlefield	500.0	500.0
Conscripted reservists MIA on the way to their units	–	500.0
POW according to Krivosheev's version	4,059.0	4,559.0
Avoided or survived captivity		
Remobilized	939.7	939.7
Of whom, former POWs	−159.0	−159.0
Set free by the Germans	1,023.2	1,023.2
Returned to the Motherland	1,836.0	1,836.0
Emigrated	180.0	180.0
Total	3,819.9	3,819.9
Remainder: those who died in captivity	239.1 (5.9%)	739.1 (16.2%)

* Former POWs are excluded from the number of remobilized MIAs as they are already included among those who were set free by the Germans.
** The number in parentheses represents the percentage of the overall number (4,059,000 or 4,559,000).

This number is not, however, mentioned again in the work, since it did not fit into the resulting casualty ratio for the opposing sides (1:1.3).

All these blatant numerical manipulations are eloquent evidence of the unreality of the claimed number of Soviet MIAs and POWs. Unsuccessfully attempting to justify the number 4,559,000, Krivosheev sometimes ties it to just POWs and other times to both POWs and MIAs. This is certainly not an accident. Doing so creates the impression that MIAs are taken into account in the calculations he presents. In fact, their number greatly exceeds the 500,000 stated in his books. MIAs are properly measured in the millions, and in no way were they not taken into account in the overall balance sheet of irrecoverable losses that the authors compiled. Also relegated to this number were those abandoned on the battlefield; those who drowned in the many rivers, lakes and marshes; those lost in caved-in trenches and dugouts, those buried by locals in shell craters, foxholes and anti-tank ditches, whom even now searchers are finding; and many other men who gave their lives for the Motherland.

Krivosheev's statements often fail to withstand even a simple comparison with his own information. For instance, he wrote:

> The casualty ratio was influenced by the fact that the number of Soviet POWs who died in Nazi camps (more than 2,500,000 men) exceeds by more than five times the number of enemy servicemen who died in Soviet captivity (420,000 men). Meanwhile, the overall number of POWs with respect to both sides was approximately the same (4,559,000 Soviet POWs and 4,376,300 German POWs).[45]

Let us immediately mention that something is clearly wrong here with the number of enemy servicemen who died in Soviet captivity (we will speak below in more detail on the number and composition of POWs from Germany and its satellites in Soviet camps). On another page of this very same book their overall number was figured to be significantly greater – 579,900, of whom 442,100 were from Germany.[46] The main discrepancy, however, is something else: how do the 939,700 men who were remobilized on territory that had been liberated by the Red Army (earlier calculated as MIAs) or who had been set free by the Germans during the war enter into the number 2,500,000, especially since Krivosheev stated the same thing elsewhere, but in more detail?

> Of the 4,559,000 Soviet servicemen who went missing in action or were captured by the Germans, only 1,836,000 (40 per cent) returned to the Motherland, while around 2.5 million men (55 per cent) died in captivity, and only a small number (more than 180,000 men) emigrated to other countries or returned to the Motherland, bypassing assembly areas.[47]

The sum obtained was 4,516,000; the remaining 43,000 inexplicably disappeared. However, the 823,230 POWs whom the Germans had set free before 1 May 1944, along with an additional 200,000 who were let go after this date and before the end of the war (a total of 1,023,230 men), were completely ignored.[48] Also not taken into account were the 939,700 who had been encircled and later remobilized into the army on liberated territory. As we have already shown, even considering the fact that a small part of those who had been remobilized had been in German captivity, the total number of

MIAs who managed to avoid it and POWs who survived it was 3,819,900 men. And, in fact, an additional 0.5 million died, not in captivity, but on the battlefield.

Therefore, the balance sheet of casualties (Table 132) also does not mention the 2.5 million who died in captivity; in no way do the numbers converge! This is not to mention the fact that 500,000 mobilized reservists, unjustifiably relegated to the country's civilian casualties, must definitely be included in the sum total of the USSR armed forces' military-operational casualties.

Now it is time to turn to the information about the overall number of Soviet POWs and the number of those among them who died, which contemporary German historians have at their disposal. Perhaps the most authoritative among them regarding this issue is Professor Christian Streit of the University of Heidelberg. It is not by chance that the official German history of the Second World War cites his book when illuminating the theme of Soviet POWs.[49] Even in his own work, Krivosheev also uses Streit's information several times.[50]

This is how the balance sheet of Soviet POWs looks, according to Streit's information. Using the number 5,734,528 as a starting point, he subtracted the following categories:

- set free by the Germans during the war: 1,023,230;
- in captivity on 1 January 1945: 930,287; and
- escaped by this time or liberated again by Soviet troops during the German withdrawal: approximately 500,000.[51]

Thus, according to Streit's information, around 3,281,000 men (57.2 per cent) perished in German captivity. He erred, however, in his computations of the number of Soviet POWs liberated by the Red Army during and after the war. This is not surprising; after all, without access to the Soviet archives, the German historian was forced to rely on what turned out to be an imprecise estimate by group IIa of the department of foreign armies 'East', dated 20 February 1945.[52]

Using Krivosheev's corresponding information, we can now refine the professor's numbers in this respect. According to him, there were 2,016,000 who had been set free (1,836,000 + 180,000 émigrés), and not Streit's 1,430,000 (930,000 + 500,000). To correctly determine the overall number of those Soviet servicemen who died in German captivity, however, it is absolutely necessary to take into account the fact that during the war some of them fell into the hands of Germany's allies. Some of these unfortunates also died there, and they numbered more than a few.

Two Romanian armies operated in the composition of Army Group South on the Soviet-German Front. In the two months of fighting for Odessa the 4th Army captured around 16,000 Red Army soldiers. By the summer of 1942, the 3rd Army had additionally captured no fewer than 87,000. The Romanians captured a total of more than 120,000 Soviet servicemen. Where Romanian troops were under direct German command, they handed over their captives to the Germans.[53] This rule applied not only to them, but also to the Hungarians, Italians, Spanish and Slovaks. Therefore, the Romanian authorities officially registered only 82,090 Soviet POWs. Of this number, 13,682 natives of Transnistria – territory annexed by Romania – were set free in 1943. A total of 5,221 POWs died in Romanian camps and 3,331 escaped, so that at the time Romania left the war (22 August 1944), 59,856 POWs were still there.[54]

Finnish forces fought independently, and all captured prisoners remained with them. During the war 64,188 Soviet POWs had fallen into Finnish hands, of whom 18,677 had died.[55]

Using Streit's data, together with this information, Krivosheev's balance sheet of Soviet troop casualties in the Great Patriotic War can be corrected, with interesting results. To better illustrate these results, we have collected them in Table 11. At the same time, we compare them with Krivosheev's analogous figures, proceeding from the number that he himself stated regarding the Red Army soldiers and officers who died in German captivity: 2.5 million men.

Table 11 demonstrates that around 2,818,000 men died in German captivity (almost half of all Soviet POWs there). This figure, distinct from Krivosheev's cunning statistics, clearly illustrates the savage ferocity with which the Nazis treated their captives.

In addition, it is immediately striking that, according to Krivosheev's results, the number of MIA servicemen is absurdly low. If we increase the number of POWs in his balance sheet to Streit's figure, then only around 305,000 were MIA. This falls considerably short of even the 0.5 million dead or wounded that Krivosheev himself mentions. Meanwhile, according to information in the TsAMO RF files, the number of MIA NCOs and soldiers alone exceeded 7 million men. Relatives and close friends still know nothing about their fate. The names of these servicemen are noted in the reports of commanders of military units (1,720,951) and in military commissariat records (5,435,311).

This number exceeds by many times the figure given by Krivosheev. It is not by chance that Streit, after becoming familiar with *The Seal of Secrecy Has Been Removed*, said that the calculation of the number of dead POWs made in

Table 11: Overall irrecoverable losses of the armed forces of the USSR, taking into account MIAs and POWs (in thousands of men)*

Type of Casualty, categories of POWs and MIAs	Using data from	
	Krivosheev	Streit
Killed and died Killed and died of wounds at stages of medical evacuation	5,226.8	5,226.8
Died of wounds in hospitals	1,102.8	1,102.8
Died of illness, perished as a result of accidents, condemned to execution	555.5	555.5
Total killed and died	6,885.1	6,885.1
MIAs and POWs MIAs, who actually died		
Actually died or, being seriously wounded, remained on the battlefield	500.0	500.0
MIA mobilized reservists	–	500.0
Total MIAs, who actually died	500.0	1,000.0**
MIAs, who avoided captivity		
Remobilized MIAs and former POWs	939.7	939.7
Of whom, former POWs	159.0	159.0
Total MIAs, who avoided captivity	780.7	780.7
POWs		
To the Germans		5,734.5
To the Romanians		82.1
To the Finns		64.2
Total POWs	5,539.2	5,880.8
Survived captivity		
Set free by the Germans	1,023.2	1,023.2
Returned to the Motherland	1,836.0	1,836.0
Emigrated	180.0	180.0
Total POWs, who survived captivity	3,039.2	3,039.2
Died in captivity		
German		2,817.7 (49.1%)
Romanian		5.2 (6.3%)
Finnish		18.7 (29.1%)
Total POWs, who died in captivity	2,500.0 (45.1%)	2,841.6 (48.3%)
Total MIAs and POWs	6,819.9	7,661.5
Difference with Krivosheev's data (4,559.0)	2,260.9	3,102.5
Total irrecoverable losses of servicemen	13,705.0	14,546.6

* Sources: *Russia and the USSR in Wars of the 20th Century*, 2001, p. 237, Table 120; Frolov, *Soviet-Finnish Captivity*, pp. 132, 307; Streit, *They Are Not Our Comrades*, pp. 258, 433; Axworthy, *Third Axis, Fourth Ally*, p. 217.

** It is very likely, in fact, that the number of the Red Army's MIAs who actually died significantly exceeds this figure. However, as of today there is not enough reliable information to accurately determine this number.

the book could not stand up to 'a more detailed verification', and reproached Krivosheev for ignoring German documents and the results of German research.[56] No work on the history of the Great Patriotic War can claim to be complete and objective without having considered this most important source of information, and without having compared information from Russian and German archives.

Most important here, however, is the obtained number of total irrecoverable losses of Soviet servicemen in the Great Patriotic War, which is 14,546,600 men. It is strikingly close to the number 14,540,700, which takes into account the uncompensated deficit of Red Army personnel losses on 1 March 1942 (3,096,000). The value of USSR irrecoverable casualties that we obtained earlier after correcting the numerical size of the USSR armed forces before and after the war, accounting for those who returned to action after injury leave, those who were remobilized from industry, local air defence and local internal security forces, and reservists who went MIA – 14,824,700 – is not at all far from it. It exceeds the total number from Table 11 by only 1.9 per cent. Crucially, all these results were obtained by completely different independent methods. Such a multifaceted coincidence cannot have come about by chance; it convincingly attests that the results of our calculations are sufficiently close to reality.

However it would be premature to take them for the ultimate truth. Judging by some information, which will be discussed later, the data for our calculations include chronic underestimation of irrecoverable losses. This is especially true regarding MIAs. Nevertheless we will base our further analysis on the results computed in Table 12 until new reliable information becomes available. Results obtained in this way should be considered a lower limit of the possible number of irrecoverable losses of the armed forces of the USSR in the Great Patriotic War.

Many historians and researchers who disagree with Krivosheev's numbers have been concerned that those numbers can be used to create a new history of the Great Patriotic War. Taking into account the ever-growing criticism of the information of his author team and in accordance with Decree no. 37 of the President of the Russian Federation, 'Issues of Memorializing Those Who Perished in Defence of the Fatherland', dated 22 January 2006, an inter-departmental commission on assessing personnel casualties and material losses during the Great Patriotic War was created in Russia. The main goal of the commission was to finally determine, by 2010, the casualties for the military and civilian population during the Great Patriotic War and to calculate material losses for the more than four years that combat operations were conducted.

Judging by everything, the authors did not intend to take the criticism into consideration and therefore refine their numbers. Suffice to say, the inter-departmental commission for computing casualties during the Great Patriotic War was formed only on 23 October 2009 by order of Russia's Minister of Defence. Representatives of the Ministry of Defence, Federal Security Service, Ministry of Internal Affairs, Federal State Statistics Service and the Federal Archive Agency were part of its composition. No changes could be detected in the calculation of armed forces casualties as compared with the earlier published numbers. Instead, under the pretext that it was necessary to stop the various types of 'speculation' on the issue of the USSR armed forces' irrecoverable losses, the military decided to turn to the country's leadership. They wanted the information about casualties that the General Staff commission had calculated to be officially fixed by a legislative act, the more so since General of the Army M.A. Gareev, President of the Academy of Military Sciences of the Russian Federation and former head of the commission for computing casualties in the war (1988), sensing the shakiness of the positions of the authors of the works, had earlier complained several times: 'All these statistical data [on casualties] have borne the character of the author and not an official one of the state. In fact, the government would not have reported to the people our personnel casualties during the war.'[57]

On 5 May 2010, according to a report by *RIA 'Novosti'*, General-Major A.V. Kirilin, Chief of the Russian Federation Ministry of Defence's Direc-torate for Memorializing Those Who Perished Defending the Fatherland, announced the following:

> The work of our interdepartmental commission is, in fact, completed. According to refined information, the USSR's overall casualties for the war period were 26.6 million men; 8,668,400 were irrecoverable combat losses for armed forces personnel, including fighting in the Far East . . . Personnel casualties of units and subunits of militias, partisan detachments and formations of civilian ministries and departments taking part in supporting the combat operations of *fronts* and naval forces were recorded in the country's overall civilian casualties.

Here, he publically declared that these numbers would be reported to the country's leadership so they could be announced on 9 May, the 65th anni-versary of the victory. Such announcements are not made without coordi-nating with the addressee, taking into consideration his high rank.

Incidentally, in a private conversation with one of the authors of this work, Kirilin, who was secretary of the interdepartmental commission, stated that, for reasons unknown to him, supposedly no armed forces casualty figures had been reported to the president and the government. It is difficult to believe this; in what form, then, must the commission have reported on its work? In favour of this assumption is the rather unexpected change in the position of Gareev, the former head of a similar commission (1988); not long before this, in a television address, he called for those who speculated on the theme of Red Army casualties in the last war to be prosecuted.

It was at this time that Gareev made a significant announcement: 'Inarguably it is necessary to speak the truth about casualties as well, without which it is not possible to assess fully the results of the war and the meaning of the victory that was achieved ... Published official information also cannot be considered unshakeable. If completely reliable information appears, then [the information] should be refined.'[58]

All of Gareev's and Krivosheev's opponents were ready to subscribe to these words. However, no real shift followed with regard to refining information about casualties. Reliable information might appear only after troop reports to the General Staff, including crucial information on the delivery of replacements to the *fronts*, on all of which Krivosheev based his calculations, were declassified.

Only by declassifying and examining this information could one come to the actual numbers for the Red Army's irrecoverable losses in the last war. However, people in the Ministry of Defence who were concerned with these documents would hardly approve of this. They did not want to be likened to the proverbial Gogol's sergeant's widow who flogged herself.

Chapter 4

Soviet armed forces' actual irrecoverable losses

The authors of the statistical study affirmed that, in addition to troop reports, they also used 'important sources such as books of district (municipal) military commissariats on notification reports (on servicemen who died and were MIA) that arrived from military units, hospitals, Glavupraform's Directorate of Personnel Records of Noncommissioned Officers and Enlisted Casualties, and military archives'.[1]

In these sources were registered 12,400,900 notifications. These added an additional 956,800 men to the overall losses that had been already recorded (11,444,100 men). However, these books sometimes contained duplicate records of the dead and MIA; two or more notifications pertaining to the same individual were sometimes sent to different military commissariats (regarding questions about relatives, in connection with their evacuation or transfer, etc.). Under this pretext, **Krivosheev's team disregarded the information in these books**.

In addition, the record books of the military commissariats also registered, among other things, notifications that had arrived from the Directorate of Personnel Casualty Records. These had been sent in response to inquiries from relatives and close friends about members of the militia, partisan detachments, destruction battalions of towns and districts, and special formations of other departments. Inasmuch as reports about combat strength and casualties from these formations were not sent to the General Staff, they were also not included in servicemen casualties.

As it became available, military commissariat information about dead and MIA servicemen was concentrated in TsAMO RF's files of irrecoverable losses. The creation of these files began when, on 9 July 1941, the department of personnel casualty records was organized as part of the Main Directorate of Organization and Recruitment of the Red Army. Among the responsibilities of the department were personnel casualty records and the compilation of an alphabetical casualty file. The department was transformed into the Central

Bureau on 5 February 1943 and into the Directorate of Personnel Casualty Records for the field forces on 19 April.

Records were kept for the following categories:

- killed, according to reports from military units;
- killed, according to reports from military commissariats;
- MIA, according to reports from military units;
- MIA, according to reports from military commissariats;
- died in German captivity;
- died from illness;
- died from wounds, according to reports from military units;
- died from wounds, according to reports from military commissariats.

At the same time, deserters, servicemen sentenced to imprisonment in forced labour camps, those sentenced to be executed, those removed from the records of irrecoverable losses as being still alive, those suspected of having served the Germans (the so-called 'signals'), and former POWs who survived their captivity were taken into account. These Red Army soldiers and NCOs were not included in the list of irrecoverable losses.

After the war the files were stored in the Archive of the Ministry of Defence of the USSR (now the Central Archive of the Ministry of Defence of the Russian Federation/TsAMO RF). The information in the files on irrecoverable losses was considerably broader than the military commissariat record books alone. The files had not only been compiled on the basis of reports from military units, notifications from military commissariats and inquiries from relatives in connection with loss of communication with soldiers at the front. Taking into account the fact that information about the fate of a large number of servicemen from military units had not arrived, a decision was made in 1946 to record irrecoverable losses according to submissions from the military commissariats.

A large proportion of the names was established by military commissariat workers during the household surveys conducted in 1946–1947 on the basis of Directive no. org/4/751524, dated 24 April 1946,[2] with the task of bringing to light all enlisted servicemen and NCOs whose fate had gone unreported.

Workers from the local military commissariats literally walked door to door and gathered information about those who had not returned from the war. The work continued 'in close association with organs of the Ministry of State Security and Ministry of Internal Affairs'. How much of this work they did conscientiously (taking into consideration that the military commissariats were poorly equipped for transportation and had to contend with a general shortage of resources) is, in the present, difficult to say. The information that

A German soldier and a dead Soviet tanker with a burning BT-5 tank in the background. Army Group South, June 1941. (*Bundesarchiv*)

crew member of a viet T-26 light tank rrenders to the rmans. Army Group ntre, August 1941. *ndesarchiv*)

Soviet POWs captured by the Germans near Stalingrad. Army Group South, summer 1942. (*Bundesarchiv*)

A Soviet POW quenches his thirst from a muddy puddle. Army Group South, July 1942. (*Bundesarchiv*)

A column of Soviet POWs captured during the Battle of Kursk. Summer 1943. (*Bundesarchiv*)

Soviet POWs transported in open freight cars. Army Group Centre, Vitebsk, 21 September 1941. (*Bundesarchiv*)

Soviet POWs in the Mauthausen concentration camp, Austria. October 1941. (*Bundesarchiv*)

German firing squad ecuting a group of viet partisans. Army oup North, September 41. (*Bundesarchiv*)

Colonel Nikolai Ilyich Lopukhovsky, commander of the 120th Howitzer Artillery Regiment of the Supreme Command Reserve. The father of one of the authors of this book, he was killed in action on 13 October 1941 while attempting to break out of the encirclement near Viaz'ma. (*Authors' archive*)

Soviet POWs captured in the Viaz'ma encirclement. October 1941. (*Authors' archive*)

A column of Soviet POWs in the Viaz'ma region. October 1941. (*Authors' archive*)

Soviet POWs captured in the Viaz'ma and Bryansk encirclements. October 1941. (*Authors' archive*)

Soviet POWs help their wounded comrades. 1941. (*Authors' archive*)

German guard hastens Soviet POWs with a stick. 1941. (*Authors' archive*)

Local women bring bread to starving Soviet POWs. 1942. (*Authors' archive*)

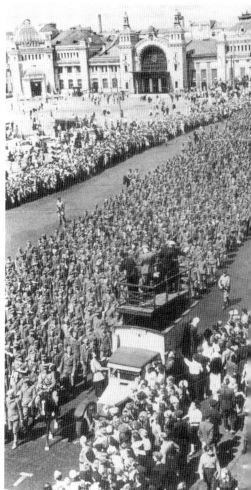

(*Left*) The infamous 'Uman' pit'. Here, in a clay quarry of a local brick factory, Germans kept 60,000–70,000 Soviet POWs surrounded near Uman', Ukraine. Army Group South, August 1941. (*Authors' archive*)

(*Right*) German POWs being marched through the streets of Moscow, 17 July 1944. (*Authors' archive*)

German POWs captured near Stalingrad. December 1942. (*Authors' archive*)

A German military cemetery in Russia. 1943. (*Authors' archive*)

(left) The registration card of a Soviet POW, Sergeant F.A. Anisov. He served in 120th Howitzer Artillery Regiment of the Supreme Command Reserve and was captured on 7 September 1941 near Elnya. He died on 26 April 1943 in Stalag X-B, located near Sandbostel, Germany. (*Authors' archive*)

(right) A Soviet soldier's plastic capsule which contained a paper insert with the soldier's personal information. It belonged to Private N.T. Prilepsky, killed in action on 13 October 1941 while attempting to break out of the encirclement near Viaz'ma. (*Authors' archive*)

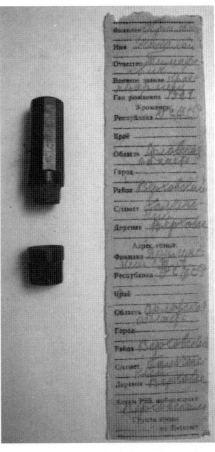

A wounded German soldier being treated by medics. A metal 'dog tag', normally worn around the neck, has been placed on top of his head, so as not to interfere with his wound dressing. France, July 1944. (*Bundesarchiv*)

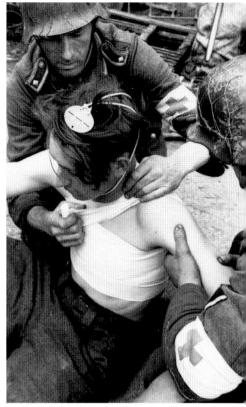

The upper half of a German soldier's 'dog tag'. Its lower half was broken off by a burial party after the owner's death. Judging by the text stamped on the 'dog tag', it belonged to soldier no. 696, who served in the 1st Company, 213th Reserve Pioneer Battalion, and had blood type B. He died in February 1942 near the village of Novye Dvory in Viaz'ma District. (*Authors' archive*)

The monument at the burial site of General-Major B.S. Bakharov. He was killed in action on 16 Ju 1944 during the liberation of Belarus and buried in Babruysk, Belarus. (*Authors' archive*)

was gathered was checked against available data and appropriate decisions were made. After processing, conclusions were included in the corresponding file. It is hard to imagine that people under frequent scrutiny by the authorities and at constant risk of being informed on by their neighbours could have reported false information about those near and dear to them. However, government information gatherers questioned only those who survived, so the information collected this way was still far from complete.

Many files in TsAMO RF were set up on the basis of studying materials from the Wehrmacht's Information Service – WASt (the Central Bureau of Military Casualty and POW Records). These held data on officer POWs and soldier POWs that the Americans handed over to the USSR soon after the war. Information collected from these sources provided a basic increase in the number of Soviet MIAs.

As of the beginning of 1990, 17.2 million such files had been set up,[3] each of which detailed the fate of a single man. Thus, the file collection exceeded twofold the number of demographic irrecoverable losses for the armed forces that Krivosheev had calculated (8,668,000), and by 1.5 times the numbers of military-operational irrecoverable losses that he published (11,444,100).

It also exceeds the number of overall losses calculated by Shtemenko's group by almost 5.8 million. Krivosheev armed himself with notification from the chief of TsAMO RF that the files had still not been processed regarding the removal of duplicate information and therefore could not be a reliable source in producing a work on casualties. The decision made to not take into account the information from the personnel casualty records was, **at that time**, completely justifiable.

In 1990 notifications on the fate of servicemen who had been taken out of action ('killed in action' notices) were finally declassified. This was done in accordance with the CC CPSU Politburo Resolution, 'On the All-Union *Book of Remembrance*', dated 17 January 1989, and as part of the planned commencement of work in district and municipal editorial boards. Starting that year, work began in TsAMO RF on putting in order the records of irrecoverable losses and eliminating duplicate information from the files. The following categories of servicemen who had been taken out of action were also excluded from the files: deserters, those who had been condemned and sent to prison, and those Soviet servicemen who had been removed from the records but who turned out to be alive, including those who had returned from captivity after the war (according to information from the repatriation organs). Also, personnel record files that had already been grouped alphabetically were counted letter-by-letter and categorized with respect to casualties.

At the same time the All-Union (now All-Russian) Scientific and Research Institute of Records Management and Archives (VNIIDAD) began to create the electronic Central Data Bank (TsBD). For this purpose, appropriate archive documents from three central Soviet archives – TsAMO RF, the Military-Medical Archive (Museum), and the Naval Archive – were delivered to the institute. By 1995 the newly created 'Fate' Scientific-Information Centre contained almost 20 million pieces of information (persons) about servicemen who had died or were MIA. This information was used in the publication of the *Book of Remembrance* in regions of Russia. In 2002 more than 40,000 people were waiting for their turn to learn at least something about the location and circumstances of the deaths of their relatives and close friends at the 'People's Remembrance' collection (the successor of the 'Fate' Scientific-Information Centre). Over twenty years of experience of work of both collections on memorializing those who had died and were MIA showed that many thousands of soldiers were not listed in any files or databases at all. Family members of those soldiers, three or four generations later, are still not able to find the graves of their relatives and close friends, or learn anything about the circumstances of their loved ones' deaths.

By 1 November 2000 TsAMO RF had processed twenty letters of the alphabet in its files. This resulted in a count of 9,524,398 people to whom the eight categories of enlisted men and NCOs were applicable. According to military commissariat reports, 116,513 men turned out to be alive and were removed from the records of irrecoverable losses. A preliminary calculation was done for the remaining six letters of the alphabet, as a result of which an additional 2,910,000 irrecoverable losses were brought to light. There was a total of 12,434,398 Red Army soldiers and noncommissioned officers (not counting casualty records for the Navy and NKVD internal and border troops) in this file. According to this method, an alphabetical file of irrecoverably lost Red Army officers was also compiled, in which there were around 1,100,000 men. Thus, as a result of the letter-by-letter calculation of the data from the two files, the Red Army's irrecoverable losses of those who were killed, went MIA or died from wounds, illness and in captivity during the war amounted to 13,534,400 soldiers and officers.[4] And these are only the demographic casualties.

Work continued on putting the records of irrecoverable losses into order and eliminating duplicate information from the files. In March 2008, according to unofficial information (results of the TsAMO RF staff's work was not made public), as a result of letter-by-letter calculation there were 13,271,269 personnel files in the registry of irrecoverable losses of armed forces enlisted men and NCOs. These were distributed in the following way, according to type of casualty (the percentage of the total number is given in parentheses):

- killed: 4,173,709 (31.45%);
- died from wounds and illness: 1,383,052 (10.42%);
- died in captivity: 495,558 (3.73%);
- MIA: 7,156,262 (53.92%); among them 1,720,951 according to information from military unit commanders and 5,435,311 according to information from military commissariats;
- sentenced to be executed (shot): 62,688 (0.47%).

Thus, according to the files, irrecoverable losses for enlisted men and NCOs were 2,896,961 men (28 per cent) greater than the figure computed by Krivosheev's team. The latter's totals amounted to 10,374,308 men, including 1,984,603 NCOs and 8,389,705 enlisted men.[5]

The nominal record of officer casualties was organized much better than that of the enlisted men and NCOs. According to the results of the letter-by-letter calculation of personnel files, as of the end of 2000, officer casualties totalled approximately 1.1 million men.[6] For various reasons, 125,232 officers had been removed from this file by the end of 2007, leaving around 970,000 men in it. At this time, however, soldiers and NCOs who had occupied officer positions had not been included in this number. According to Krivosheev's information, irrecoverable losses for officers, taking into account the 122,905 servicemen who had not attained officer rank but still occupied officer positions, amounted to 1,023,088 men.[7] This convincingly attests to an adequate degree of reliability on the files' part.

One can find a clear comparison of the precision of different methods of loss calculation in the chapter in Krivosheev's book devoted to the Soviet-Finnish War (1939–1940). According to the summary table, which was compiled based on troop reports, Soviet armed forces' irrecoverable losses there amounted to 84,994 men, of whom 65,384 were killed or died during stages of medical evacuation, while 19,610 were MIA.[8] These figures were then made more precise, mainly because of the inclusion of Air Force personnel losses, as well as of those who died from wounds or illness in hospitals after March 1940. The new casualty figure increased to 95,348 men;[9] however, it was not the final one. Subsequent prolonged and meticulous work by the officers of the USSR Ministry of Defence's Main Personnel Directorate and the Ground Forces Main Staff in 1949–1951 made it possible to substantially refine this information. After the nominal lists of Red Army servicemen who were killed, died or went MIA in the Soviet-Finnish War were compiled, it turned out that actual casualties had reached 126,875 men: 71,314 were killed or died during stages of medical evacuation, 16,292 died from wounds and illness in hospitals, and 39,369 went MIA.[10] Thus, the total number of irrecoverable losses increased by 1.5 times! This was mainly because of MIAs that had been incorrectly recorded earlier. In the opinion of Krivosheev's team, this latter figure 'more fully reflects the country's demographic irrecoverable losses in the War against Finland'.[11] Is this not convincing proof of the advantage of the nominal method of calculating casualties as compared with estimating them on the basis of the troop reports that Krivosheev used for calculating casualties in the Great Patriotic War?

Using information from TsAMO RF's files on irrecoverable losses and Krivosheev's information on casualties for other personnel categories, one can calculate the USSR armed forces' overall irrecoverable losses during the Great Patriotic War. For clarity, the figures from the files are compared with the information in Table 120 from Krivosheev's book.

The total of demographic servicemen casualties in this case amounts to 14,554,100 men. At first glance this number almost exactly matches the total number of irrecoverable casualties of Soviet servicemen in the Great Patriotic War (14,546,600) that we obtained in Table 11. The difference between them is all of .05 per cent! In reality, they differ considerably, because the number from Table 11 represents the **total** irrecoverable losses of the USSR armed forces while the one from Table 12 only shows their **demographic casualties**. After all, Soviet servicemen who returned from captivity after the war and who were remobilized into the army on liberated territory were excluded from the TsAMO RF files (if they survived the war, of course). After adding these figures to the demographic casualties' number, however, we can determine the total irrecoverable casualties of the USSR armed forces based on the information from TsAMO RF files.

However, it is not as easy as it may seem, and here is why. Unfortunately, there are no actual data on the number of former servicemen who were remobilized on liberated territory and survived the war, so it needs to be calculated. To do this, first of all, one should find out how many Soviet servicemen were killed at the front during the whole war. This information can be obtained from Krivosheev's statistical study. It includes 6,329,600 who were killed or died of wounds, 555,500 noncombat casualties and 500,000 MIAs who actually died, which gives us altogether 7,385,100 men. It turns out that of the total 34,476,700 men who served in the Soviet armed forces during the Great Patriotic war,[12] 21.42 per cent died at the front. However, the overwhelming majority of those who were remobilized into the army on liberated territory made it to the front in the second half of the war, and not all of them right away. During that period, the probability of their being captured, and dying in captivity, was not large enough to factor into our calculations, especially since it is more than compensated for by a constant decrease in average Red Army losses over the course of the war. As a result, for those who came to the front at the end of the war, the chances of dying had dropped significantly below average, even without taking into account the time those soldiers spent there. Therefore, we will not deviate too far from the truth if, based on the duration of returning troops' stays at the front, we assume that the likelihood of their dying there was two times lower than the average for the whole war, i.e., 10.71 per cent. From these considerations, it turns out that out of the 939,700 who were remobilized on liberated territory perhaps 100,600 died at the front, and the remaining 839,100 survived the war. We used this estimated number in Table 12.

This count of the USSR armed forces' demographic casualties, obtained according to the information in the TsAMO RF files, exceeds Krivosheev's calculated demographic casualties by almost 6 million men, or by 1.7 times. To ignore such a large difference is totally unacceptable. Moreover, there is no reason to consider our figure significantly exaggerated, if only because, according to Ivlev's information, the work of putting into order the file on enlisted and NCO casualties was completed at the end of 2010. All files were sorted alphabetically and according to type of casualty. As a result, a total of 15.3 million men was obtained for Soviet soldier and NCO demographic casualties,[13] comprising 88 per cent of the overall size of the file at the beginning of 1990. This is a full 2 million more than the number we used! The total irrecoverable losses of servicemen should also increase correspondingly. By how many? Let us wait until the Ministry of Defence deigns to publish the information from the TsAMO RF files of irrecoverable losses.

There is also nothing new or surprising in the fact that the troop report information on which Krivosheev's team built its statistics is far from complete and strikingly differs from the information in TsAMO RF files on irrecoverable losses. In People's Commissar of Defence Order no. 0270, 'On Personnel Records of Irrecoverable Losses at the Fronts', dated 12 April 1942, the following was openly said: 'At present, no more than one-third of the actual number of killed are in the personnel records. Personnel record information of those who are missing in action and prisoners of war is even further from the truth.'[14]

The shortcomings pointed out in the order were not even completely eliminated before the very end of the war. Tens of thousands of those who were mobilized but not listed in a single document will outweigh by far some number of possible 'duplicates' remaining in the TsAMO RF files. Ivlev cites a characteristic example: during the Memorial Watch on the territory of the

Table 12: Comparison of information on the USSR armed forces' irrecoverable losses and their demographic casualties, obtained from different sources (in thousands of men)*

According to information from Krivosheev's team	Number	Difference between information from Krivosheev and TsAMO RF Files	According to information from TsAMO RF Files (as of March 2008)	Number
Type of casualty			Type of casualty	Soldiers and NCOs
Killed or died from wounds during stages of medical evacuation	5,226.8	1,053.1 more	Killed	4,173.7
Died from wounds in hospitals	1,102.8	280.2 fewer	Died of wounds and illness	1,383.0
Total	6,329.6	772.9 more	Total	5,556.7
Noncombat casualties: died of illness or accidents; sentenced to be executed	555.5	492.8 more	Sentenced to be executed	62.7
MIAs, POWs	3,396.4	3,759.9 fewer	MIAs	7,156.3
Unrecorded casualties of the first months of the war	1,162.6	667.0 more	Died in captivity	495.6
Total	4,559.0	3,092.9 fewer	Total	7,651.9
			Total, soldiers and NCOs	13,271.3
			Other casualties:	
			– officers	970.0
			– seamen	153.7
			– Border and KGB troops	61.4
			– Ministry of the Interior internal troops	97.7
Total servicemen irrecoverable losses	11,444.1	5,785.1 fewer	After adding former servicemen who were remobilized on liberated territory and survived the war and those who returned from captivity after the war	17,229.2

Former servicemen who were remobilized on liberated territory	939.7	100.6 more	839.1	Former servicemen who were remobilized on liberated territory and survived the war
Servicemen who returned from captivity after the war	1,836.0	–	1,836.0	Servicemen who returned from captivity after the war
Total excluded from the number of irrecoverable losses	2,775.7	100.6 more	2,675.1	Total excluded from the number of irrecoverable losses
Demographic casualties of roster-strength servicemen**	8,668.4	5,885.7 fewer	14,554.1	Demographic servicemen casualties (see previous note)

* *Russia and the USSR in Wars of the 20th Century*, 2001, p. 237, Table 120; p. 389, Table 146; p. 434, Table 167; information from TsAMO RF files of irrecoverable losses (as of March 2008).

**What is meant here is not only those servicemen who were killed and died from wounds, but also all those who were taken out of action (excluded from the roster); died from illness, died as a result of accidents and mishaps, those who were condemned to execution (noncombat casualties), and those who were still MIA after the war and did not return from captivity.

Yartsevsky District (Smolensk *Oblast*) from 25 August 2010 to 23 August 2011, the bodies of 548 Soviet servicemen were found and buried with military honours. Of the sixty persons identified by dog-tag forms, they were recorded as follows:

- in unit combat casualty reports: 4 men (7%)
- in regional military commissariat reports on place of residence of relatives, as those who had not returned and were MIA: 33 men (55%);
- in other sources: 3 men (5%);
- not recorded at all: 20 men (33%).[15]

It is not at all by chance that Krivosheev made the reservation 'demographic casualties of **roster strength** servicemen' in the corresponding place.[16] Those who were mobilized but who were not included in the unit lists for various reasons (including because of an irresponsible attitude toward personnel records) were simply listed among the losses of the USSR civilian population.

There is another mind-boggling number in these already grievous statistics – they were able to identify only 11 per cent of the 548 discovered remains of Soviet soldiers. This is due to the fact that the Red Army's identification system performed rather poorly. A soldier's identification tag consisted of a small plastic capsule, closed by a screw cap, containing a paper insert. This insert was to be filled in by its owner with basic data about himself and his family. However, this information did not always survive. A capsule could be easily destroyed by fire or penetrated by groundwater, thereby ruining the fragile insert inside or washing out its text. In addition, many soldiers did not even fill in their inserts. Many underestimated their importance, and others considered filling them in a bad omen and refused to do so because of superstition. Furthermore, not all soldiers had identification tags – they were adopted by the Red Army shortly before the war, on 15 March 1941[17], and were abolished on 17 November 1942 without any equivalent replacement.[18] For all of these reasons, it is understandable why millions of missing Soviet servicemen have remained unidentified. The metal dog tags used in the Wehrmacht were much more effective in identifying those killed in action.

The following argument was made to cast doubt on the information in TsAMO RF's irrecoverable losses files: there was no information on the military service of conscripted persons in the majority of reports from the military commissariats and People's Commissariat of Defence's Directorate of Personnel Casualty Records (compiled on the basis of inquiries from relatives). Therefore, those reports may contain information on persons who 'did not serve in the forces, but were sent by the military commissariats to formations of civilian departments (maritime and riverine fleets, civil aviation, railway transport, defence industry factories, etc.). Those who died were subsequently calculated in the overall number of the country's human casualties (26.6 million men).'[19]

This is, however, a matter of almost 3 million men. It is known that 5,039,600 men were sent as replacements for NKVD troops and organs and for formations and units of allied armies, for work in industry, and to military formations of other departments.[20] Could 3 million of them have died or gone missing in action? Where, when, and in what situation could there have been such reservist casualties in formations of civilian departments and in the defence industry? Where were they recorded? Furthermore, as we have already mentioned, reservists were periodically withdrawn from industry and NKVD formations by having their special draft exemptions taken away.

It should be noted that one could check, if one so desired, which relatives of MIA soldiers and NCOs received a military pension. The Soviet government paid out allowances to soldiers' parents and children, the latter until they were 18 (or until graduation for those who were studying at colleges and universities).

How, then, could those who **were conscripted and did not return from the war** not be taken into account? Are all those people, whom they did not want to acknowledge as defenders of the Motherland, really damned by the fact that personnel records in units and formations were not organized as they should have been? Why were 500,000 men who had been conscripted but who did not reach their units not recorded as servicemen casualties? After all, their service began from the moment they were conscripted and sent to their units!

The fact is that, owing to the great numerical difference, acknowledging the information in the TsAMO RF files would place in doubt both the numbers of irrecoverable military-operational casualties of the armed forces of the USSR (11,444,100) and the demographic servicemen casualties (8,668,400).[21] It would be necessary to re-examine the results of the calculations of the authors of *Russia and the USSR in Wars of the 20th Century* and adjust the numbers upward. However, the appropriate departments, for well known reasons, do not wish to do this; after all, this would then change the overall ratio of irrecoverable personnel losses of the opposing sides. It is for this reason that TsAMO RF's files of irrecoverable losses are like thorns in the sides of certain persons. Owing to this, we have seen recent published declarations from some of the military's top brass that they themselves are still listed in the files as dead or MIA. Such declarations are an attempt to undermine trust in the files' information. It is not for no reason that in 1995, when the fifty-year storage period had expired, there were recommendations to destroy the files. It is entirely possible that these attempts may be realized today under the pretext of the expiration of the time set for their storage, or, for example, during a reorganization of the archives or while transferring the files from one establishment to another.

The unwillingness of the appropriate authorities to take into account the information in TsAMO RF's records of irrecoverable losses is yet another piece of evidence of the presence of a political injunction: to in no case allow a sharp imbalance in the ratio of irrecoverable losses of the opposing sides in the Great Patriotic War, and to reduce any such imbalance to a minimum. Most likely this directive was expressed privately (such decisions and instructions were, as a rule, not formulated officially) when the General Staff departments and commissions were only beginning to prepare casualty information. The influence of this order can be seen especially clearly in numerous examples of the reduction of casualties in unsuccessful Red Army operations.

MIA and POW servicemen comprise a considerable part of the USSR's irrecoverable losses – around 54 per cent, as recorded in TsAMO RF files. The difference of several million men between Krivosheev's information and ours emerged largely because of this type of casualty. The authors of the work on casualties complain that they did not manage to find German documents that contained complete information about the number of Soviet POWs captured before the beginning of 1942. They explain this using the fact that in 1941 it was not obligatory for Wehrmacht units to report the number of Soviet servicemen they captured. Only in January 1942 did the Supreme High Command of the German Army issue instructions regarding this issue to the troops.[22]

Apparently, the authors did not look very hard. Let us turn to German information for 1941, the hardest year for the USSR (essentially, six months of combat operations). Addressing the Reichstag on 11 December 1941, Hitler reported that for the five months of the war, from 22 June to 1 December, 17,332 Soviet combat aircraft, 21,391 tanks and 32,541 artillery pieces had been captured or destroyed.[23] Naturally, Soviet *agitprop* declared that these figures were fabrications of Goebbels and the delirium of the demonic Fuehrer. This line was adhered to even after the war – for more than fifty years.

Now, Krivosheev's team had computed that in 1941 the Red Army had lost 20,500 tanks (of which 3,200 were medium and heavy), 17,900 combat aircraft and 101,100 artillery pieces and mortars (including 38,000 50mm mortars).[24] These figures do not differ greatly from those that Hitler had declared.[25] As an aside, let us mention that by December 1941 there remained

1,958 tanks, of which 1,393 were light, in the Red Army field forces.[26] This takes into account the 361 British tanks that had arrived in the Soviet Union from October to December.[27]

At the same time the Fuehrer proclaimed that, by 1 December, 3,806,865 Soviet soldiers and officers had been captured. On 19 February 1942 Mansfeld, the head of the Four-Year Plan Directorate's task team on the use of the labour force, announced an even larger number – 3.9 million – in the Reichstag's Economic Chamber.[28] It was based on German troop reports, according to which 3,906,765 men (including 15,196 officers) had been captured since the beginning of the war.[29] However, on 20 December 1941, after subsequent refinement, the total number decreased to 3,350,639 (of whom 15,179 were officers), including those who by this time had died, escaped or been set free.[30] Apparently this occurred due to the elimination of duplicate records and the exclusion of civilians from the number of POWs.

The official German history of the Second World War notes:

> Of 3,350,000 prisoners taken in 1941, almost 60 per cent had died by 1 February 1942, including over 600,000 since the beginning of December 1941. Mortality was especially high in the Reich (18.5 per cent as of December 1941), with about 47 per cent of Soviet prisoners of war there dying of starvation and typhus by the beginning of April 1942. This fact alone proves that the prisoners did not die as the result of an unavoidable 'emergency situation', but fell victim to a ruthless starvation policy.[31]

These numbers have much in common with the information we already know from Streit: of the 3,350,639 Soviet POWs, only 1,020,531 men were still alive by 1 February 1942, and an additional 280,108 had been set free. The more than 2 million remaining men were victims of executions, epidemics, starvation and cold.[32] Let us mention that the principal number of Soviet POWs perished in 1941 and the beginning of 1942. After the Wehrmacht's defeat at Moscow, the ultimate blitzkrieg failure that shifted the war to its attrition phase, the Germans' need for prisoners to serve as a cheap labour force increased significantly. Consequently, the attitude toward prisoners changed: the Nazis stopped consciously and purposefully creating unbearable living conditions for them. Therefore, for those POWs who had been able to stay alive until this time, and for those who were captured by the Germans later, the chances of survival increased considerably.

Streit also provided information about the overall number of Soviet POWs captured by the Wehrmacht. According to data from the Supreme Command of the German Armed Forces' department of POW affairs, there were

5,163,381 men in German captivity on 1 May 1944; in December 1944 there were 5.6 million. According to information from the Supreme Command of the German Ground Forces, dated 20 February 1945, there were 5,734,528 POWs as of 31 January 1945.[33] Let us mention that this figure is not a final one; after all, the Germans continued to capture Soviet servicemen right up to the very end of the war. For example, even in the last ten days of April 1945, as a result of the counterstrike by Army Group Centre under the command of F. Schörner, some of the troops of the 2nd Polish Army and the 52nd Soviet Army were encircled in the region of Bautzen and suffered considerable casualties. Some 600 soldiers and officers from their composition wound up in German hands.[34] However, information about the number of Soviet POWs captured by the Wehrmacht in the last three months of the war suffers from incompleteness and unreliability; therefore, we will not take those POWs into account. Fortunately, they in no way change the overall picture.

More relevant are the Red Army servicemen who were captured by the Romanians and Finns. We have already cited precise information about their numbers. Taking them into account when determining Soviet military-operational casualties, we must add the 146,300 men captured by Germany's satellites to the number of Red Army servicemen captured by the German army. Thus, the overall number of Soviet POWs captured by the Germans and their allies amounts to no fewer than 5,880,000 men, which is 1,320,000 more than the number computed by Krivosheev's team.

Having basically acknowledged the German information about Red Army losses of war materiel, the authors of *Russia and the USSR in Wars of the 20th Century* categorically dispute the number of Soviet POWs. With regard to this, we must once again return to Krivosheev's talk at the meeting of the Association of Historians of the Second World War:

> The results of research of the materials, including archival documents of the German military command, confirm that 4,559,000 Soviet servicemen had been captured. Around 450,000–500,000 servicemen from those who were MIA died, remained on occupied territory or joined the partisans.
>
> These facts are basically confirmed by information from Germany's Main Ground Forces Command, published in a war diary, according to which, by 20 December 1942, 3,350,639 Soviet servicemen had been captured.[35]

Apparently, someone misinformed Krivosheev about this issue.

It is strange how the authors researched archival documents of the German military command because these very numbers apply to December 1941, rather than 1942. As we have mentioned already, according to the combat journal of the Supreme Command of the German Ground Forces, the overall number of Soviet POWs on 20 December 1941, as refined by the Germans, totalled 3,350,639 men, including those who by that time had died, escaped or been set free (see Appendix D).

The authors dispute the German information about the number of POWs, arguing also that, in addition to servicemen, 'in the POW camps were a large number of Soviet civilians who were not servicemen and were captured by the Germans in violation of the Hague and Geneva Conventions'.[36] Reports about them were not sent to army and navy headquarters or to the General Staff. Therefore, in Krivosheev's opinion, information published in the foreign press about the number of POWs cannot be accepted as a basis for determining the actual number of Soviet servicemen who wound up in German captivity. Of course, such reports were not sent to the Red Army General Staff, but what does German information have to do with it? One must verify the count's reliability by comparing facts from various sources, and on the basis of this, one must attempt to determine, at least approximately, a more accurate number of Soviet servicemen captured by the Germans.

Actually, when computing captured POWs the Germans did not pay attention to which department their prisoners belonged. For example, among the captured were many military builders. Using the example of the Baltic Special Military District, one can judge their numbers in the territory of the border districts. On the eve of the Great Patriotic War, a total of 87 construction, 35 combat engineer and 8 motor vehicle battalions from interior areas worked in the zone of this district.[37] These subunits, formed from those who had been called up for the six-month military training sessions in March–May 1941, were sent from all USSR military districts to the Soviet-German state border to build fortifications. Their personnel had not been recorded as mobilized;[38] therefore, they were not entered into the military commissariats' conscription book for mobilization, although the appropriate mention of mobilized reservists was made in their record files and their documents were put into a separate filing system.[39]

According to the TOE, battalions had the following in their composition: construction battalions: 1,000 men; combat engineer battalions: 455 men; motor vehicle battalions: 529 men.[40] Thus, according to Ivlev's calculations, the number of military builders involved in site construction for the Baltic Special Military District (soon to become the Northwestern Front) could have been no fewer than 107,000 men. During the fighting, these men were often used to replenish unit and formation casualties. Only a small part (no more than 30 per cent) of these soldiers left Northwestern Front subordination in the composition of construction units taken to the near rear area for the construction of defensive lines.

On 19 September 1941 9 separate construction battalions were involved in construction in the Western Front zone, and 129 more of these battalions were doing the same in the Reserve and Briansk Front zones. There were 85,336 men in construction battalions building the fortifications of the Rzhev-Viaz'ma line. They suffered heavy casualties. Of the 100,000 builders of the Western Directorate of Defensive Work, only 42,000 were transferred to new lines.[41]

If, in mid-September, the field construction capacity of the Main Directorate of Defensive Work comprised 1.2 million men, then by 10 October 700,000 of them remained. Military builder casualties (dead, wounded, MIA, POW) numbered 500,000 men.[42] How many among them were servicemen who were registered with the NKVD and People's Commissariat of Defence? In addition, 6 sapper armies comprising 33 sapper brigades were formed in October–December 1941.[43] They were relegated to the field forces, worked in the *fronts*' rear areas, and were often directly involved in combat. Even more servicemen were among those there who were killed or captured during repeated withdrawals or encirclements. There is probably corresponding information at the General Staff. Were these men also not taken into account?

The authors of the work about casualties also did not want to take into account the militiamen, many of whom died, went MIA or were POWs. They were counted in the overall casualties of the country's population. Meanwhile, according to a State Defence Committee resolution, their mobilization into the people's militia of, for example, the capital was conducted by the district committees of the Party (200,000 Muscovites) and of the Moscow *Oblast'* (50,000 collective farmers), under the leadership of the Moscow Military District headquarters **with the subsequent processing of those who were mobilized through the district military committees. Here, volunteers were promised that they would enjoy the rights of servicemen**. In particular, State Defence Committee Resolution no. 10, dated 4 July 1941, stated that 'in case of disability and/or death of one who was mobilized, he and his family enjoy the right to obtain a pension equal to that of a Red Army conscript'.[44]

Here, the deadlines for the conduct of mobilization were very strict. The above-mentioned State Defence Committee resolution required the formation of the first twelve divisions by 7 July,[45] that is, in only three days. Therefore, in the majority of cases, the military commissariats did not manage to register mobilized militiamen. Moreover, the lists of those who had been mobilized were destroyed in many of Moscow's district Party committees during the 16 October 1941 panic. None of this was the fault of the militiamen.

Up to now, the councils of veterans of militia divisions have been, with rare exceptions, unsuccessful in regenerating the lists of their brothers-in-arms. For instance, workers and employees of a minimum of twenty-six factories, organizations and schools of Moscow's Rostokino district volunteered for the 13th People's Militia Rifle Division (soon to become the 140th Rifle Division). By the 65th anniversary of victory, the veterans' council had succeeded in establishing the names of 488 militiamen of the division's more than 11,000 soldiers and officers.[46]

After the mobilization of the first twelve people's militia divisions (initially numbering in the order of 150,000 men) the districts of Moscow *Oblast'* continued to create separate subunits and units. Militia formations were also created in other cities, although not all of them were included in the composition of the field forces. What can we say about the men mobilized by the field military commissariats on territory liberated from the enemy? Sometimes they were thrown into battle not only without having been registered in subunits, but also without having changed into a military uniform or been completely armed.

Krivosheev has justly pointed out that these were not the only men in the camps for Soviet POWs; there were also 'captured partisans, underground fighters and personnel from incomplete people's militia formations, local air defence, destruction battalions, and police, as well as militarized formations from civilian departments and some of the people who had been deported for forced labour'.[47] Here, though, one must keep in mind that the Germans, as a rule, did not consider captured underground fighters and partisans to be POWs, and executed them without delay, especially during the first half of the war.

The authors of the statistical study did not include any of the categories listed above in their calculation of irrecoverable losses for the USSR armed forces so as not to exceed in any way the number of them that had been determined earlier.

The fate of the men who were MIA during the Great Patriotic War concerns millions of families in Russia and the former republics of the Soviet Union. According to Krivosheev's information, around 2.5 million men died in captivity.[48] However, as of 2008 the TsAMO RF files had documented (by last name) only 495,600 POWs as having died in captivity. The Germans, known for their precision and their liking for order, began a file for each POW that, in addition to the usual information about the man himself, also indicated his military unit, place of capture, place of birth and parents. In the POW concentration camps (Stalags and Oflags) the captives were photographed and fingerprinted. According to available information, one of the TsAMO RF repositories still contains around 500,000 packed and unsorted files, transferred there by the Germans, concerning Soviet POWs who died in captivity. Many of these men are still most certainly listed as MIA. These files have not even been translated into Russian. What can explain this? Is it a lack of resources or an unforgivable unwillingness to shed light on the fate of MIA soldiers? Who is responsible for this?

The opposite trend can be seen in the determination of irrecoverable losses for the German armed forces. In this regard, the composition of German POWs who were in Soviet captivity is of unquestionable interest. Among them were also groups of men similar to those whom Krivosheev had pointed out. For example, to the POWs are relegated auxiliary personnel of Germany's air defence system and personnel from military-labour service detachments, police units and subunits, Hitler Youth, the *Volkssturm* (German national militia) and the militarized construction organization *Todt*. In short: all Germans captured by Soviet troops and wearing what looked like military uniforms. Most often men from these categories were not held separately, but rather kept in the usual POW camps, which notably increased the overall number of German POWs.

Moreover, at the end of the war, an acute need for labour forced the Soviet leadership to take extreme measures. On 16 December 1944 Stalin signed State Defence Committee Resolution no. 7161ss, which said:

1. Mobilize, intern, and send to work in the USSR all able-bodied Germans – men 17–45 years old, women 18–30 years old – who are located in the territories of Romania, Yugoslavia, Bulgaria and Czechoslovakia that have been liberated by the Red Army.

    Establish that Germans of German and Hungarian citizenship, as well as Germans who are citizens of Romania, Yugoslavia, Bulgaria and Czechoslovakia, are subject to mobilization.
2. The NKVD USSR (comrade Beria) is in charge of the mobilization.[49]

This was only the beginning of the forced emigration of the German labour force to the USSR. At the end of January 1945 the Red Army crossed the border of the Third Reich and without delay State Defence Committee Resolution no. 7467ss appeared on 3 February. It prescribed that the 1st, 2nd and 3rd Belorussian Fronts and the 1st Ukrainian Front conduct the next mobilization of the German civilian population, this time on German territory. Subject to mobilization were:

> ... all German men 17–50 years old who are fit for physical labour and capable of carrying weapons. Germans regarding whom it will be established that they served in the German army or in '*Volkssturm*' units are to be considered prisoners of war and sent to NKVD camps for prisoners of war. From the remaining Germans who can be mobilized, form labour battalions of 750–1,200 men each to be used for work in the Soviet Union, first and foremost, in the Ukrainian SSR and Belorussian SSR.[50]

All these campaigns were conducted within the framework of the so-called 'reparation by labour' which had been levied on the still-fighting Germany in advance. As a result, from January to May 1945 as many as 303,489 people, of whom at least 51,787 were women, were deported to the USSR.[51] First and foremost, those who were interned were assigned to be used in the industry of the USSR as part of the labour battalions. Some of them, however, as is obvious from the text of the State Defence Committee resolution, were seen as POWs and therefore sent to the appropriate NKVD camps. These numbered as many as 10,263 men.[52] But, in fact, they had no relationship whatsoever to the Wehrmacht servicemen captured during combat. The fact was that these were civilians who had been demobilized or who had deserted before the Red Army's arrival. They came not only from the Wehrmacht, but also from the *Volkssturm* – a direct analogy with the Soviet people's militia itself, to whose soldiers Krivosheev categorically denied the right to be considered servicemen.

This matter, however, goes further. For various reasons, a number of those who were interned, together with POW trains, arrived at NKVD camps to which they had not been assigned. In order to correct this mistake, Special Directive no. 28/35 from the NKVD's Main Directorate for Prisoner-of-War and Internal Affairs (Glavnoe upravlenie po delam voennoplennykh i internirovannykh, hereafter cited as GUPVI), dated 6 June 1945, 'On the Introduction of Separate Accounting for Prisoners of War and Interns in NKVD Camps for Prisoners of War', was needed. It strictly prescribed the following:

1. ... Identify all interned citizens – members of various enemy organizations; leaders of district and provincial councils; administrators, mayors and managers of economic and administrative organizations; editors of newspapers and magazines; authors of

anti-Soviet publications, and all others, and from now on, in muster rolls submitted for prisoners of war, do not report them as not associated with the prisoners of war …

…

3. All interned citizens identified in camps and special hospitals are to be listed in the next prisoner-of-war muster roll in the column 'Removed to intern record', and, regarding the muster roll for interns, register them in the column 'Came from a prisoner-of-war record'.[53]

It turned out that there were quite a few citizens identified this way, who had wound up by chance in camps intended for captured servicemen. Moreover, they found themselves not only among Germans. In accordance with a GUPVI NKVD document dated 1 January 1949, 25,318 former POWs from Germany and its allies were transferred to the intern records. Another 21,411 were sent to GULAG camps. This in no way reflects on those who were condemned by military tribunals; those were allocated a separate column, as were those who were sent to prisons.[54] Of course, they all continued to figure in the overall balance sheet of POWs in the Soviet Union, which inflated the sum total.

However, this is still far from everything that affected the POW count. After the Red Army arrived on the territory of the states of Hitler's bloc, a decision was made to clear out potentially hostile elements from areas at the army's rear. Among them were, first and foremost, the former leaders of the Third Reich; functionaries and activists of the Nazi Party and other Nazi organizations; members of the police, the *Sicherheitsdienst* (German security service), Gestapo and other law enforcement agencies; prison and concentration camp guards; judicial officers and prosecutors; mass media editors and well known journalists, etc. All these people that could be found were subject to arrest, and a network of NKVD special camps was set up on German territory to hold them. However, far from all of them were sent there. Thus, on 18 April 1945 USSR NKVD Order no. 00315, signed by Beria, was issued. In particular, it required the following:

The command-political and enlisted personnel of the enemy army, as well as of the militarized '*Volkssturm*', SS and SA organizations, as well as personnel from prisons, concentration camps, military commandants, military prosecution offices and courts, are to be sent to USSR NKVD camps for prisoners-of-war, as established by procedure.[55]

Thus, 68,451 men were counted in the overall totals, while an additional 6,680 were sent to POW camps, having first been in NKVD special camps.[56]

As we see, men who had not served in the German armed forces were arbitrarily recorded as POWs, numbered alongside Wehrmacht and Waffen SS soldiers and officers.

Similar cases occurred not only with the Germans, but also with their former allies. Thus, after Budapest was captured, the 3rd Ukrainian Front forces energetically purged it of suspicious persons. How this was implemented in practice can be discerned from a top secret letter from M. Rákosi, General Secretary of the Hungarian Communist Party Central Committee, to G.M. Dimitrov, Head of the Party Central Committee's Department of International Information, about Hungary's domestic political and economic situation, sent on 17 March 1945:

> We are experiencing great difficulties because raids are becoming more frequent on the streets of Budapest. Sometimes it happens that thousands of workers going to the factories or returning from there are stopped on the streets and sent to various camps as prisoners of war. These measures are justified by the fact that there are many Fascist soldiers in Budapest dressed in civilian clothes. As a result, hundreds of comrades are disappearing. Our people are laying siege literally every day to the House of the Central Committee, complaining about this.[57]

The reason for sending to POW camps peaceful citizens who had been seized on the streets of a rear-area town was not some outrageous arbitrariness on the part of the 3rd Ukrainian Front's command. It was acting in strict accordance with instructions from authorities, summarized in telegram no. 100 088/III/42.[58] It should be mentioned that, in the final analysis, among people, who suffered because of this edict, many got off comparatively easily. Apparently, Rákosi's letter to Moscow may have had some effect, or perhaps it was for some other reason, but by the beginning of August no fewer than 10,352 of them had been released to their homes directly from front camps.[59]

Even after their release, however, they were not excluded from the Soviet POW statistics, which was also true for those who had been interned. In the overall balance sheet, these Hungarians were simply allocated a separate column: 'Released in Budapest during the Raids'. At the same time they were conveniently included in the sum total of POWs,[60] listed precisely among those who had already been captured during combat.

Women were yet another category of the civilian population that the USSR unjustifiably counted among the POWs. With the rarest exceptions, women did not serve in the Wehrmacht, but were used there only as service staff. Nevertheless, around 20,000 of these women were taken into Soviet captivity on the Soviet-German Front and sent to the appropriate NKVD camps.[61]

Characteristically, Krivosheev's team did not even try to somehow distinguish all these people from the overall number of Wehrmacht POWs. If that is to be the approach, however, this should also not be done for Soviet POWs, otherwise comparing the two totals would not make any sense. It is for this reason that, in subsequent computations, we will use both the German information we have about the number of Soviet POWs (5,734,528, according to Streit) and the complete Soviet information from NKVD statistics on the number of servicemen from Germany and its allies that the Soviets captured during the war, without the unjustified exclusion of any individual categories from them.

At the same time Krivosheev frankly did not observe the elementary, albeit very important requirement for any objective comparison: consistent criteria for the values being compared. It is not by chance that he did this. On the one hand, he completely rejected the German count of Soviet POWs and tried in any way possible to reduce this number. On the other hand, by hook or by crook he inflated the number of POWs from the Nazi coalition countries. All this was mainly the result of nothing other than his constantly manifested desire to decrease the disproportion in the ratio of irrecoverable losses between the opposing sides on the Soviet-German Front.

Chapter 5

Irrecoverable casualties of the German armed forces on the Soviet-German Front

Thus, we discover a constant and clear attempt on the part of Krivosheev's team to reduce the USSR armed forces' irrecoverable losses so as not to exceed the number reported by the Central Committee of the CPSU: 11,444,100. The opposite trend can be seen in their determination of the enemy's irrecoverable losses, above all those of the Red Army's main adversary, the Wehrmacht. Here the authors of the statistical study indulged in increasing the irrecoverable losses of the German armed forces in any way they could.

In ascertaining and publicizing the ratio of irrecoverable losses of the opposing sides in the Great Patriotic War, exacting standards must be applied. Only the most reliable information must be used, sources must be indicated without exception, every doubtful number must be carefully analysed, and all figures must be scrupulously rechecked and compared. Unfortunately, the authors of the statistical study consistently demonstrated a completely different approach.

Everything began with the basic initial balance sheet of the personnel strength of the armed forces of Nazi Germany during the Second World War. Computing the overall number of German servicemen who served in the Wehrmacht and Waffen SS, the authors made an egregious error, whether deliberately or unintentionally, which substantially affected the end results of their work. The authors added to the number of those who had been mobilized since 1 June 1939 (17,893,000 men) another 3,214,000 who had supposedly been serving on 1 March 1939,[1] thereby increasing the initial number for all their subsequent calculations by 18 per cent. Characteristically, however, for Krivosheev's team the overall balance sheet for the change in personnel strength of the German armed forces converged right on the nose. Is this not a model of shameless manipulation of the numbers? After this, how can one trust the rest of their calculations?

As we have established, this figure has no relation whatsoever to reality. First of all, in fact, on 1 March 1939 there were 730,000 men serving as German peacetime ground forces personnel,[2] 300,000 in the Air Force,

78,000 in the Navy and 23,000 in the Waffen SS,[3] for a total of 1,131,000. From where did Krivosheev obtain a number that was almost three times as large? After all, he based it by citing this very same Müller-Hillebrand.[4] This puzzle is easily solved: in the German mobilization plan, which had just been adopted on 1 March 1939, the overall strength of the ground field forces and the reserve army minus the number of conscripts was set at 3,214,104 men.[5] This purely planned number, however, has nothing in common with the actual personnel strength of the German armed forces on 1 March 1939, despite Krivosheev's claims to the contrary.

Second of all, and much more importantly, Müller-Hillebrand included all men who served in the German armed forces throughout the Second World War in the overall balance sheet. For greater clarity, he rendered his results in graphic form and put it into his famous book. His graph demonstrates more than clearly that there were altogether 17,893,200 men.[6] Hence, this number takes into account all servicemen, without exception, including those who were mobilized before the beginning of the war.

We would like to pause here to address one very important matter. The fact is, an annoying misprint slipped into the Russian translation of Müller-Hillebrand's classic work, one which might inadvertently mislead and confuse many of its readers. It concerns the exact temporal framework of the period in which men serving in the German armed forces during the Second World War were taken into account. In the Russian-language edition of *Germany's Ground Forces* this begins, for some strange reason, on 1 June 1939, when, as is known, the war started exactly three months later. Many different specula- tions and theories can be built on this discrepancy, but it is much more pro- ductive to simply find out just what the origin of this seemingly inexplicable date was. To do this one must know the history of the writing of Müller-Hillebrand's book and the sources used in its creation. The book's immediate predecessor was *Statistics Systems*, written by the same author in collaboration with seven other former German officers in 1949. This work was done under the aegis of the US Army's Department of History within the framework of studying the experience of the recent war. Therein, at the very place where in the Russian-language edition '1 June 1939' is printed, the date '1 Sep 1939' (i.e. 1 September 1939) is given.[7] Thus, everything immediately falls into place, and the issue born of a simple misprint is put to rest once and for all.

To fully confirm the correctness of the number we researched, we can compare it with the figures of other reliable independent sources on this subject. In his book *Fighting Power*, Martin van Creveld, a well known military historian, used the number already familiar to us: 'From September 1939 to April 1945 17,893,200 men passed through the Wehrmacht and Waffen SS.'[8]

In volume 2 of *Waffen und Geheimwaffen* ('Weapons and Secret Weapons') Fritz Hahn, a reputable German author, states the same: 'A total of 17,893,200 men served in the Wehrmacht and Waffen SS during the Second World War.'[9] In an authoritative statistical publication chock-full with the most detailed information on the Second World War, the total number of men who served in the German armed forces at that time is given as 17.9 million.[10]

All these sources are in complete concurrence with Müller-Hillebrand's corresponding number, and there are more at our disposal. We can turn to the well known work of Rüdiger Overmans, researcher at the Federal Republic of Germany's Military History Research Institute, which was completely devoted to Wehrmacht casualties. According to this work, a total of 18.2 million men served in Germany's ground forces, Air Force, Navy and Waffen SS during the Second World War.[11] This is slightly more than Müller-Hillebrand's number, but there is no major difference here – less than 2 per cent. Moreover, all of Overmans' information was calculated and, according to the majority of specialists, somewhat overstated. In general and on the whole, his completely independent research agreed quite well with Müller-Hillebrand's results, and once again only served to positively confirm its correctness.

Thus, the total personnel resources that Germany's military leadership had at its disposal during the entire Second World War were fewer than Krivosheev's number by the very 3,214,000 men whom he had completely groundlessly added. A totally logical question then arises: in which item in Krivosheev's table, which reflects the dynamics of change in the personnel strength of Germany's armed forces during the Second World War, were these 3.2 million ghost soldiers included? The answer to this lies on the surface: in the irrecoverable losses, of course. After all, the German servicemen who were still in the ranks at the end of the war and who were convalescing at that time, as well as the deserters, those who had been discharged because of wounds and illness, and those who had been demobilized and sent to work in industry before the end of the war, had been documented much better than the casualties, especially at the end of military operations. Essentially, the German armed forces' irrecoverable losses in the statistical study were obtained by subtracting all the above-mentioned categories from the overall mobilization resources.

It turns out that, in fact, the Wehrmacht's total irrecoverable losses for the period of the Second World War numbered 8,630,000 men, not the 11,844,000 that Krivosheev calculated. Accordingly, we must also correct his count of casualties on the Soviet-German Front. To do this it is necessary to reduce the count proportionally to its share in the distribution of Germany's irrecoverable losses among the different theatres of military operations. According to Krivosheev's information, during the Great Patriotic War the Germans irrecoverably lost 7,181,100 men (60.63 per cent of all losses) on the Soviet-German Front.[12] Therefore, taking into account the corrected number of total German irrecoverable losses, the Soviet-German Front portion amounts to 60.63 per cent of 8,630,000, which is equal to 5,232,400 men, or 37 per cent fewer than Krivosheev's calculation.

This, however, is far from the only example in the book of open inflation of the casualties of the USSR's enemies. Let us take, for example, the table of information about Nazi Germany's irrecoverable armed forces personnel losses on the Soviet-German Front from 22 June 1941 to 9 May 1945.[13] Its content immediately gives rise to a number of questions.

First and foremost, the absence of citations of sources is noteworthy. Although this is completely customary for Krivosheev's team, in this case the authors undoubtedly used not information from the Soviet archives, but rather some German document they mentioned in passing,[14] and likely not just one. They did not, however, wish to identify these sources. One can understand why: to make it easier to engage in distortions and fabrications. Nevertheless, we will try to analyse some of these numbers.

Let us take the Air Force and air defence casualties as a starting point. In Germany these belonged to the same department: Goering's. Krivosheev arbitrarily relegated 75 per cent of their casualties to the Soviet-German Front. Meanwhile, according to Overmans' information, 45.26 per cent of Luftwaffe personnel were killed there. This ratio does not take into account casualties at the end of the war or those who died in captivity, but there is no strong basis to assume that it could change so dramatically with these added. The same applies to German Navy losses. According to Overmans, only 9.72 per cent of Kriegsmarine seamen died in the East (also excluding the last period of the war and POW fatalities), while Krivosheev, of his own volition, increased this to 32 per cent. In this simple way he added as many as 165,800 men to the irrecoverable German losses.[15]

It is not at all clear from where the authors of the statistical study obtained the Wehrmacht's noncombat casualties and how the authors divided those casualties among the different theatres of military operations. Moreover, a complete absurdity is created by their numbers that reflect the fate of the wounded in German hospitals on the Soviet-German Front. According to Krivosheev's team, during the last nine days of the war, 152,800 German servicemen died there out of the total 484,100 who died during the war's entire 1,418 days and nights.[16] Thus, it turns out that in May 1945 the daily fatality rate of wounded in German hospitals in the East increased from 235 to 16,978 men, or by more than 72 times! Apparently, Krivosheev and his team did not realize (or perhaps did not wish to realize) that some people, on the basis of these clumsily falsified statistics, would eventually accuse the Red Army of the mass extermination of the German wounded who had fallen into their hands during the very last days of the war.

Further on, this manipulation becomes even more outrageous. The presence in the table of German armed forces casualties on the Soviet-German Front of information about military formations and installations that were not part of the Wehrmacht or the Waffen SS causes legitimate confusion. After all, the authors of the statistical study themselves intentionally disregarded casualties of similar categories in the balance sheet of USSR armed forces' irrecoverable losses. Casualties of these kinds were simply ignored on the basis that they were not operationally taken into account in the monthly troop reports. Therefore, casualties of similar Soviet armed formations were relegated to the country's civilian population losses. However, such logic demands that the casualties of any German organizations not relegated to the Wehrmacht or the Waffen SS – as many as 777,800 men – must also be likewise removed from the list of German armed forces' irrecoverable losses.

The statistics of enemy servicemen captured by the Red Army during the Great Patriotic War are treated even more illogically. To compute them, Krivosheev's book uses information about the number of POWs from Germany and its allies in NKVD camps, calculated as of 22 April 1956.[17] This is a completely reliable document; after all, it was intended as information for only a few high-ranking officials and even bore the seal 'Of Special Importance'.[18] However, one need only turn one's attention to the date in the title of the table made on the document's basis – **22 April 1956** – and it becomes immediately clear that the document concerns all POWs from the Nazi Axis countries, including those that capitulated **after** 9 May 1945. Krivosheev, however, unabashedly listed them all as captured **before** this date.

At the same time, he reported that, after 9 May 1945, 1,591,121 soldiers and officers (only from Germany's armed forces) laid down their arms to Soviet troops.[19] However, there were others who surrendered – the Hungarians, for example. Did the authors of the statistical study really have in mind that all these men were inexplicably able to elude Soviet POW camps? Of course not, and we will demonstrate this later. Moreover, even later the influx of new prisoners into the numerous installations of the GUPVI system in no way dried up. In all, 3,250,151 POWs from the armed forces of Germany and its satellites came there from the very beginning of the Great Patriotic War until the end of 1945. In the following year another 32,779 were added,[20] and the total number as of 22 April 1956 had reached 3,486,206.[21] Thus, over the following ten years the number increased by 236,055 men. The main reason for this increase was the fact that POW camps in the USSR were used extensively to punish various types of Nazi criminals and their accomplices, as well as to force them to work for the good of the country. In addition to them, a large number of random men also wound up in these camps. One can argue at length whether or not they all deserved the status of POW, but in this case it is not particularly important. The main thing is this: all these men wound up in POW camps following the capitulation of their countries, and therefore in no way should have been counted among the irrecoverable losses those countries' armed forces suffered during the war. Krivosheev, however, did not shy away from putting these prisoners there along with the almost 1.6 million men who surrendered after 9 May. By doing so he unjustifiably inflated the number of enemy POWs captured by the Red Army during the war by more than 1.8 million men!

The abundance of factual distortions and patent misrepresentations, the obvious miscalculation of Soviet armed forces losses, the chronic additions to enemy casualties, the clear internal contradictions and the elementary mistakes in Krivosheev's work all lead to the conclusion that we should, by and large, reject all his arithmetic and proceed by another, independent path. This promises results that correspond much better to reality.

Of course, we must also approach his foundational information with a certain degree of caution. The most substantive shortcoming is the widespread absence of citations, making it quite impossible to verify sources. This circumstance results in legitimate distrust of Krivosheev's numbers, further exacerbated by the obvious prejudice of the authors of the statistical study. Therefore, we must try to find more reliable information that can be verified.

Today, Overmans' aforementioned book contains the fullest and most trustworthy information about fallen German armed forces servicemen during the Second World War. The figures in this book are of a calculation nature and based on an extensive card file of German servicemen who were killed, died or MIA and were subsequently acknowledged as dead. Essentially, they represent the maximum of all possible casualties; therefore, they can be considered slightly overstated in comparison with reality. Furthermore, they include casualties of civilian personnel of the Wehrmacht, organizations providing services to it, the *Volkssturm*, the police, etc.[22] Therefore, there can be no talk whatsoever of undercalculation here.

According to Overmans' calculations, the Germans had lost 2,742,909 killed on the Soviet-German Front by the end of 1944, and an additional

1,230,045 by the end of the war on all fronts.[23] It is not known precisely how many of them died fighting against the Red Army in 1945, but their number can be approximately calculated. One need only proceed from the completely sensible assumption that German casualties in 1945 were distributed among the various theatres of military operations in the same proportion as the losses in the second half of 1944, which we know. According to Overmans' information, 1,162,966 Germans were killed from the beginning of July to the end of December 1944, of which 740,821 (63.7 per cent) were on the Soviet-German Front.[24] From this we can deduce that 783,600 men in the German armed forces died in the East in 1945 and 3,526,500 during the entire Great Patriotic War.

Now only the number of German POWs captured on the Soviet-German Front is required to compute the overall number of German armed forces irrecoverable losses there. The most reliable information about them can be found in the large-format book *POWs in the USSR. 1939–1956. Documents and Materials.* According to a document published there, 664,188 POWs from the German army arrived at Soviet MVD camps in 1941–1944, with an additional 1,856,126, including Spaniards, in 1945.[25]

The existence of a front-line network of POW camps subordinate to the Red Army command also cannot be forgotten. It was from these camps that enemy servicemen captured during combat were sent to rear area NKVD camps, and only from then on were they registered in its statistics. By November 1945 the front-line camps had basically been dismantled,[26] but by 30 December there were still 14,730 German POWs there and an additional 4,416 on their way to the rear area camps.[27]

Thus, from 22 June 1941 until the end of 1945 there were 2,539,440 German armed forces servicemen in Soviet captivity. However, far from all of them had been captured before Germany's unconditional surrender on 9 May 1945. According to a 27 June 1945 document from A.N. Bronnikov, Chief of the GUPVI's 2nd section (records), these numbered 1,390,516 men.[28] Only 1,320,500 of them, however, were associated with the German armed forces; the remaining 70,000 were serving in the Hungarian army.[29] In addition to them, it is necessary to exclude from the general list those POWs whom the Red Army had not captured, but rather who had wound up in Soviet hands for other reasons. There was a sizeable number of these, among whom were:

- around 3,000 Wehrmacht servicemen interned during the war in Sweden and sent to the USSR at the latter's request on 16 June 1945; and

- around 25,000 German POWs, including 5,000 officers, whom the Americans bequeathed to the Red Army, together with camps and assembly points, in Thuringia after this territory had been transferred to Soviet control at the beginning of July 1945.[30]

In turn, the USSR transferred 50,000 German POWs to Poland in September 1945, and an additional 3,000 to Czechoslovakia in November to work in the Jachymov uranium mines. However, these prisoners all managed to enter the general Soviet POW statistics, namely into the number of those captured by the Red Army and then repatriated.[31] Therefore, their removal from the NKVD camps has no effect at all on our calculations.

From all these numbers it follows that during the war Soviet POW camps accepted 1,190,900 German army soldiers and officers captured during combat. However, the overall number of POWs from the Third Reich captured by the Red Army is in no way encompassed by this figure; there were others as well. This is what Krivosheev wrote about them:

> ... according to reports from the *fronts* and individual armies, which the General Staff of the USSR armed forces has summarized, our forces captured 4,377,300 German servicemen, of whom around 600,000 were, after the appropriate verification, released directly at the front lines. Generally, they were persons of non-German nationality who had been forcibly conscripted into the Wehrmacht and armies of its allies (Poles, Czechs, Slovaks, Romanians, Slovenians, Bulgarians, Moldavians, *Volksdeutsche*, and others), as well as disabled persons who could not be transported. These persons were not sent to the rear area POW camps on USSR territory, and were not included in the registration data.[32]

To start with, let us note that the issue here does not only concern German servicemen. Krivosheev once again unintentionally contradicts himself, because one learns from his book that the casualties of those captured from the German armed forces and the armies of its allies – Hungary, Italy, Romania, Finland and Slovakia – amounted to a total of 4,376,300 men.[33] This is a whole thousand fewer than for the Germans alone, about whom he writes here. Further, one cannot help but note that many of the persons of non-German nationality he describes here were clearly not associated with the servicemen of the Wehrmacht and its allied armies, but rather with service personnel. And according to Krivosheev himself, this category should not have been entered as POWs.

We will not, however, split hairs here. It is much more interesting and useful to determine who these people were, why they were released and, most importantly, when they were released. After all, as is known, neither the *front* command nor even the GUPVI had the right by its own authority to release those captured who were at their disposal. This absolutely required the appropriate approval of the USSR's higher political leadership, and such approval was received.

First, State Defence Committee Resolution no. 8921ss, 'On the Distribution of Prisoners of War and Measures to Improve Their Use as Labour', dated 4 June 1945, was issued. In particular, it stated:

> The NKVD is permitted to release from camps and special hospitals and send to their homeland prisoners of war who cannot be used for work because of their physical condition: the disabled, chronically sick, extremely weak – those who will be unable to work for a long time – a total of as many as 225,000 men.
>
> Prisoners of war who cannot work are to be sent from camps and special hospitals during June–July 1945 by trains delivering prisoners of war from the front lines on their return trips.[34]

NKVD Order no. 00698, dated 4 June 1945, for the execution of this decision, explained that the lists of those to be sent home should include 'the disabled, those ill with tuberculosis, the chronically ill with surgical diseases, those with 1st and 2nd degree dystrophy, and all those who will be unable to work for a long time'.[35] The Soviet leadership had decided to get rid of unnecessary ballast among the POWs. Only those who could effectively work in industry and construction for the recovery of the war-torn USSR economy remained in the GUPVI camps. Those who could not work were sent home.

Continuing on this course with regard to POWs, one more State Defence Committee resolution – no. 9843ss, dated 13 August 1945 – was issued. In accordance with it, the NKVD was authorized 'to release and send to their homeland prisoners of war from those enlisted and NCOs who are in the USSR in regions of former front lines, a total of 708,000 men ...', among whom were '412,000 disabled Germans and others unable to work'.[36] The next day People's Commissar of the NKVD L. Beria signed Order no. 00955, 'On the Release of Some of the Prisoners of War from NKVD Camps and Special Hospitals'. Therein it was clarified that by the end of the year '419,000 men from camps of the former front network and 289,000 men from rear area camps and special hospitals, [including] ill and disabled German prisoners of war and those who will be unable to work for a long time, totalling 412,000 men, of whom 301,000 men are at the fronts,' would be subject to release. The task 'to complete the transport of released prisoners of war from rear area camps and special hospitals to transfer points before

15 October 1945' was assigned. Incidentally, in addition to those unable to work, those to be released also included those very persons of non-German nationality whom Krivosheev mentions in the book: Poles, Czechs, Slovaks, Romanians, Slovenians, Bulgarians and many others. We should mention that among them were 150,000 Hungarians who were serving in their own country's army, not in the Wehrmacht.[37] In addition to them, in accordance with State Defence Committee resolution no. 8921ss, yet another 24,909 Hungarian POWs had just earlier been released.[38]

In sum, by the end of the year the planned numbers of those who could be released with respect to both State Defence Committee resolutions had been somewhat exceeded. A total of 950,514 POWs were sent home, of whom 408,248 were from rear area camps and the remaining 542,266 from front-line camps.[39]

In the statistical study one can find both the total number of the Wehrmacht POWs who were freed from Soviet captivity (2,910,400) and the number of those who were released from NKVD camps (2,352,700).[40] The difference between these numbers (557,700) tells us how many German POWs were released from Soviet front-line camps, according to Krivosheev's information. He still preferred to slightly exaggerate this figure by writing that 'around 600,000 were, after the appropriate verification, released directly at the front lines'. At the same time, he concealed the main reasons why they were sent home. The key detail here is that, whether by mistake or deliberately, he misled his readers regarding the time of those prisoners' release. This is of fundamental importance to determining the actual ratio of the irrecoverable losses of the opposing sides for the entire period of the Great Patriotic War. Apparently, it was for this reason that Krivosheev portrayed them all as part of those captured during combat. Meanwhile, judging by the time and reasons for their release, the majority of these prisoners were associated with those who had surrendered after 9 May 1945.

Of all POWs who were freed from the front-line camps at that time, 126,451 were Hungarians and 4,835 were Romanians,[41] so 410,980 men from the German armed forces remained in this category. How many of them had been captured before the end of the war? It is possible to answer this complex question, albeit only approximately. Judging by a document about the movement of POWs as of 21 May 1945, from 9 to 19 May 1,239,950 enemy soldiers and officers had surrendered to the Red Army. By the end of this period there were an additional 1,505,006 men at Red Army front assembly points and camps, in hospitals and in rear area camps.[42] Hence, at the moment of Germany's capitulation, there were 265,056 POWs (21.4 per cent of those who had been captured) in front-line camps. If we proceed from the fact that

German POWs released from front-line camps were evenly distributed among all the remaining ones, then it turns out that approximately 87,900 were among those who had been captured during combat. Adding this number to our already calculated number of captured German servicemen who arrived at the GUPVI camps during the war (1,190,900), we see that Soviet front-line and rear area POW camps received a total of 1,278,800 men.

Our calculations, however, do not end here. Krivosheev mentioned the following categories among the enemy soldiers captured by the Red Army who did not arrive in Soviet POW camps:

- around 57,000 who died of wounds, illnesses and frostbite on the way, thus never reaching the rear area camps;
- more than 220,000 Soviet citizens who had served in the Wehrmacht or who had taken part in the war on the side of Nazi Germany; and
- 14,100 military criminals, who had been sent to special camps.[43]

We would like to delve into the latter in a little more detail. The fact is that both military criminals sentenced by Soviet tribunals and those who for various reasons were sent to prison were entered into the overall statistics of enemy POWs in the USSR. A 28 January 1949 GUPVI document allotted separate columns for them and noted the reasons for their removal from the general list.[44] At the same time, special NKVD camps and prisons for military criminals also existed. They had been organized on German territory, but Beria had signed Order no. 00461 about this on 10 May 1945, after the war had ended.[45] Those of these prisoners' potential contingent who had been arrested even earlier and who had been associated with the command and political personnel of the Wehrmacht, Waffen SS and the *Volkssturm*, together with many others, had been sent to general POW camps,[46] and, accordingly, had been included in their statistics.

Thus, the total enemy POWs who had not arrived at Soviet camps numbered 277,000 men. Among these men, however, as well as among all remaining POWs in Krivosheev's statistics, were both those who had been taken captive during combat and those who had surrendered after 9 May 1945. To find out the numbers of the former and the latter, we will use an analogous proportion between the numbers of German POWs we know to have arrived in Soviet camps before victory (1,278,800) and after it (1,320,500). The proportion of those captured before the war ended was 49.2 per cent; consequently, the calculated number of those German POWs who for various reasons did not arrive at Soviet camps equals 136,300.

Adding this to our calculated total of German POWs in Soviet front-line and rear area camps (1,278,800), we obtain a sum total of 1,415,100 German armed forces servicemen whom the Red Army had captured during the Great Patriotic War before Germany's surrender.

We would like to pause here to discuss a very important detail. In their attempt to overstate the Red Army's military successes while smoothing over its blunders, Krivosheev's team unduly increased the number of German POWs that had been captured before 9 May 1945. Any such stretching of the truth in statistical balance sheets inevitably creates bizarre implications, which sooner or later become impossible to ignore. In this case, Krivosheev's authors have managed to completely discredit the Soviet GUPVI camp system and, inadvertently or not, accused it of unjustifiable cruelty.

We have already demonstrated this with the example of the fatality rate of Soviet POWs in German camps; now we will do the same for German POWs in Soviet camps. Using only Krivosheev's information for this calculation once again leads to, put delicately, unexpected results. According to his claim, 3,576,300 servicemen from the German armed forces had been captured before 9 May 1945; after this date an additional 1,591,125 were brought in,[47] totalling around 5,167,400. If we subtract from this number the 600,000 who were released directly at the front lines, 220,000 Soviet citizens who served in the Wehrmacht or took part in the war on the side of Nazi Germany, 14,100 military criminals sent to special camps, and around 57,000 who died on the way of wounds, illness or frostbite, then we are left with the figure of 4,276,300 German servicemen who arrived at Soviet POW camps.

But how many of them eventually returned home? According to Krivosheev's information, 2,352,671 Wehrmacht POWs were released and repatriated.[48] It appears that the missing 1,923,600 did not survive captivity. Moreover, taking into account the 57,000 who died on the way from wounds, illness and frostbite, it turns out that of the 4,333,300 Wehrmacht and Waffen SS soldiers and officers imprisoned in the USSR, 1,980,600 (a little less than half – 45.7 per cent) died in the NKVD camps or on the way to them. Such a devastating fatality rate has no rational justification and, like it or not, recalls the single-minded policy of genocide to which Soviet POWs in Nazi camps were subjected. These are the conclusions – not just absurd, but dangerous – to which trust in Krivosheev's conniving arithmetic leads!

In truth, the overall number of POWs who died in NKVD camps has been precisely known for a long time already: 518,520 of the 3,486,206 men who arrived there.[49] Taking into account the additional 57,000 who died on the way and never reached these camps, we see that the fatality rate in Soviet captivity was actually 16.2 per cent, that is, almost three times lower than the figure we arrived at when uncritically relying on the information from the statistical study.

In sum, we can determine the irrecoverable losses for the German armed forces on the Soviet-German Front during the Great Patriotic War by adding the overall number of killed, dead or MIA (but subsequently acknowledged as having died) servicemen (3,526,500) to the total number of German POWs (1,415,100). As a result, we obtain a total number of 4,941,600 men, or **almost 1.5 times fewer** than the 7,181,100 whom Krivosheev's team calculated.

Chapter 6

Irrecoverable casualties of the German and Soviet allies on the Soviet-German Front

According to information from Krivosheev's team, the total irrecoverable losses for the armed forces of Germany and its allies on the Soviet-German Front amounted to 8,649,300 men.[1] Judging by everything, this information is noticeably overstated. First and foremost, legitimate doubts are raised by the obvious discrepancy in the numbers of irrecoverable personnel losses for Germany and its allies on the Soviet-German Front when comparing the 1993 work[2] with the 2001 work.[3] Unlike the USSR, the other warring countries conducted a census soon after the war (no later than 1951);[4] therefore, work on determining their actual casualty figures relied on a considerably more precise demographic base than in the USSR. Although this base in no way changed during the eight years that had passed between Krivosheev's publications, for some reason he reported the total irrecoverable losses for Germany's satellites differently. Suddenly these were reduced by 257,600 men (while the number of men reported as captured increased by 33,200), despite the addition of Slovaks to the statistics. Even more surprising, however, is that Germany's irrecoverable losses also increased by this same number, and the number of German POWs increased at the same time by 1,004,700.

We have an extremely interesting phenomenon: the composition of the allies changed, and the numbers with respect to types of casualty in both works 'ramble', but as a result the total number of irrecoverable losses remained practically unchanged. Accordingly, their ratio – 1:1.3 – also stays unchanged. Is this not yet another piece of clear evidence of a target number coordinated beforehand with a 'higher authority'?

Heated discussions around the extensive information published by Krivosheev's team have not abated since the appearance of the first edition in 1993. However, they argue mainly about the magnitude of the casualties of the principal participants on the battlefields of the Great Patriotic War – the Red Army and the Wehrmacht. At the same time, their allies, who fought shoulder-to-shoulder with them, generally remain in the shadows. Nevertheless, their contribution to the fierce fighting on the Soviet-German Front was not small. This especially applies to Germany's satellites. From practically the very first days of the war troops from Hungary, Romania, Slovakia and Finland fought on Germany's side. They sent out against the Soviet Union a total of 31 divisions and 18 brigades, which comprised more than 30 per cent of the Wehrmacht formations fighting on the front line.[5] A few weeks later an Italian expeditionary corps also joined them.

The military contingents of all these states were operationally subordinate to the German command. However, they still maintained relative independence and kept their own records of successes, failures and casualties. Red Army soldiers and officers who fell into the hands of the Finns and in part the Romanians remained in their POW camps until the very time that these countries left the war. The remaining foreign citizens who fought on the German side on the Soviet-German Front, as well as the subunits, units and formations that had been organized from them, were organically part of the Wehrmacht; therefore their casualties were entered into the calculation of its losses.

However, these armies' irrecoverable losses noticeably affected the general level of casualties of the USSR's enemies. Krivosheev did not pass over them. In his book there is a table on page 514, 'Irrecoverable Personnel Casualties of the Armed Forces of Germany's Allies on the Soviet-German Front from 22 June 1941 to 9 May 1945'. Two circumstances associated with this are immediately evident: firstly, the surprising detail and precision of the figures there – the overwhelming majority of data are calculated down to a single man; secondly, there is not a single citation there, foreign or Soviet.

Apparently, a large part of the information included there was obtained from *front* (army) reports on the results of operations that had been conducted. Those who directly worked with the original TsAMO RF documents saw these fantastic numbers. If we put them together, then by the beginning of 1944 there should have been no ground forces, in general, remaining in Germany. The only exception here is the information on the number of POWs who turned up in Soviet camps and their subsequent fate. Therefore, we must seek reliable figures regarding the casualties of the German satellites in the works of respected historians who have devoted substantial monographs to the participation of these countries in the war. Of course, there are such historians, and they are well known to all who are interested in this important topic.

First and foremost among them is Mark Axworthy. His monograph, *Third Axis Fourth Ally. Romanian Armed Forces in the European War, 1941–1945*, became a universally recognized classic immediately after its publication in 1995. Since then there has not been a serious work on this subject that has not cited it. When *Axis Slovakia: Hitler's Slavic Wedge, 1938–1945*, a fundamental work on the Slovak armed forces during this same period, appeared seven years later, it occupied a similar place in its own right with respect to the book's theme, which before this had not been studied much.

Issues concerning the participation of the Hungarian armed forces on Germany's side in battles on the Soviet-German Front were illuminated best of all by well known historian Leo Niehorster in his most detailed work, *The Royal Hungarian Army, 1920–1945*. Hungarian scholar Tamás Stark elaborated on Niehorster's work in *Hungary's Human Losses in World War II*, a book on this theme in particular. One could find a reliable figure on the casualties of the Italian expeditionary corps in the USSR in the authoritative statistical publication, *The World War II Databook*, prepared by John Ellis. And *POWs in the USSR. 1939–1965*, a voluminous collection of documents and materials, made it possible to refine the number of POWs from these armies who were held captive by the Soviets.

Finally, Finnish Army casualties in 1941–1945 are most comprehensively reflected in *Jatkosodan historia*, a six-volume publication of the official history of this war, published in Helsinki in 1988–1994. Here one can find the overall number of Finnish POWs captured by the Red Army in Professor D.D. Frolov's solid monograph, *Soviet-Finnish Captivity. 1939–1944. On Both Sides of the Barbed Wire*. Frolov did a great deal of work in both the Soviet archives and the National Archive of Finland and essentially refined earlier information on the number and fate of Finnish servicemen in Soviet captivity. Thus, while Krivosheev counted 2,377 Finnish prisoners in Soviet captivity, of whom 403 (17 per cent) died, Frolov calculated 3,114 captive Finns, of whom 997 (32 per cent) did not survive the war.[6]

Information from the sources enumerated above is collected in Table 13.

A serious discrepancy is more than obvious between the number of the table's computed irrecoverable losses of the armed forces of Germany's allies and Krivosheev's information. His result was 1,468,145 men (41 per cent greater).[7] We indicated earlier one of the main reasons for such a significant difference. True to itself, Krivosheev's team, without further ado, as in the case with the Germans, included in the number of POWs captured by the Red Army before 9 May 1945 everyone, without distinction, including servicemen who surrendered after the war ended and even some interned civilians.

Krivosheev's information about the irrecoverable losses of the armed forces of Germany's allies on the Soviet-German Front is also far from reliable.

Table 13: Irrecoverable losses of the armed forces of Germany's allies on the Soviet-German Front*

Country	Period	Killed and died of wounds	MIA	POW	Total
Hungary	1941–1945	120,000		415,764**	535,764
Italy	1941–1943	35,887		48,943	84,830
Romania	1941–1944	72,291	116,790	166,532	355,613
Slovakia	1941–1944	1,235	2,243	294	3,772
Finland	1941–1944	51,879	3,722	3,114	58,715
Totals	1941–1945	404,047		634,647	1,038,694

*Sources: Axworthy, *Third Axis Fourth Ally*, p. 216; M.W.A. Axworthy, *Axis Slovakia: Hitler's Slavic Wedge, 1938–1945* (Bayside, NY: Axis Europa Books, 2002), p. 211; J. Ellis, *The World War II Databook* (London: Aurum Press Ltd, 1995), p. 255; *Jatkosodan historia. Osa 6* (Helsinki: National Defence College, 1994); L.W.G. Niehorster, *The Royal Hungarian Army, 1920–1945* (Bayside, NY: Axis Europa Books, 1998), p. 157; T. Stark, *Hungary's Human Losses in World War II* (Uppsala: Reprocentralen, HSC, 1995), p. 33; *POWs in the USSR*, pp. 331–3, 1041; Frolov, *Soviet-Finnish Captivity*, p. 292.

**Excluded from the number of Hungarian POWs are 10,352 men who were released after being captured in Budapest during the raids and 70,000 men who surrendered after the end of the war.

Above all, this is in regard to Romania's casualties. Moreover, he does not reflect Finland's participation in the war against Germany at all, despite the fact that Finland fought against the Germans on the Soviet side for almost seven months, from 1 October 1944 to 25 April 1945.[8] It is interesting that Krivosheev conscientiously calculated the 72 Mongolian servicemen who were casualties of the war against Japan, but for some reason preferred to completely ignore the 1,036 Finns who were killed, captured or went MIA in the fighting against the Wehrmacht on the extreme northern flank of the Soviet-German Front. After all, in addition to everything else, they captured 2,600 Germans and, in accordance with their agreement, transferred them to the Soviet Union.[9]

The data summarized in the table about the irrecoverable losses of the armed forces of Soviet allies on the Soviet-German Front during the Great Patriotic War differs from Krivosheev's number (76,122 men)[10] by more than 1.5 times. While he substantially overstated the casualties of Germany's satellites, he reduced the casualties of the USSR's allies to an even greater degree.

The reasons for this distortion are more than understandable: Krivosheev's team diligently solved their assigned problem to adjust the total ratio of

Table 14: Irrecoverable losses of the armed forces of Soviet allies on the Soviet-German Front*

Country	Period	Killed and died of wounds	MIA	POW	Total
Bulgaria	1945	10,124			10,124
Poland	1943–1945	24,707			24,707
Romania	1944–1945	21,035	58,443		79,478
Finland	1944–1945	774	224	38	1,036
Czechoslovakia	1943–1945	4,011			4,011
Total					119,356

* Sources: Axworthy, *Third Axis Fourth Ally*, p. 216; *Jatkosodan historia*; *Russia and the USSR in Wars of the 20th Century*, 2001, p. 450.

irrecoverable losses of the opposing sides on the Soviet-German Front to a more or less acceptable value. After all, carrying out a political order has nothing in common with searching for the truth, although the latter is what should occupy the honest historian.

Overall ratio of irrecoverable losses of the opposing sides in the Great Patriotic War

It is finally time to summarize our discussions about the irrecoverable losses of the opposing sides on the Soviet-German Front and **to determine their ratio**.

To begin with, however, let us recall that the irrecoverable losses of the armed forces refer to those who were killed, died of wounds and illnesses, died as a result of accidents, were executed by their own people according to sentences of tribunals and in combat, MIAs and captured servicemen, regardless of their subsequent fate (whether or not they returned to the Motherland after the war). In other words, we refer to all of those who were lost during the war and were excluded from the armed forces personnel rosters.

Together with the results of combat, battles, operations and the war itself, this integral statistical parameter has very important significance for assessing the effectiveness of the armed forces during combat. It quite objectively demonstrates both the results of troop combat training and the quality of their command and control at all levels. Each of the components of irrecoverable losses has its own importance. Whereas the number of enemy soldiers and officers killed better characterizes the tactical ability of soldiers and their junior, mid-level and senior officers, the number of captured POWs depends, to a greater degree, on the operational skill of the generals and the strategic expertise of the Supreme Command. The percentage of those who died of wounds and illnesses is an objective indicator of the general level of medical and health services for the troops. The number of those executed by their own people clearly reflects their combat spirit and political-moral condition.

The statistic of the irrecoverable losses for the armed forces acquires particular value because of its independence from various types of secondary factor. Let us say that one can kill all enemy captives, but this does not change the level of his enemy's irrecoverable losses, simply because the POWs have already been taken into account in these losses, so that their subsequent fate is irrelevant. Civilian casualties also do not affect the irrecoverable losses of the armed forces. There is only one real path to increase them: kill or capture enemy troops. This is easy to say, but, in fact, with weapons in hand, they do everything to hinder this and even, on the contrary, attempt to inflict the greatest possible casualties on the side fighting against them.

However, irrecoverable losses, in and of themselves, as distinct from all others, are not easy to assess; after all, everything is relative. Therefore, the ratio of the irrecoverable losses for the warring enemies is much more persuasive. It is this ratio that makes it possible to clarify what price was paid for the results of combat. Using this analysis, one can judge who fought using numbers and who fought using skill. It also demonstrates whose political leadership better prepared his armed forces for war and provided them the optimal initial conditions to enter it.

Judging by everything, the author team under Krivosheev's leadership understood quite well the true importance of the ratio of irrecoverable losses between the Soviet and German armed forces and those of their allies. It is for this reason that they did everything, by hook or by crook, to make it as favourable for the Red Army as possible. Nor did they stop at direct fabrications: they ascribed 3,214,000 men as having served in the Wehrmacht who never had been there, and calculated 2,326,600 POWs as having been captured by Soviet forces in combat who had actually been captured after Germany surrendered. There is no reason to be surprised at such dishonest methods on the part of the authors of the statistical study; after all, an obvious desire to justify at any cost the actions of the Soviet military and political leadership at that time and reduce the importance and consequences of their mistakes and blunders is transparent in their work. The main result of their calculations was that 'the ratio between German and Soviet irrecoverable [losses] is 1:1.3'.[1] However, all this clever arithmetic, built on numerous distortions of the facts, does not deserve to be trusted. In addition to all the other reasons, their computed ratio does not take into account that during the war the Germans succeeded in capturing 2.8 times more men than Soviet forces before Germany's surrender, which, of course, seriously affected the overall ratio of irrecoverable losses. To admit now to a cover-up of the truth and manipulation by those who prepared and announced the official casualty figures is tantamount to political suicide. One can only commiserate with them.

Taking into account the figure we validated above, the ratio of irrecoverable losses between the opposing sides on the Soviet-German Front during the Great Patriotic War looks completely different. It is shown in Table 15.

It should be mentioned that some information in the table was distributed according to year using certain assumptions and proportions; therefore, in the future they may be refined, although we do not anticipate any substantial

Table 15: Yearly ratios of irrecoverable losses between the armed forces of the USSR and its allies and the armed forces of Germany and its allies on the Soviet-German Front (in thousands of men)

Year	Type of irrecoverable loss	Countries						Ratio
		USSR*	Allies of the USSR**	Total	Germany	Allies of Germany	Total	
1941	Died and MIA	1,313.1 (27.4%)		1,313.1 (27.4%)	302.5 (96.8%)	80.9 (99.3%)	383.4 (97.3%)	3.4:1
	Captured	3,478.2 (72.6%)		3,478.2 (72.6%)	10.1 (3.2%)	0.6 (0.7%)	10.7 (2.7%)	325.1:1
	Total	4,791.3		4,791.3	312.6	81.5	394.1	12.2:1
1942	Died and MIA	2,273.5 (57.7%)		2,273.5 (57.7%)	506.8 (85.3%)	135.7 (72.6%)	642.5 (82.3%)	3.5:1
	Captured	1,668.6 (42.3%)		1,668.6 (42.3%)	87.4 (14.7%)	51.1 (27.4%)	138.5 (17.7%)	12.0:1
	Total	3,942.1		3,942.1	594.2	186.8	781.0	5.0:1
1943	Died and MIA	2,321.1 (79.4%)	2.9	2,324.0 (79.4%)	700.7 (86.1%)	49.0 (59.0%)	749.7 (83.6%)	3.1:1
	Captured	603.9 (20.6%)		603.9 (20.6%)	113.5 (13.9%)	34.0 (41.0%)	147.5 (16.4%)	4.1:1
	Total	2,925.0	2.9	2,927.9	814.2	83.0	897.2	3.3:1
1944	Died and MIA	1,883.5 (93.5%)	55.1	1,938.6 (93.7%)	1,232.9 (70.2%)	110.2 (32.6%)	1,343.1 (64.1%)	1.4:1
	Captured	130.1 (6.5%)		130.1 (6.3%)	523.9 (29.8%)	227.6 (67.4%)	751.5 (35.9%)	1:5.8
	Total	2,013.6	55.1	2,068.7	1,756.8	337.8	2,094.6	1:1
1945	Died and MIA	862.6 (100%)	61.4	924.0 (100%)	783.6 (53.5%)	28.3 (8.1%)	811.9 (44.8%)	1.1:1
	Captured				680.2 (46.5%)	321.3 (91.9%)	1,001.5 (55.2%)	
	Total	862.6	61.4	924.0	1,463.8	349.6	1,813.4	1:2
Total	Died and MIA	8,653.8 (59.5%)		8,773.2 (59.9%)	3,526.5 (71.4%)	404.1 (38.9%)	3,930.6 (65.7%)	2.2:1
	Captured	5,880.8 (40.5%)		5,880.8 (40.1%)	1,415.1 (28.6%)	634.6 (61.1%)	2,049.7 (34.3%)	2.9:1
	Total	14,534.6	119.4	14,654.0	4,941,6	1,038.7	5,980.3	2.5:1

* 12,000 men who died and were MIA during the war against Japan are excluded from the number of irrecoverable losses of the Soviet armed forces calculated in Table 11. See *Russia and the USSR in Wars of the 20th Century*, 2001, p.309.

** There is not enough reliable information to divide irrecoverable losses of the Soviet allies into 'died/MIA' and 'captured'.

changes here. That being said, we computed all the total figures, so the cumulative ratio we calculated thereby has completely acceptable precision.

Having compared the irrecoverable losses of the opposing sides on the Soviet-German Front, we are forced, most unfortunately, to admit that **during the Great Patriotic War the armed forces of the USSR and its allies, according to the most conservative calculations, lost 2.5 times more men than the Wehrmacht and the armies of Germany's satellites. After taking into consideration the information from TsAMO RF files shown in Table 12 this ratio can grow up to 3:1.**

In our opinion, this casualty ratio corresponds more to the actual nature of military operations during the last war, especially taking into account its initial period, which developed extremely unsuccessfully for the Soviet Union and its armed forces. In this regard it is fitting to recall the words of Marshal G.K. Zhukov (and he certainly knew the German army):

> It will be necessary to face the truth and, without restraint, say how it was indeed. It will be necessary to assess the true worth of the German army against which we had to fight from the very beginning of the war. We certainly did not withdraw thousands of kilometres before fools, but rather before the world's most powerful army. It is necessary to say that at the beginning of the war the German army was better trained, educated and armed and more psychologically ready for war and involved in it than our army. It had war experience, and of a victorious war besides. This plays an enormous role. It is also necessary to admit that the German General Staff and German staffs at that time in general worked better than our General Staff and our staffs in general, that the German high commanders at that time thought better and deeper than our high commanders. During the war we studied and learned and began to beat the Germans, but this was a long process. And this process began from the fact that the Germans had superiority in all respects.[2]

On 22 August 1944 Zhukov wrote a letter to General F.I. Golikov, Chief of the People's Commissariat of Defence's Main Personnel Directorate. In it was a very perceptive analysis of the training of Soviet military personnel, based on the fresh experience of military operations during the Great Patriotic War, which at that time was at its height. The marshal's conclusions have not lost their relevance even today; therefore, we have decided to reproduce them here in full:

> In developing a plan for using and creating Red Army personnel after the war it is necessary, above all, to proceed from the experience that we have obtained during the initial period of the Patriotic War.

What has this experience taught us?

Firstly, we did not have beforehand selected and well trained *front*, army, corps and division commanders. In charge of *fronts* were men who had made a mess of one thing after another (Pavlov, Kuznetsov, Popov, Budyonny, Cherevichenko, Tyulenev, Ryabyshev, Timoshenko, etc.).

Poorly educated and trained men were also placed in charge of armies. And it could not have been otherwise, because there were no candidates for the *fronts*, armies and formations who had already been trained before the war. They did not know men well. In peacetime the People's Commissariat of Defence not only did not train candidates, but also did not even train officers to command *fronts* and armies.

The matter was even worse with division, brigade and regimental commanders. Officers who were not suited to their task were placed in charge of divisions, brigades and regiments, especially the less important ones. In short, each of us knows the consequences of the command of these men and what our Motherland experienced putting its fate in the hands of such officers and commanders.

Conclusion: if we do not want to repeat the mistakes of the past and want to successfully wage war in the future, then it is necessary in peacetime to train commanders for the *fronts*, armies, corps and divisions without sparing any resources.

Resources expended will be compensated for by successes in war.

Obviously, in peacetime it is necessary to have two or three sets of both division and regimental commanders who would provide for the complete deployment of the army and three or four months of conducting a war.

Each *front* and army commander should have a selected and trained deputy.

Secondly, there is no argument that we had not trained reserve personnel. All officers who were mobilized from the reserve were, as a rule, unable to command regiments, battalions, companies or platoons. **All these officers learned war in the war, paying for this with the blood of our people.**

Thirdly, we did not have educated staff officers and, as a result, did not have well knit staffs.

Fourthly, with regard to education, our officers were inadequately suited to the requirements of modern war. Modern war is 8/10 a war of equipment against an enemy's equipment, and this means that it is necessary to be an educated man in order to be able to quickly understand one's own equipment and the enemy's equipment, and, having done so, to intelligently employ one's own equipment.

It is necessary to tell the truth: because of the ignorance and lack of education of our people, we very often suffered great losses in equipment and personnel without having achieved potential success.

Fifthly, our peacetime system of training and educating our personnel did not provide us with a model and competent officer cadre for the war.

Our academies, schools and courses did not properly teach our officers, namely:

1. Theoretical training clearly proceeded to the damage of practical training. The experience of the war demonstrated that only those officers who grew up on field work, and not in offices, turned out to be good commanders.

   Consequently, training officers – working in the field in situations close to combat – should be the main emphasis in the future.

2. Our officers did not and do not know our equipment (aviation, artillery, tanks, etc.) very well. It is absolutely necessary in the future to assign every officer, from battalion command up, to special units for 6–10 months for fundamental study of the heart of equipment.

3. The volitional qualities of our officers – initiative and the ability to take responsibility upon themselves – have clearly been inadequately developed, and this was calamitously reflected during the war in the initial period. Consequently, this most important issue must be resolved determinedly.

   As for your considerations of keeping a possibly larger officer cadre in the ranks of the peacetime army, I think that this is basically correct, but I am in favour of keeping only needed and capable personnel, and not those such as we had, who made a mess of things.[3]

This opinion from the celebrated military leader once again confirms the correctness of the ratio that we obtained of the irrecoverable personnel losses of the opposing sides on the Soviet-German Front, and explains, to a great extent, why it turned out that way. We can still cite many similar ideas and testimonies of veterans of former battles, from famous marshals to simple soldiers, who carried on their shoulders the undue weight of the war, poured out much sweat and blood there, and lost many, many friends and brothers-in-arms. Veterans remember for ever the enormous sacrifices that the country had to lay on the altar of Victory.

Unfortunately, however, there are still many who strive to be holier than the Pope. These people stop at nothing, even openly distorting history, in an attempt to attach a mellow character to the results of the Great Patriotic War. They want to wipe out from the people's memory the consequences of the numerous mistakes and blunders made at that time by the USSR's political and military leadership. And after all, it was because of this that the long-awaited victory came to the Soviet people at such a dear cost.

One of the main goals of such people was to distort the actual ratio of the irrecoverable losses of the opposing sides on the Soviet-German Front in favour of the Red Army. And no wonder: after all, it is this ratio that clearly quantifies the effectiveness of a state's administration and its armed forces' command and control on the eve of a war and during it. Krivosheev's team came out as the heavy artillery for the apologists of the leaders of the Soviet Union at that time. They tried to underpin their arguments with a peculiar scientific base and supported their claims by any means necessary. We have already said much about these improper methods, with the help of which this general of history, together with his team, tried to prove that the irrecoverable losses of the armed forces of the USSR and its allies were only 30 per cent greater than the losses of Hitler's coalition.

As it turned out, however, he did not stop at what had been achieved. The latest edition of his popular book presented to the readers a clear example of forthright swindle. During its revision, instead of correcting numerous distortions of numbers and facts, Krivosheev contrived to adjust his former cumulative ratio of the irrecoverable losses in the Great Patriotic War, making it even more favourable for the USSR. He succeeded in doing so by means of a very simple trick. In order to grasp the essence of it, it is best to present the words of the authors themselves:

> . . . after the year 2000 German scholars, headed by the historian Professor Rüdiger Overmas [sic.], spent many years working on a careful analysis of reports and statistical documents that were kept in Germany's archives. As a result of the research it was established that **the Wehrmacht's total irrecoverable losses amounted to 5,300,000 soldiers and officers**. This information was published in Munich in the book, *German Military Casualties during the Second World War*.
>
> Taking into account the results of the research by the German scholars, the authors of this current work introduced the appropriate corrections into the information that was previously available about the irrecoverable losses of the countries of the Fascist bloc on the Soviet-German Front.[4]

After this, without a moment's doubt, they adjusted the irrecoverable losses of the German armed forces (killed, died, captured and MIA) to 8,876,300, thereby increasing them by 1,695,200 men at one stroke. Correspondingly, the ratio of irrecoverable losses decreased from the former 1:1.3 (which was a strain to begin with) to an even more flattering 1:1.1. And from there it was not at all far to complete parity. After all, judging by the clear trend that had unfolded in the works of the authors and their readiness, demonstrated many times, to do everything for the sake of achieving certain goals, one cannot exclude the possibility that in subsequent editions of their books this ratio will make a complete turn in favour of the USSR.

It must be said that at first glance the above-mentioned change looks completely justified, especially in light of the use of a well known contemporary German historian to correct the German casualties. In fact, however, everything relied on people not being familiar with Overmans' book and blindly trusting every word of the authors of *The Book of Casualties*. But for the most part they do not deserve any trust, especially after having substantially misrepresented the very content of the book they cited. Judging by everything, this was done intentionally and consciously.

We would like to ask directly: if, as Krivosheev himself seriously claims, 5.3 million is 'the sum total of the Wehrmacht's irrecoverable losses', then why at the very point in his own table where these irrecoverable losses for the German armed forces are figured, calculated operationally during the war as the totals increased, is there the number 8,876,300?[5] In fact, with Overmans the issue is not about the Wehrmacht's irrecoverable losses, but rather about the statistics of those German servicemen who were killed or died, or were MIA but subsequently acknowledged to have died, so that in this case it is valid to add to them 3,576,300 POWs. Still, in reality, they were much fewer – namely, 1,415,100. After all, as we have already shown above, Krivosheev shamelessly ascribed to those who had been in Soviet captivity during the war the more than 2 million who arrived there after Germany's surrender.

However, another matter is even more inexcusable. According to Overmans' information, 314,000 Waffen SS soldiers and officers and 4,826,000 Wehrmacht soldiers and officers, including 53,000 civilians employed by the military, died during the entire period of the Second World War. In addition to them, he calculated 78,000 from the *Volkssturm*, 63,000 police officers and 37,000 members of other organizations. Summing them up, we get 5,318,000 men,[6] and not Krivosheev's 5,300,000.[7] In addition, the overall losses of the German armed forces as calculated by Overmans here include 459,000 who died in captivity.[8] In no way can they be added to the irrecoverable losses when they were already calculated as POWs.

In this regard, a legitimate question arises: why, taking into account German casualties from the *Volkssturm*, police and other similar organizations, did the authors of the newly appearing sensation deliberately ignore the casualties of the Soviet people's home guard, militia, destruction detachments and other formations that were completely similar to the German ones? Where is the logic here? But what have the rules of logic to do with the authors' work of proving the unprovable!

The main thing, however, is that the above-enumerated German casualties refer **to all fronts**, without exception, and not to the Soviet-German Front alone. It is not without reason that the authors of the new inflated sensation did not directly refer to Overmans' book, so that the readers could not check their false arguments. And after all, the German historian left not the slightest doubt in this regard, having cited the overall distribution of those German servicemen who died during the Second World War according to theatres of military operations and principal places where they died (Table 16).

Overmans himself did not indicate how the 1,230,000 Germans who died in 1945 were distributed with respect to the different theatres of military operations. As we calculated earlier on the basis of his information, however, during the Great Patriotic War 3,526,500 German armed forces servicemen died or went permanently MIA on the Soviet-German Front; in no way was it the 5,300,000 that Krivosheev shamelessly ascribed here.

Thus, using Overmans' book as an example, we became very familiar with how anti-scientifically Krivosheev's team worked with sources and how they unashamedly distorted them in favour of their own goals. Then, however, the questions inevitably arise: How did the team treat documents from the Soviet archives? How can we trust the statements and calculations of people who substantially distorted the information even from sources that are easily checked? What prevented them from doing the same thing with information

Table 16: Place of death of German armed forces servicemen during the Second World War*

Place of death	Number of dead	Percentage
Balkans	104,000	2.0%
Italy	151,000	2.8%
Western Theatre of military operations	340,000	6.4%
Eastern Theatre of military operations	2,743,000	51.6%
Other theatres of military operations	291,000	5.5%
End of the war (1945)	1,230,000	23.1%
Captivity	459,000	8.6%
Total	5,318,000	100.0%

* Overmans, p. 265.

from closed archives? After all, in manipulating data according to their own wishes, they did not have to worry about being caught in the act. Therefore, the numerous misrepresentations, blunders and mistakes (if not more) that have been noted in their works by attentive and knowledgeable readers are not at all surprising.

When the first edition of Krivosheev's statistical study, *The Seal of Secrecy Has Been Removed*, was published in 1993, it was a real breakthrough in the history of the Great Patriotic War. Finally, professionals, experts and aficionados of military history were able to become familiar with the enormous factual material that had not been accessible to anyone before. For this long-awaited opportunity they were ready to close their eyes to all the book's shortcomings, both those that were immediately obvious and those that the authors had skilfully hidden. It would have been simply naïve to expect perfection from the first attempt to create such a wide-ranging work, so completely filled with the most valuable information, on a theme that had before been poorly developed.

The general euphoria ended in 2001 after the publication of the second edition, entitled *Russia and the USSR in Wars of the 20th Century*. It soon became clear that this time the issue was not the annoying deficiencies and random flaws of the first edition – after all, in the eight years that had passed between the publications one could have got rid of most of them. The far-from-candid position of Krivosheev's team became even more obvious. For the unprejudiced readers valid suspicions began to arise willy-nilly that the issue here was clearly a single-minded policy of embellishing history and glossing over its shortcomings. And as independent researchers became more familiar with the archive materials that they then found, studied and published, these suspicions multiplied and strengthened.

Meanwhile, it is interesting to follow how casualty figures for the opposing sides changed, starting from 16 December 1988. On that day Minister of Defence D.T. Yazov addressed the Central Committee of the CPSU with a request to examine information on Soviet armed forces casualties during the Great Patriotic War, proposing to publish it in the open press **after approving the presented information**. It was just then that the enormous Red Army and Navy irrecoverable losses – 11,444,100 men – were announced (it took a whole forty-three years after the end of the war to do it). What is surprising is that almost a quarter of a century after the leaders of the country decided to publish this information, the original figure did not change by a single person. Is this because the figure had been approved (read 'confirmed') in due course by the Central Committee of the CPSU? For a long time already there has been neither a ruling CPSU nor an all-powerful Central

Committee, but no official has decided to doubt the figures that were prepared by General of the Army S.M. Shtemenko's commission under conditions of confrontation between two political systems and a fierce ideological struggle. In those times, to give any trump cards to the 'Western falsifiers' of the history of the Second World War was considered ill-advised. Since then a long time has passed, but the cart is still not moving . . .

At that time Yazov announced not only Soviet casualties, but also the irrecoverable losses for the Fascist bloc on the Soviet-German Front: 7,168,000 men. The ratio between them was 1.6:1, not in the Red Army's favour. However, there was no desire to spare enemies here! And as a result of further research, the team increased the irrecoverable losses of the armed forces of Germany and its satellites by almost 1.5 million men, to 8,649,300. Correspondingly, the ratio of irrecoverable losses became more favourable for the USSR at 1.3:1, although still in favour of the Germans.

However, even this was obviously not acceptable for someone. The next edition of Krivosheev's work, which appeared in 2010, dotted the final 'i's. In it the authors were not even squeamish about openly falsifying information about German armed forces casualties published by Overmans, bringing their irrecoverable losses to 8,876,300 men. And how did all these tricks for increasing German casualties affect the general balance sheet of Germany's personnel losses? It did not; for more than twenty years it remained unchanged for the authors of the statistical study, because they had made it with a large reserve or 'with room for growth'. Having added an additional 1,695,200 men to the irrecoverable losses for the armed forces of the countries of the Fascist bloc, they reduced the ratio to 1.1:1 (11,520,200:10,344,500). It is fitting to recall the prewar Soviet song: 'We will defeat the enemy with little blood, with a powerful blow!'

In order to better illustrate the unsavoury means by which they achieved their newest ratio, we have added their table,[9] in which that ratio was derived using much more reliable information, and compared it with Krivosheev's latest figures (Table 17).

Close acquaintance with Krivosheev's books makes it clear that his methods were extremely simple. At first he produces an appropriate impression on his readers, with both his place of work and his high scholarly and military ranks and posts, earning their attention and trust. Then he blinds them with a smokescreen made of huge volumes of figures. And under the reliable cover of this information avalanche he demonstrates with the skill of a circus magician an artful substitution of concepts, a contradictory approach to similar phenomena on different sides of the front line, and a frank disregard of

Table 17: Overall ratios of irrecoverable and demographic losses between the armed forces of the USSR and its allies and the armed forces of Germany and its allies on the Soviet-German Front (in thousands of men)

Type of casualty		Armed forces of the USSR and its allies			Armed forces of Germany and its allies			Ratio
		USSR	Allied*	Total	Germany	Allied**	Total	
1. Irrecoverable losses, reported operationally during the war by an increasing sum	According to Krivosheev	11,432.1***	76.1	11,508.2	8,876.3	1,468.2	10,344.5	1.1:1
	Actual	14,534.6	119.4	14,654.0	4,941.6	1,038.7	5,980.3	2.5:1
	Difference	−3,102.5	−43.3	−3,145.8	+3,934.7	+429.5	+4,364.2	
Including:- killed, died of wounds and illnesses, MIA and noncombat casualties	According to Krivosheev	6,873.1	76.1	6,949.2	5,300.0	668.2	5,968.2	
	Actual	6,873.1	119.4	6,992.5	3,526.5	404.1	3,930.6	
	Difference	0.0	−43.3	−43.3	+1,773.5	+264.1	+2,037.6	
− MIA†	According to Krivosheev	0.0		0.0				
	Actual	1,780.7		1,780.7				
	Difference	−1,780.7		−1,780.7				
− captured	According to Krivosheev	4,559.0		4,559.0	3,576.3	800.0	4,376.3	
	Actual	5,880.8		5,880.8	1,415.1	634.6	2,049.7	
	Difference	−1,321.8		−1,321.8	+2,161.2	+165.4	+2,326.6	
Of whom:- died in captivity	According to Krivosheev	2,543.0		2,543.0††	442.1	137.8	579.9	
	Actual	2,841.6		2,841.6	438.1	137.8	575.9	
	Difference	−298.6		−298.6	+4.0	0.0	+4.0	
− released by the Germans†††	According to Krivosheev	823.2		823.2				
	Actual	1,023.2		1,023.2				
	Difference	−200.0		−200.0				
− emigrated to other countries	According to Krivosheev	180.0		180.0				
	Actual	180.0		180.0				
	Difference	0.0		0.0				

– returned from captivity§	According to Krivosheev			1,836.0	2,910.4§§	662.2	3,572.6	
	Actual			1,836.0	2,895.0	615.0	3,510.0	
	Difference			0.0	+15.4	+47.2	+62.6	
– former servicemen remobilized on liberated territory who had previously been reported as captive or MIA	According to Krivosheev			939.7			939.7	
	Actual			939.7			939.7	
	Difference			0.0			0.0	
2. Demographic casualties (after subtracting those who returned from captivity and those who were remobilized)	According to Krivosheev	8,656.4	76.1	8,732.5	5,965.9	806.0	6,771.9	1.3:1
	Actual§§§	11,758.9	119.4	11,878.3	3,964.6	541.9	4,506.5	2.6:1
	Difference	−3,102.5	−43.3	−3,145.8	+2,001.3	+264.1	+2,265.4	

* Bulgarian, Polish, Romanian, Czechoslovak and Finnish forces. Here Krivosheev in his balance sheet completely ignored Finnish casualties during the time that Finland fought on the Soviet side.

** Hungarian, Italian, Romanian, Finnish and Slovak forces.

*** Excluding the 12,000 Soviet servicemen who were irrecoverably lost in the war against Japan. See *Russia and the USSR in Wars of the 20th Century*, 2001, p. 309.

† Of whom, 500,000 remained on the battlefield and 500,000 were mobilized reservists. An additional 780,700 were included in the number of 939,700 who had been remobilized on liberated territory, the remaining 159,000 being POWs whom the Germans released. Here Krivosheev did not include all these 939,700 who were MIA at the beginning of the war and then remobilized in the overall number of MIAs and captured. Moreover, he mentioned in his book another 450,000–500,000 Soviet servicemen who in fact had died or, having been seriously wounded, remained on the battlefield that had been captured by the enemy; however, as Tables 10 and 11 show, he completely ignored them in his balance sheet. Still, even taking them into account, the total number of Soviet POWs who died in German captivity does not add up to 2.5 million, the number he provides in his statistical study. Thus, at least according to Krivosheev's information, it turned out that the Red Army in general did not leave any MIAs on the battlefield. By the same token, he in no way explains whose bodies the searchers keep finding and burying with honours even today.

†† Krivosheev cited the number 2,500,000 Soviet POWs who died in captivity. In fact, taking into account the 1,836,000 who returned from captivity and the 180,000 who immigrated to other countries, this number should be 2,543,000 (4,559,000 − 1,836,000 − 180,000 = 2,543,000).

††† Krivosheev mentioned in his book 823,230 POWs released by the Germans before 1 May 1944, but he completely ignored them in his balance sheet.

§ Here are taken into account those POWs who returned, without exception, including those who surrendered after Germany's capitulation.

§§ Not counting those POWs who were Soviet citizens serving in the Wehrmacht.

§§§ For Germany and its allies, this is the total number of those who were killed, died of wounds or illnesses and in captivity, MIA and noncombat casualties.

inconvenient facts while using far-fetched, albeit somehow fitting information, as well as several misrepresentations, right up to direct forgeries. To say the least, such disregard for the truth has no place in a serious scholarly work, especially one that claims official status. Moreover, it completely discredits the work itself and its authors.

After all, General-Colonel Krivosheev and his formidable team are not just any men off the street who represent only themselves. In annotations to their books it was written that they are researchers from the General Staff and Military-Memorial Centre of the Russian Federation Armed Forces. Even if they did not value their own reputation as scholar-historians, they must surely have thought about the honour of the organizations in which they worked. After all, the devious actions of clumsy and reckless workers tarnish these organizations themselves. Whatever motivated Krivosheev and his team, by their deliberate distortion of reality they undermined the authority of all Russian science, and of Russia itself, in the eyes of the entire world.

Chapter 8

Conclusion

In our work, we have striven to show the inconsistency of the calculations of the team of authors under the leadership of G.F. Krivosheev and to prove the unsuitability of using those calculations in the new twelve-volume history of the Great Patriotic War. We do not at all claim to have determined the precise numerical values of the USSR's personnel casualties on the Soviet-German Front. It is, unfortunately, unfeasible to decisively close this issue now.

This is hindered chiefly by the lack of reliable information, especially about the number of Red Army soldiers and officers who went MIA, who number in the millions. It would be advisable, however, to replace all our calculated numbers with the actual ones, which still have yet to be found. In addition, it is necessary to find and add to the number of dead and MIA the number of soldiers of militarized formations of different civilian departments (People's Commissariats of Transportation, Communication, Maritime and River Fleets, and Civil Aviation; the Directorate of Defence Construction of the USSR Council of People's Commissars; and NKVD), a number of people's militia formations, and municipal and regional destruction detachments and battalions. After all, they fought with weapons in hand against the Germans and their henchmen, and inflicted considerable casualties on them. Moreover, German casualties in the same categories were taken into account in our calculations.

The contribution of Soviet partisans and members of the underground to the ultimate victory was even more weighty. Here is what Krivosheev himself wrote about this:

> The patriots inflicted enormous material and personnel losses on the Nazi army and the occupation administration. They destroyed, wounded and captured more than 1 million soldiers and officers of the Wehrmacht and military-construction formations, officials, settlers, etc. Partisans and members of the underground killed 67 generals from the ground forces and Waffen SS as well as a number of other high-ranking officers, and captured about 45,000 soldiers and officers, including 5 generals.[1]

It is possible, of course, that their real achievement was somewhat more modest. However, even with a correction for the embellishment of one's own successes (usual for any war), these people still made an impression. In addition, the partisans and members of the underground in no way operated on their own: their formations were supported, supplied and led by the Central Headquarters of the Partisan Movement, which was located in Moscow. Many Red Army officers who had been sent specially into the enemy's rear fought alongside them. By valiantly disorganizing the Soviet-German Front's rear area and disrupting its lines of communication, the partisans continuously diverted major enemy forces from the front to themselves. In addition, they conducted several operations that were closely coordinated with regular Red Army operations. Finally, they deservedly received state combat awards for their great service. Most importantly, a significant percentage of the irrecoverable losses for the Wehrmacht and its allies were caused by the partisans and members of the underground. How, then, can their own casualties not be taken into account here? Unfortunately, what is known about them today is clearly inadequate.

In short, much long and painstaking work is still necessary to definitively dot all the 'i's and cross all the 't's regarding the subject of the Soviet Union's irrecoverable losses in the Great Patriotic War. It is, however, completely possible, as far as our current knowledge allows, to come nearer to a solution of the many problems associated with determining them. Therefore, we sincerely hope that other historians and researchers continue this work and eventually, collectively, complete it.

It is necessary to do this; many independent military history specialists and experts have noted numerous weak points in the work of Krivosheev's team. At the beginning of 2011, well known researcher I.I. Ivlev was compelled to write the president of the Russian Federation a letter in which he expressed doubt as to the reliability of the calculation of personnel losses for servicemen in the Great Patriotic War and proposed the creation of a special programme to calculate the casualties of Soviet servicemen and civilians. In response, he received nothing more than a meaningless form letter from the Ministry of Defence Directorate for Memorializing Those Who Died Defending the Fatherland.

One of the authors of this work wrote a similar letter to the president of the Russian Federation in November 2011. In it, he expressed serious concern that the information about Soviet armed forces casualties that were calculated by Krivosheev's team and that did not correspond to reality might be used in the new edition of the history of the Great Patriotic War without careful verification or appropriate corrections. In addition, he expressed his bewilderment that Russian Federation Ministry of Defence officials were hiding from the public the final result of the letter-by-letter calculation of personnel information about soldiers who died or went MIA, which was kept in the Ministry of Defence's Central Archive in card files of irrecoverable losses.

The letter, registered on 18 November 2011, spent more than two months in the president's office. Having received no instructive response about the handling of the letter or information about where it had been sent to be examined, on 2 February 2012 the author filed a complaint about the violation of the law by administration officials. Only after this did the officials begin to stir, responding to the author on 3 February with two identical formal replies that the letter had been sent on to the Ministry. In fact, only the complaint had been readdressed and promptly faxed there, while the letter was sent to the Ministry in the usual way. So, after receiving the complaint, the officials telephoned the author and asked him to send them a copy of the letter for the president. General-Major A.V. Kirilin, Chief of the Ministry of Defence's Directorate for Memorializing Those Who Died Defending the Fatherland, reported that he had agreed with Professor O.A. Rzheshevsky to discuss the issues raised at one of the sessions of the Association of Historians of the Second World War in March-April of that year, with an invitation to interested persons.

This meeting took place on 20 April 2012. All hopes that, finally, the authors of this book might succeed in engaging in a direct argument with representatives of Krivosheev's team were, however, unfounded. Kirilin, having spoken about the tasks and successes of his directorate, began to explain in detail to the audience, which was composed of qualified military historians, what was meant by irrecoverable and demographic casualties, and by combat and noncombat casualties. He then spent a long time rehashing the latest edition of the well known work on casualties without even mentioning the issues about which his listeners were currently concerned. Kirilin ended his talk with a report about the latest 'discovery' – a ratio of 1.1:1 with regard to the irrecoverable losses of the opposing sides on the Soviet-German Front. Those who were gathered did not hear a distinct explanation of what basis for German casualties in all fronts and theatres of military action the authors used to compute their ratio on the Soviet-German Front. The discussion that the many historians invited to the session had been counting on never began: critics of the works of Krivosheev's team were simply not allowed to speak.

The false figures for Soviet and German casualties ultimately found their way into the new twelve-volume history of the Great Patriotic War. The authors of the first volume followed the lead of careless 'researchers', thereby giving those incorrect totals official status. In 2010 Russia's political leadership refused to satisfy a similar request from the chief of the General Staff. However, in order not to attract attention to the scandalous figures, they shamefully left out a conclusion about the ratio of irrecoverable losses of the opposing sides, leaving a ratio which was impossible to validate and in which no serious historian believed.

A legitimate question arises in this regard: where did the experts from the Main Editorial Commission of the twelve-volume work and their leader, Professor Rzheshevsky, look? They undoubtedly knew that the cited calculations were incorrect, and even that direct fabrication was used to produce them (if they did not know, then what kind of experts were they?). In light of what has been written, the behaviour of Professor Rzheshevsky, President of the Association of Historians of the Second World War, who at the 20 April 2012 session did everything possible to prevent a public discussion of Kirilin's talk, was understandable. The fact that he was the Chief of Research at the Centre of War History and Geopolitics of the Russian Academy of Sciences' Institute of General History, Vice President of the International Committee of the History of the Second World War, and even a member of the joint commission of German and Russian historians adds a special piquancy to the position the professor took.

After all, it was the Research Centre for the Military History of the Bundeswehr (Militärgeschichtliche Forschungsamt der Bundeswehr) that translated *The Seal of Secrecy Has Been Removed*, edited by Krivosheev, for internal use. After reading it more closely, German historians decided to refuse to publish it due to the use of information distorted in the old Soviet tradition. Thus, in some battles the Germans captured more prisoners than were officially declared as the Red Army's total losses.[2] The Research Centre's reaction to the 'latest achievement' of Russian military 'researchers' is not known. Taking into account the policy of the German leadership with regard to past Nazi Germany, German official institutions would hardly engage in a dispute with Russian historians regarding who killed more and captured more of their enemies during the war.

It is possible that the authors of this work will be accused of trying to reduce the magnitude of the heroic deeds of Soviet soldiers and officers, diminish the merits of military leaders and, in the final analysis, devalue the Soviet victory itself. Such accusations have happened more than once; it has often been the case that, instead of offering an answer to some problematic and unresolved questions posed by independent researches, the voices of those who have made patriotism their profession thundered about attempts to rewrite the results of the war. No one (with rare exception) intends to rewrite them. Our interest is not revisionism, but rather a re-evaluation of some events of the war in light of newly discovered facts, hitherto carefully hidden in the remote depths of archives and restricted sections of libraries. Russia's military history must be liberated from the false dogmas and stratification resulting from the ideological tenets of the Central Committee of the CPSU. It is time, finally, to understand why the Red Army's victory march to Berlin began from the walls of Moscow, why this path ran across the Caucasus, Stalingrad and Kharkov, and why the price of victory was so unreasonably high. Without such an analysis, research into the Great Patriotic War cannot be considered complete, and the war's objective history is impossible to create.

There is no doubt that sooner or later the official casualty figures for servicemen in the Great Patriotic War will have to be re-examined. We hope that the facts we have cited and the assessment we have offered will be used by other researchers, or will at least attract their attention. If some day a decision is to be made to verify the armed forces' casualty figures in the last war, then it would be better if the work on a serious correction of the positions and conclusions relative to casualties is conducted not by a restricted group of people using information prepared during the Cold War, but rather by the joint efforts of many historians and researchers with access to the best available data. For this, it is necessary to create the appropriate conditions: first and foremost, to open the remaining closed archive collections, particularly the General Staff collection; to digitize all archive materials for better storage and ease of access for all; and to actively continue to publish collections of archive documents.

Unfortunately, those participating in the creation and reanimation of myths about the Great Patriotic War are hindering in any way possible the publication of the most important documents about the war, including those that concern casualties. In its time, the Institute of Military History has published at least a dozen statistical studies on the Red Army's and Navy's order of battle and personnel strength, but it printed ridiculously few copies of them, practically restricting these documents to the Institute's own internal use. However, Russian taxpayers contributed a great deal of money to this enormous and useful endeavour. Therefore, all these studies should be published immediately and offered for sale so that they benefit both the public and the state, rather than funding the underground businessmen who now live off under-the-counter sales of illegal copies.

As we have seen, the lack of reliable information creates fertile ground for myth-making, especially in the field of history. It is not surprising to see the multiplication of amateurs and professionals of this worthless pursuit, who, on the back of their wild fantasies, are trying to solicit money and fame from the easily persuaded and inadequately knowledgeable people. What is more

dangerous, however, is when well known and competent historians partici-
pate in the same unseemly business – all the more so when they hide behind
high ranks and awards while exploiting monopolistic access to secret treasures
in archives that are closed to other people, all the while receiving a salary from
the government. It must be said with great regret that the authors of the
statistical study being criticized here have been so occupied for a long time.
In the latest editions of their works, the bias, prejudgement and sloppiness
inherent in the earlier editions have been especially prominent. As a result, in
our opinion, those authors have substantially discredited their own scholarly
reputations and, to a considerable degree, have lost the trust of those people
who are seriously interested in the history of the Great Patriotic War.

It is sometimes naively assumed that the nation and its patriots can only be
nurtured by victories, successes and positive examples. This is wrong. On
the contrary, bitter but truthful facts and honest descriptions of ambiguous
historical events spark awareness more quickly and leave a deeper imprint on
the soul, especially for the young. The great Russian poet Pushkin said that
the moral basis of a state begins with a love for the graves of its fathers. The
true history of the Great Patriotic War has not yet been written. Thus, it is
perhaps the time to stop lying to ourselves and tell the truth about what it cost
the Soviet Union and its armed forces to succeed in defeating the Nazi war
machine. The Russian people have the full right to know this, a right that was
won with the blood of their fathers and grandfathers.

The harsh truth about Soviet casualties in no way belittles the significance
of the great victory over a powerful and pernicious enemy. Several 'super-
patriots', however, take the efforts of independent researchers to refine the
casualty numbers in the past war as attempts to diminish the victory's importance and besmirch and destroy its shining image as a symbol of national
unity. Jingoists and their supporters agree to consider as a patriot only one
who adamantly refuses to see any of his country's shortcomings, one who
strives not only to whitewash but also to paint over the past and turn history
into just popular literature.

During the war the Soviet Union lost 26.6 million citizens. Of them, more
than half were not simple victims, but people who participated, to some
degree or another, in the armed struggle against the Nazis. Krivosheev's
team, however, completely unjustifiably excluded millions of these people
from the casualties the Soviet armed forces suffered during the Great
Patriotic War. After all, they made the gravest contribution – their own lives
– to the defeat of Nazism. Depriving them of the status of soldiers who died
for the Motherland is not only the blackest ingratitude, but also a sacrilege to
their shining memory.

Appendix A

Information on Red Army Personnel Combat Casualties during the Great Patriotic War[1]

1. Killed or died of wounds
- Killed in battle (according to troop reports)   5,141,000
- Died of wounds in hospitals (according to reports)   1,190,000

     6,331,000

2. Wounded casualties

Overall number of wounded (after subtracting those who died of wounds in hospitals) according to troop reports   13,960,000
- of whom, disabled soldiers from the Great Patriotic War   2,576,000

Note: Number of wounded includes not only those who were wounded once, but also those who were repeatedly wounded (two, three and more times).

3. MIA and captured
- overall number of captured recorded by repatriation organs   2,015,000
- MIA (according to troop reports)   1,196,000
- unrecorded losses of men that must be related to casualties in the initial period of the war   133,000

Total captured and MIA casualties   3,344,000

Totals   23,635,000

June 1945
Colonel Podolsky, Chief of the Directorate for Accounting and Control of the Numerical Strength of the Armed Forces

Appendix B

**Information on the Numerical Strength of the Red Army,
Replacements and Casualties from the Beginning of the War
to 1 March 1942[1]**

By the beginning of the war, the Red Army's overall numerical strength was 4,924,000 men, of whom 668,000 had been called up for large training sessions before mobilization had been announced.

As of 1 August 1941, that is, forty days after the war had begun, the Red Army's actual numerical strength was 6,713,000 men, of whom 3,242,000 were at field *fronts* and 3,464,000 were in military districts. Casualties for this period were 667,000 men.

If we take into account the casualties, the Red Army's numerical strength on 1 August would have been 7,380,000.

From the beginning of the war until 1 August, 2,456,000 men joined the Red Army, of whom 126,000 were field replacements and 2,330,000 were in formations and units.[2]

From the beginning of the war until 1 December, 2,130,000 men were used as field replacements. The monthly totals were as follows: 126,000 in July, 627,000 in August, 494,000 in September, 585,000 in October and 299,000 in November.

On 1 December the numerical strength of the Red Army was 7,734,000 men, of whom 3,267,000 were on the front lines and 4,527,000 were in the military districts.

Overall casualties from 1 August to 1 December were approximately 3,337,000 men (there is no precise information); November casualties were (approximately) 875,000 men (27 per cent of the numerical strength of the field *fronts*).

If we do not take casualties into account for this period, the numerical strength of the field *fronts* on 1 December would be $7,735,000 + 875,000 = 8,608,000$ men.

Conclusion: With regard to records, especially casualty records, the period from 1 August to 1 December is the most unclear. One can state with complete certainty that the Organization and Staff Directorate's information regarding casualties for October and November does not at all correspond to reality. According to this information, in each of these months 374,000 men were lost, while, in fact, the troops suffered their greatest casualties during October and November.

At the beginning of the offensive (1 December), the Red Army's numerical strength was 7,733,000 men, of whom 3,207,000 were at the front lines and 4,526,000 were in the military districts. During the entire period from 1 December to 1 March, the overall number of replacements was 3,220,000 men, of whom 2,074,000 arrived as part of the field replacements and 1,146,000 in the composition of formations. The monthly distribution of replacements is as follows:

- field replacements: December – 550,000; January – 751,000; February – 770,000 men;
- in the composition of formations: December – 756,000; January – ?; February – 453,000 men.

Overall casualties for this period were 1,638,000 men, of whom there were 552,000 in December, 558,000 in January, and 528,000 in February. The average monthly casualties were 546,000 men.

The overall number (since the beginning of the war) of wounded and contused, frostbitten or ill was 1,665,000 (12 per cent); the number of those who returned to action according to information from the medical directorate was approximately 1,000,000 men.

The overall totals regarding numerical strength for the last period: at the beginning of the war the Red Army numbered 4,924,000. Before 1 January 1942, according to information from the Directorate of Mobilization, 11,790,000 men had been mobilized, and from 1 January to 1 March 1942, 700,000 men were mobilized into the army. A total of 12,490,000 men had been mobilized.

Proceeding from this information, the total manpower in the army on 1 March 1942 was 17,414,000 men.

What are the facts? Front-line casualties were 4,217,000 men, of whom 1,000,000 returned to action. The total irrecoverable losses numbered 3,217,000. Taking into account casualties, there should have been a total of 14,197,000 men in the Red Army. In fact, according to information from the Organization and Staff Directorate, on 1 March 1942 the Red Army numbered 9,315,000 men.

1 May 1942
Colonel Efremov, Chief of the Organization and Records Department,
Operations Directorate of the General Staff of the Red Army

Appendix C

Report on Mobilization Resources and their Use during the War
(1 September 1942)[1]
To the Chairman of the USSR State Defence Committee
Comrade J.V. Stalin

1. Conduct of Mobilization

1. Before mobilization into the armed forces there were three draft ages
   (1919–1921 year of birth) and those called up to training sessions from
   other age groups, with an overall numerical strength (including NKVD
   troops) totalling around 5,000,000 men (4,275,713 in the Red Army and
   374,608 in the Navy) . . .

   After full mobilization the numerical strength of the armed forces
   (including 531,524 in the Navy and an unknown quantity in the NKVD
   troops) reached around 10,000,000 men. A detailed calculation of the
   composition of the armed forces before and after full mobilization is
   provided in the attached Table 1 . . .

2. Use of Resources during the War

4. From the beginning [of the war] until 1 September 1942 the following
   resources were required:

Goal for which resources were required	Men
1. Part of the composition of the fully mobilized armed forces	10,000,000
2. For replacements of field *fronts*, Navy and NKVD units	8,574,500
3. For formation of rifle divisions, brigades, artillery regiments, armoured and other units	6,450,000
Total	**25,024,500**

5. This resource requirement was covered by:	Men
Removing resources from the country	18,069,000
Using recuperated wounded	3,174,200
Using those who had returned from encirclement	114,000

Freeing up resources by reducing the TOEs of rear establishments and units of military districts and *fronts*	3,667,300
Total	**25,024,500**

Detailed calculations are found in attached Tables 3 and 4.

3. Availability of Resources and Their Expenditure

6. Overall resources of persons liable for military service are listed:

a. According to information from the 1940 registration of persons liable for military service throughout the entire territory of the USSR, born in 1890–1921 (thirty-two age groups) on 1 January 1941	20,023,800
b. Reserve officers	893,200
c. In the ranks of the armed forces (three age groups, born in 1919–1921)	3,679,200
d. Cadre officers	554,200
e. Conscripts born in 1922 and 1923	2,118,600
f. Conscripts born in 1924 and 1925	1,450,000
Total	28,719,000
g. Special draft exemptions	2,781,000
Total	**31,500,000**

All calculated resources of servicemen and persons liable for military service comprised 16.4 per cent of the total population of the country at the beginning of the war.

7. Resources expended during the war:

a. Lost on territory temporarily occupied by the enemy	5,631,000
– Fifteen age groups not mobilized (born in 1890–1904)	3,628,000
– Untrained persons not conscripted from mobilized fourteen age groups	822,000
– Persons from the Baltic Republics and Moldavian SSR not conscripted from mobilized fourteen age groups	668,000
– Conscripts not mobilized who were born in 1922 and 1923	513,000
Total	**5,631,000**

b. Excluded from the number of contingents of persons liable for military service of nationalities fighting against us (Volga Germans, Germans from other regions, Romanians, etc.)	250,000

c. Transferred into the composition of the Red Army, Navy, and NKVD for the entire war (including availability on 1 June 1941)   18,069,000

c. Transferred by State Defence Committee Resolution no. 2100 on organizational measures conducted in September 1942 (including 880,000 from the country's resources being used repeatedly)[2]   1,380,000

Total resources used and lost on territory temporarily occupied by the enemy   **24,830,000**

By 1 September 1942 resources that had been used comprised 12.7 per cent of the total population of the USSR within the prewar borders.

8. Remainder of unused resources:
   a. Special draft exemption for the national economy   2,781,000
   b. In labour columns[3]   1,321,000
   c. Conscripts born in 1925 (with a 20 per cent allowance for rejection)   700,000
   d. Remainder of those fit for military service up to 45 years old in the Central Asian Military District   600,000
   e. Remainder of those fit for service in the rear area and older than 45 (not including the Far Eastern Front, Transbaikal Front and Transcaucasian Front; including 277,000 of Central Asian nationalities in the Central Asian Military District)   500,000
   f. In the Far Eastern, Transbaikal and Transcaucasian Fronts (including 200,000 men fit for noncombat service and 207,000 men older than 45)   505,000
   g. Reserve officers   156,000
   h. Recovered wounded expected to return from hospitals in three months (including more than 180,000 used directly by the *fronts*[4])   350,000

Total   **6,973,000**

Additionally, those from 17 to 45 years old who were in the GULAG and prisons   1,156,000

9. From the overall remaining resources of persons liable for military service, in the next six–seven months of war, i.e., until spring 1943, under persistent pressure the following numbers can be obtained for manning the Red Army:

a. Cancellation of special draft exemptions   270,000
b. From labour columns   230,000
c. Conscription of citizens born in 1925   700,000
d. Remainder of those fit for military service up to 45 years
   old of Central Asian nationality from the Central Asian
   Military District   200,000
e. Recovered wounded (fit for service) expected to return
   from hospitals in six months   600,000
f. Released from the GULAG and prisons   100,000
g. Those older than 45 (including 100,000 of Central Asian
   Military District nationalities) who are fit for service in
   the rear area   200,000

Total   **2,300,000**

10. The 18,069,000 men taken from the country during the war to man the
    armed forces numbered as follows as of 1 September 1942:
    a. In the Red Army, Navy and NKVD   11,055,700
    b. Wounded, recuperating in hospitals   766,000
    c. Released from the ranks as being unfit for military
       service   1,150,000
    d. Died of wounds in hospitals   177,000
    e. Killed, captured, MIA   4,920,300

   Total   **18,069,000**

10 September 1942   E. Shchadenko[5]
no. 178/83ss

**Table 1. Calculation of the composition of the country's armed forces
before and after mobilization (in thousands of men)**

	Before mobilization			After mobilization			
	In the Red Army				In the Red Army		
Resources	Total	Including in the Far Eastern Front, Transbaikal Front, Transcaucasian Military District	In the Navy	Total	Inc. in the field army	Including in the Far Eastern Front, Transbaikal Front, Transcaucasian Military District	In the Navy
Men	4,275.7	876.7	374.6	9,005.7	3,544.05	876.75	531.5

Table 3.[6] Calculation of the removal from the country of human, horse and motor vehicle resources to support the requirements of the armed forces (including the NKVD) for the entire period of the war to 1 September 1942

	Men
1. Comprising the mobilized armed forces (including the NKVD)	10,000,000
Including	
Ground forces	9,005,713
Navy	531,524
2. Transferred field replacements	8,217,570
3. Used for new formations	6,450,003
4. Transferred for manning the Navy	77,000
5. Transferred for manning the NKVD	280,000
Total	**25,024,573**
Including those who were reused	6,955,573
Of whom	
– recovered wounded	3,174,243
– released after the reduction of auxiliary units	3,667,330
– returned from encirclement	114,000
Actual number removed from the country (minus those who were reused)	18,069,000[7]

Table 4. Calculation of the removal of personnel under State Defence Committee Resolution no. 2100 for the Conduct of Organizational Measures in August–September 1942

1. Conscription of citizens born in 1924	650,000
2. Cancellation of special draft exemption (including the NKVD)	135,000
3. Transfer from labour columns, liberated from the GULAG and labour deportees	95,000
Total	**880,000**
Reused:	
1. Transferred to the Red Army from the Navy	100,000
2. Transfer of those released because of a reduction in service and rear area units	400,000
Total	**500,000**
Overall total	**1,380,000**

Appendix D

Information on the Number of Soviet POWs Captured by German Forces from 22 June 1941 to 10 January 1942[1]

Year	Month	Ten-day period	Number of POWs perten-day period[2] Total	Of which, officers	Cumulative total Total	Of which, officers	Corrected number[3] Total	Of which, officers
1941	June	22–30	112,784	645	112,784	645		
	July	01–10	253,588	1,324	366,372	1,969		
		11–20	234,366	405	600,738	2,374		
		21–31	213,092	648	813,830	3,022		
	August	01–10	271,714	1,625	1,085,544	4,647		
		11–20	211,225	647	1,296,769	5,294		
		21–31	215,641	552	1,512,410	5,846		
	September	01–10	203,668	749	1,716,078	6,595		
		11–20	234,574[4]	605	1,950,652	7,200		
		21–30	550,961	1,553	2,501,613	8,753		
	October	01–10	288,485	861	2,790,098	9,614		
		11–20	499,476	3,392	3,289,574	13,006		
		21–31	249,817	931	3,539,391	13,937		
	November	01–10	152,296	742	3,691,687	14,679		
		11–20	85,786	312	3,777,473	14,991		
		21–30	53,852	64	3,831,325	15,055		
	December	01–10	39,596	74	3,870,921	15,129		
		11–20	19,277	0	3,890,198	15,129	3,350,639	15,179
		21–31	16,567	67	3,906,765	15,196	3,367,206	15,246
1942	January	01–10	11,383	25	3,918,148	15,221	3,378,589	15,271

Notes

Chapter 1: Circumstances governing the publication of loss data in the Great Patriotic War

1. Tsentral'nyi arkhiv Ministerstva oborony [Central archive of the Ministry of Defence of the Russian Federation, hereafter cited as TsAMO RF], f. 14, op. 3028, d. 8, ll. 1–2, cited in A.A. Shabaev and S.N. Mikhalev, *Tragediia protivostoianiia. Poteri vooruzhennykh sil SSSR i Germanii v Velikoi Otechestvennoi voine 1941–1945 gg. (Istoriko-statisticheskoe issledovanie)* [The tragedy of opposition. Casualties for the armed forces of the USSR and Germany in the Great Patriotic War, 1941–1945 (historical and statistical research), hereafter cited as Shabaev and Mikhalev, *The Tragedy of Opposition*] (Moscow: Moskovsky gorodskoi fond 'Veteran Moskvy', 2006), p. 214.

2. V.A. Vsevolodov, *'Stupaite s mirom': k istorii repatriatsii nemetskikh voennoplennykh iz SSSR (1945–1958 gg.)* ['Go in peace': on the history of the repatriation of German prisoners of war from the USSR (1945–1958), hereafter cited as Vsevolodov, *Go in peace*] (Moscow: MID, 2010), pp. 84, 209.

3. M.A. Gareev, 'O mifakh starykh i novykh' [On myths, old and new], *Voenno-istorichesky zhurnal* [Military-historical journal, hereafter cited as VIZh], 1991 (4), p. 47.

4. Ibid.

5. R.G. Pikhoia, 'Chekhoslovakiia, 1968 god. Vzgliad iz Moskvy. Po dokumentam TsK KPSS' [Czechoslovakia, 1968. The view from Moscow. From CC CPSU documents], *Novaia i noveishaia istoriia* [New and most recent history], 1994 (6), p. 8.

6. Translator's note: when the term 'front' (Russian фронт) refers to a formation size (above an army), it will be italicized.

7. Unless otherwise indicated, emphasis (bold font) is always the authors'.

8. AP RF, f. 3, op. 102, d. 1117, ll. 57–73, 79, 83, cited in Z. Vodop'ianova, T. Domracheva and G. Meshcheriakov, 'Sformirovalos' mnenie, chto poteri sostavili 20 millionov chelovek' [An opinion has been formed that

casualties amount to 20 million people], *Istochnik* [Source, hereafter cited as *Istochnik*], 1994 (5), pp. 88–90.

9. Ibid., p. 90.
10. Note: in the document the number of Nazi Germany's irrecoverable losses does not include foreigners who were in rear units and establishments, and who were doing construction and other work. (There are no records of this category in German documents.)
11. *Istochnik*, 1994 (5), pp. 90–91.
12. Ibid., p. 91.
13. Ibid., p. 94.
14. Ibid.
15. Ibid.
16. *Izvestiia*, 9 May 1990.
17. This referred not only to servicemen who had been killed in action or died of wounds, but also to all who had died as a result of accidents, had been executed (noncombat losses), MIAs and POWs.
18. Excluded from the overall casualties here were 1,836,000 men who had returned from captivity after the war (according to data from repatriation organs) and 939,700 men who had earlier been considered MIAs and were drafted again on territory liberated by Soviet forces.

Chapter 2: Soviet troop casualties in certain strategic operations

1. *Grif sekretnosti sniat. Poteri vooruzhennykh sil SSR v voinakh, boevykh deistviiakh i voennykh konfliktakh. Statisticheskoe issledovanie* [The seal of secrecy has been removed. USSR armed forces' casualties in wars, combat operations and military conflicts. Statistical research, hereafter cited as *The Seal of Secrecy Has Been Removed*], under the general editorship of General-Colonel G.F. Krivosheev (Moscow: Voenizdat, 1993).
2. *Rossiia i SSSR v voinakh XX veka: Poteri vooruzhennykh sil. Statisticheskoe issledovanie* [Russia and the USSR in wars of the 20th century: armed forces casualties. Statistical research, hereafter cited as *Russia and the USSR in Wars of the 20th Century*, 2001], under the general editorship of General-Colonel G.F. Krivosheev (Moscow: OLMA-PRESS, 2001).
3. TsAMO RF, f. 48a, op. 1640, d. 180, l. 275.
4. Translator's note: Ставка Верховного Главнокомандования hereafter cited as *Stavka*.
5. These instructions were in force from the beginning of the war until 4 February 1944, when they were replaced by the *Instructions on Red*

Army Personnel Records (in Wartime), which had been developed with combat experience taken into account.

6. H. Schustereit, *Vabanque. Hitlers Angriff auf die Sowjetunion 1941 als Versuch, durch den Sieg im Osten den Westen zu bezwingen* [Vabanque. Hitler's attack on the Soviet Union in 1941 as an attempt to defeat the West by victory in the East, hereafter cited as Schustereit] (Herford: Mittler & Sohn, 1988), p. 73.

7. L.N. Lopukhovsky and B.K. Kavalerchik, *Iiun' 1941. Zaprogrammirovannoe porazhenie* [June 1941. Preprogrammed defeat, hereafter cited as Lopukhovsky and Kavalerchik] (Moscow: Iauza-Eksmo, 2010).

8. *Russia and the USSR in Wars of the 20th Century*, 2001, p. 484, Table 189.

9. Klenov's fate ended tragically: after being removed as Northwestern Front chief of staff, he was arrested soon after, and on 23 February 1942 he was executed without a trial, together with a large group of generals and top executives of the war industry (see V.E. Zviagintsev, *Voina na vesakh Femidy. Voina 1941–1945 gg. v materialakh sledstvenno-sudebnykh del* [War on the scales of Themis. The 1941–1945 war in materials of investigative and trial cases] (Moscow: TERRA, 2006), pp. 47–8).

10. *Velikaia Otechestvennaia voina 1941–1945 gg. Deistvuiushchaia armiia* [The Great Patriotic War, 1941–1945. Field forces] (Moscow: Kuchkovo pole, 2005), p. 328.

11. I.I. Ivlev, 'A v otvet tishina – on vchera ne vernulsia iz boia!' [And the answer was silence – he did not return from battle yesterday], *Voennaia arkheologiia* [Military archaeology, hereafter cited as Ivlev, *Military Archaeology*], 2011 (5), p. 17.

12. Igor' Ivanovich Ivlev, active member of MIA search team, creator of the very informative and popular site *soldat.ru* (www.soldat.ru).

13. Electronic Archives – the main contractor, as ordered by the Ministry of Defence of the Russian Federation, of work on the creation of the Joint Data Base [hereafter cited as JDB] 'Memorial' and 'Exploits of the Nation'.

14. According to data from the medical department of Northwestern Front headquarters from the beginning of the war to 14 July 1941 (Ivlev, *Military Archaeology*, 2012 (2), p. 13).

15. Ivlev, *Military Archaeology*, 2011 (4), pp. 16–17.

16. Ivlev, *Military Archaeology*, 2011 (6), p. 12.

17. Ibid.

18. *Russia and the USSR in Wars of the 20th Century*, 2001, p. 266.

19. Tsentral'noe upravlenie voennykh soobshcheny RKKA (Red Army Central Directorate of Military Transportation), hereafter cited as VOSO.

20. Ivlev, *Military Archaeology*, 2012 (2), p. 12. Table 10 (note 4).

21. Ivlev, *Military Archaeology*, 2011 (5), p. 10.

22. Ibid.

23. Ibid.

24. Ibid.

25. Ivlev, *Military Archaeology*, 2012 (2), p. 13. Table 11.

26. *Russia and the USSR in Wars of the 20th Century*, 2001, p. 270.

27. A.V. Isaev, *'Kotly' 1941-go. Istoriia VOV, kotoruiu my ne znali* [The encirclements of 1941. The History of the GPW that we did not know] (Moscow: Iauza, Eksmo, 2005), p. 197.

28. dr-guillotin.livejournal.com/62623.html.

29. *Kriegstagebuch des Oberkommandos der Wehrmacht* [War Diary of the Armed Forces Supreme Command], Vol. 1: August 1940–31 December 1941. (Frankfurt am Main: Bernard & Graefe Verlag, 1965), p. 661.

30. *Russia and the USSR in Wars of the 20th Century*, 2001, p. 250, Table 133.

31. Ibid., pp. 268, 270.

32. Ibid., p. 330.

33. Ibid., pp. 273, 276.

34. Ibid., p. 310.

35. B.I. Nevzorov, *Moskovskaia bitva: fenomen Vtoroi mirovoi* [The Battle of Moscow: phenomenon of the Second World War, hereafter cited as Nevzorov, *The Battle of Moscow*] (Moscow: SiDiPress, 2001), p. 48.

36. TsAMO RF, f. 500, op. 12462, d. 165, l. 1. Bundesarchiv Rv. 6/V. 556. S.40, cited in *Statistical Analysis*, Book 1.

37. Calculated according to ten-day Supreme Army Command casualty reports (http://ww2stats.com/cas_ger_okh_dec41.html).

38. *Bitva pod Moskvoi. Khronika, fakty, liudi*. Book 1 [The Battle of Moscow. Chronicle, Facts, Men] (Moscow: OLMA-PRESS, 2001), p. 14.

39. For the numbers of formations and units encircled in the regions of Elnya, Spas-Demiansk, Viaz'ma, and Sychevka, see L.N. Lopukhovsky, *Viazemskaia katastrofa* [The Viaz'ma catastrophe, hereafter cited as Lopukhovsky, *The Viaz'ma Catastrophe*] (Moscow: Iauza, Eksmo, 2008), p. 321 (Sketch 23). See also Lopukhovsky L., *The Viaz'ma Catastrophe, 1941: The Red Army's Disastrous Stand against Operation Typhoon* (West Midlands, England: Helion & Company, 2013).

40. B.I. Nevzorov, 'Pylaiushchee Podmoskov'e' [Blazing Moscow suburbs], *VIZh*, 1991 (11), p. 22.

41. Fedor von Bock, *The War Diary. 1939–1945* (Atglen, PA: Schiffer Military History, 1996), p. 336. These very numbers of POWs and war materiel captured by the Germans in the Viaz'ma and Briansk area are also cited in the 19 October 1941 report of Army Group Centre's Intelligence department (TsAMO RF, f. 500, op. 12454, d. 246, l. 56).

42. TsAMO RF, f. 14, op. 113, d. 1, ll. 228–38, cited in Shabaev and Mikhalev, *The Tragedy of Opposition*.

43. *Russia and the USSR in Wars of the 20th Century*, 2001, p. 235.

44. TsAMO RF, f. 500, op. 12462, d. 548, ll. 181–258.

45. National Archives and Records Administration [hereafter cited as NARA], t. 312, r. 150, f. 7689805.

46. Bundesarchiv-Militärarchiv [Federal archive-military archive], RH 20-4/1198, KTB no. 9, pp. 260–5.

47. Now the Field of Memory at the village of Krasnye Kholmy.

48. NARA, t. 312, r. 150. ff. 7689806, 7689812.

49. TsAMO RF, f. 500, op. 12462, d. 320, l. 57.

50. Ibid., f. 288, op. 2524, d. 15, l. 7.

51. *Statistical Analysis*, Book 1, pp. 314, 315.

52. Seven *front* operations were conducted within the framework of the strategic defensive operation: Orel-Briansk, Viaz'ma, Kalinin, Mozhaisk-Maloyaroslavets, Tula, Klin-Solnechnogorsk, and Naro-Fominsk.

53. *Velikaia Otechestvennaia voina 1941–1945. Voenno-istoricheskie ocherki v 4 kn.* [The Great Patriotic War, 1941–1945. Military-historical essays in four books], Kn. 1, *Surovye ispytaniia* [Book 1, *Severe Trials*] (Moscow: Nauka, 1998), p. 226 [hereafter cited as *Severe Trials*].

54. TsAMO RF, f. 208, op. 2511, d. 11, l. 125.

55. Nevzorov, *The Battle of Moscow*, pp. 60, 61.

56. V.T. Eliseev, *Dokumenty TsAMO o Viazemskom okruzhenii, poteriakh v Moskovskoi bitve* [TsAMO documents on the Viaz'ma encirclement, casualties in the Battle of Moscow, hereafter cited as Eliseev, *Dokumenty TsAMO*], *Voenno-istorichesky arkhiv* [Military-historical archive], 2006 (12), pp. 59–60.

57. M. Khodarenok and B. Nevzorov, 'Chernyi oktiabr' 1941-go goda' [Black October 1941], *Nezavisimoe voennoe obozrenie* [Independent military review], 2002 (20).

58. Shabaev and Mikhalev, *The Tragedy of Opposition*, p. 21.

59. *The Seal of Secrecy Has Been Removed*, p. 171. The figures on the *fronts'* strength from the authors of the official research 'wander', but the sum total – 1,250,000 men – never changes.
60. TsAMO RF, f. 202, op. 5, d. 40, l. 1.
61. Ibid., f. 208, op. 2513, d. 82, l. 185.
62. *Russia and the USSR in Wars of the 20th Century*, 2001, p. 274.
63. TsAMO RF, f. 500, op. 12454, d. 165 (225), ll. 1–5, cited in *Statistical analysis*, Book 1, p. 333.
64. K. Reinhardt, *Povorot pod Moskvoi* [The turning point at Moscow] (Moscow: Veche, 2010), p. 65.
65. TsAMO RF, f. 500, op. 12462, d. 548, l. 248 (from Operations Report of the Supreme High Command no. 121, dated 14 October 1941).
66. NARA, t. 312. r. 150. f. 7689415 (order regarding 12th Army Corps of Army Group Centre's 4th Army).
67. State Archive of the Smolensk *Oblast'*, f. 2361, op. 5c, sv. 3, d. 12, l. 47. According to some information, the Smolensk *Oblast'* Military Commissariat archive was burned in the Volokolamsk Forest in connection with the threat of enemy capture.
68. TsAMO RF, f. 127, op. 12915, d. 49, l. 18.
69. P. Polian, *Ne po svoei vole … Istoriia i geografiia prinuditel'nykh migratsy v SSSR* [Not of their own will … History and geography of forced migration in the USSR] (Moscow: OGI – Memorial, 2001), p. 211.
70. Schustereit, p. 73.
71. Ibid.
72. A.V. Isaev, Viaz'minsky kotel. Aktual'naia istoriia [The Viaz'ma encirclement, Actual history, hereafter cited as Isaev, *The Viaz'ma encirclement*], http://actualhistory.ru/wiazma_kessel.
73. *Sovetskaia voennaia entsiklopediia* [Soviet military encyclopedia], Vol. 1 (Moscow: Voenizdat, 1976), p. 495.
74. Isaev, *The Viaz'ma Encirclement*.
75. *Statistical Analysis*, Book 1, p. 317.
76. Lopukhovsky, *The Viaz'ma Catastrophe*, p. 621.
77. TsAMO RF, f. 388, op. 8712, d. 4, ll. 1, 5.
78. Lopukhovsky, *The Viaz'ma Catastrophe*, p. 621.
79. TsAMO RF, f. 386, op. 8583, d. 9, ll. 26, 27.
80. Shibaev and Mikhalev, *The Tragedy of Opposition*, p. 218.
81. B.I. Nevzorov, *Moskovskaia bitva 1941–1942* [The Battle of Moscow 1941–1942] (Moscow: Patriot: 2006), pp. 221–3.
82. *Russia and the USSR in Wars of the 20th Century*, 2001, p. 273.
83. Isaev, *The Viaz'ma Encirclement*.

84. TsAMO RF, f. 219, op. 679, d. 25, l. 26.

85. *Russia and the USSR in Wars of the 20th Century*, 2001, p. 484, Table 189.

86. Shabaev and Mikhalev, *The Tragedy of Opposition*, p. 216.

87. Ibid., p. 214.

88. *Russia and the USSR in Wars of the 20th Century*, 2001, p. 261, Table 138. Casualties for January–February 1942 are taken as two-thirds of the 1,791,441 casualties for the first quarter.

89. Ibid., p. 246, Table 130.

90. Ibid., p. 237, Table 120.

91. Shabaev and Mikhalev, *The Tragedy of Opposition*, p. 216.

92. Ibid., p. 222.

93. Ibid., p. 219.

94. *Russia and the USSR in Wars of the 20th Century*, 2001, p. 261, Table 138.

95. Ibid., p. 237, Table 120.

96. *The Seal of Secrecy Has Been Removed*, p. 130, Table 56. See also *Russia and the USSR in Wars of the 20th Century*, 2001, p. 237, Table 120.

97. *Russia and the USSR in Wars of the 20th Century*, 2001, p. 237, Table 120.

98. G.F. Krivosheev, 'Nekotorye novye dannye analiza sil i poter' na sovetsko-germanskom fronte' [Some new data analysis of forces and losses on the Soviet-German Front]. *Mir istorii* [The world of history], 1999 (1).

99. *Russia and the USSR in Wars of the 20th Century*, 2001, pp. 235, 236.

100. Ibid., p. 236.

101. Ibid., p. 237, Table 120.

102. *Statistical Analysis*, p. 335.

103. *Russia and the USSR in Wars of the 20th Century*, 2001, pp. 258, 268, 272, 273, 276.

104. M.V. Zakharov, *General'nyi shtab v predvoennye gody* [The General Staff in the prewar years] (Moscow: ACT, 2005), pp. 475–6.

105. Ibid., p. 472.

106. *The Seal of Secrecy Has Been Removed*, p. 139.

107. *Russia and the USSR in Wars of the 20th Century*, 2001, p. 245.

108. *Spravochnye materialy po organizatsionnoj structure strelkovoy divizii Sovetskoy Armii v period Velikoj Otechestvennoy Voyny 1941–1945* [Reference materials on TOE of the Soviet Army's rifle division during the Great Patriotic War] (Moscow: VIU GVNU GSh Sovetskoi Armii, 1951), pp. 4–5, 18, 21.

109. Register no. 5 of Rifle, Mountain-Rifle, Motorized Rifle and Motorized Divisions that were in the Composition of the Field Forces during the Great Patriotic War, 1941–1945, p. 29.
110. With the exception of two temporary breaks (4 February–6 March and 31 July–6 September 1943), when the division was in the strategic reserve.
111. TsAMO RF, f. 208, op. 2511, d. 216, l. 123.
112. Ibid., f. 48a, op. 1640, d. 180, l. 275.
113. Eliseev, *Dokumenty TsAMO*, pp. 60, 62.
114. Shabaev and Mikhalev, *The Tragedy of Opposition*, pp. 221, 222.
115. *Russia and the USSR in Wars of the 20th Century*, 2001, Table 189, pp. 273, 275–6, 484.
116. Ibid., pp. 273, 276.
117. www.soldat.ru/doc/nko/text/1941-00123.html.
118. TsAMO RF, f. 2, op. 795437, d. 1, ll. 442–3 (a copy of the order is in *Voenno-istorichesky arkhiv*, 2006 (12), p. 66).
119. *Velikaia Otechestvennaia voina 1941–1945: sobytiia, liudi, dokumenty (kratky istorichesky spravochnik)* [The Great Patriotic War: Events, Men, Documents (short historical reference handbook)], (Moscow: Politizdat, 1990), p. 76.
120. R.V. Mazurkevich, 'Plany i real'nost'' [The plans and the reality], *VIZh*, 1992 (2), p. 23.
121. *The Seal of Secrecy Has Been Removed*, p. 143, Table 67. *Russia and the USSR in Wars of the 20th Century*, 2001, p. 252, Table 134.
122. *Russia and the USSR in Wars of the 20th Century*, 2001, p. 285.
123. Ibid.
124. TsAMO RF, f. 240, op. 2795, d. 38, l. 1.
125. TsAMO RF, f. 1262, op. 1, d. 28, ll. 2–7; d. 11, ll. 11–33. The combat strength of a rifle division is defined as the combined strength of all its rifle, reconnaissance and combat engineer battalions.
126. Ibid., f. 240, op. 2795, d. 35, l. 123.
127. TsAMO RF, f. 203, op. 2870, d. 44, l. 931.
128. Steppe Front's personnel strength on 20 July 1943 was 451,524 men on the roster (TOE of 572,683). This included the following: 4th Guards Army – 83,391 (83,385); 7th Guards Army – 80,637 (118,919); 47th Army – 82,831 (93,807); 53rd Army – 72,035 (85,480); 69th Army – 70,028 (111,562); 5th Air Army – 16,316 (18,220); units of *front* subordination (not including state bank institutions, etc.) – 46,556 (61,310). Figures are from TsAMO RF, f. 240, op. 2795, d. 38, l. 1.

129. E. Manstein, *Uteriannye pobedy* [Lost victories] (Moscow: ACT, 1999), pp. 532, 535.

130. For a detailed explanation of army and *front* casualties, see L.N. Lopukhovsky, *Prokhorovka. Bez grifa sekretnosti* [Prokhorovka. Without the seal of secrecy, hereafter cited as Lopukhovsky, *Prokhorovka. Without the Seal of Secrecy*] (Moscow: Iauza-Eksmo, 2008), pp. 503–14.

131. For more detail, see ibid., pp. 521–3.

132. *The Seal of Secrecy Has Been Removed*, pp. 188, 189.

133. *Russky arkhiv: Velikaia Otechestvennaia. Kurskaia bitva. Dokumenty i materialy. 27 marta–23 avgusta 1943 g.* [Russian archive: Great Patriotic War. Battle of Kursk. Documents and materials. 27 March–23 August 1943], Vol. 15 (4-4) (Moscow: TERRA, 1997), pp. 394, 395, 401.

134. For more detail, see Lopukhovsky, *Prokhorovka. Without the Seal of Secrecy*, pp. 524–5.

135. G.F. Krivosheev, V.M. Andronikov, P.D. Burikov, et al., *Rossiia i SSSR v voinakh XX veka. Kniga poter'* [Russia and the USSR in Wars of the 20th Century. Book of Casualties, hereafter cited as *Russia and the USSR in Wars of the 20th Century. Book of Casualties*, 2010] (Moscow: Veche, 2010), pp. 299–301.

136. For more detail, see Lopukhovsky, *Prokhorovka. Without the Seal of Secrecy*, p. 549.

137. K.H. Frieser, Paper: 'The German Offensive against Kursk. Illusions and Legends.'

138. *Voennaia entsiklopediia* [Military encyclopedia], Vol. 4 (Moscow: IVI, 1999), p. 361.

139. N.M. Ramanichev, 'Bitva pod Kurskom. Doklad na simpoziume v Ingol'shtadte' [The Battle of Kursk. Lecture at the symposium in Ingolstadt], Vortrage zur Militargeschichte [Series of lectures on military history], Vol. 15. (Hamburg, Berlin, Bonn: Verlag E.S. Mittler und Sohn: 1996), p. 62.

140. TsAMO RF, f. 236, op. 2673, d. 6, ll. 48–51; f. 203, op. 2843, d. 301, l. 204.

141. *Russia and the USSR in Wars of the 20th Century*, 2001, p. 485.

142. K.H. Frieser, 'Schlagen aus der Nachhand – Schlagen aus der Vorhand. Die Schlachten von Charkov und Kursk 1943' [Backhand blow, forehand blow. The Battles of Kharkov and Kursk, 1943], Series of Lectures on Military History, Vol. 15, p. 129, note 57.

143. For more detail, see Lopukhovsky, *Prokhorovka. Without the Seal of Secrecy*, pp. 488–92, 501, 502.

144. I.N. Venkov, 'Doklad na simposiume v Ingol'stadte' [Lecture at the symposium in Ingolstadt], Series of Lectures on Military History, Vol. 15, p. 238.
145. *Russia and the USSR in Wars of the 20th Century*, 2001, pp. 250–1, Table 133.

Chapter 3: Results of the computation of Soviet troop casualties by the authors of *Russia and the USSR in Wars of the 20th Century*

1. Ibid.
2. Ibid., p. 281.
3. Ibid., p. 292.
4. See Table 1.
5. TsAMO RF, f. 500, op. 12462, d. 165, l. 1.
6. Ivlev, *Military Archaeology*, 2012 (2), p. 13, Table 11.
7. Eliseev, *Dokumenty TsAMO*, p. 59.
8. *Voennoplennye v SSSR. 1939–1956. Dokumenty i materialy* [Prisoners of war in the USSR. 1939–1956. Documents and materials, hereafter cited as *POWs in the USSR*] (Moscow: Logos, 2000), p. 1041.
9. *Russia and the USSR in Wars of the 20th Century*, 2001, p. 511, Table 197.
10. *POWs in the USSR*, p. 1040.
11. *The Seal of Secrecy Has Been Removed*, p. 393.
12. *Russia and the USSR in Wars of the 20th Century*, 2001, p. 518.
13. TsAMO RF, f. 2, op. 795437s, d. 5, l. 573.
14. *Russia and the USSR in Wars of the 20th Century*, 2001, p. 236.
15. Ibid., p. 514, Table 200.
16. Ibid., p. 515, Table 201.
17. Ibid., p. 463.
18. Ibid., p. 237, Table 120.
19. Ibid., pp. 247–8, Table 132.
20. Shabaev and Mikhalev, *The Tragedy of Opposition*, p. 35.
21. Ibid., p. 36.
22. S.N. Mikhalev, *Liudskie poteri v Velikoi Otechestvennoi voine 1941–1945 (Statisticheskoe issledovanie)* [Human casualties in the Great Patriotic War, 1941–1945 (statistical study)] (Krasnoyarsk: RIO KGPU, 2000), p. 28.
23. *Russia and the USSR in Wars of the 20th Century*, 2001, p. 237, Table 120.
24. Ibid.

25. According to Table 120, those troops who died or went missing in action, but had not been reported, were entered here, although in explanations the authors relegated the casualties unrecorded because of this to the number of MIAs.

26. *Russia and the USSR in Wars of the 20th Century*, 2001, p. 237, Table 120.

27. Ibid., p. 461.

28. Ibid., p. 462.

29. Ibid., p. 237, Table 120.

30. Ibid., p. 248, Table 132.

31. G.F. Krivosheev, 'Nekotorye novye dannye analiza sil i poter' na sovetsko-germanskom fronte' [Some new data of the analysis of forces and casualties on the Soviet-German Front]. *Mir istorii* [World of history], 1999 (2).

32. *Russia and the USSR in Wars of the 20th Century*, 2001, p. 515, Table 201.

33. Ibid., p. 458. As shown below, this in no way is the complete number of Soviet POWs whom the Germans freed during the war.

34. Ibid., p. 237, Table 120.

35. Ibid., p. 463.

36. Ibid., p. 458.

37. Translator's note: from the German *hilfswilliger*, 'willing to help'.

38. Streit, *They Are Not Our Comrades*, p. 433.

39. Ibid., pp. 194–5, 197.

40. Ibid., p. 258.

41. Ibid., pp. 256, 433.

42. *Russia and the USSR in Wars of the 20th Century*, 2001, p. 512, Table 198.

43. Ibid., p. 511.

44. Ibid., p. 246, Table 130.

45. Ibid., p. 518.

46. Ibid., p. 515, Table 201.

47. Ibid., p. 511.

48. Streit, *They Are Not Our Comrades*, p. 258.

49. *Germany and the Second World War*, Vol. IV. *The Attack on the Soviet Union* (New York, NY: Oxford University Press, 1999), p. 1177.

50. *Russia and the USSR in Wars of the 20th Century*, 2001, pp. 455, 456, 457.

51. Streit, *They Are Not Our Comrades*, pp. 258, 433.

52. Ibid., p. 434.

53. A. Shneer, *Plen. Sovetskie voennoeplennye v Germanii. 1941–1945* [Captivity. Soviet prisoners of war in Germany 1941–1945] (Moscow, Jerusalem: Mosty kul'tury, 2005), p. 233.

54. M. Axworthy, C. Scafes and C. Craciunoiu, *Third Axis Fourth Ally. Romanian Armed Forces in the European War, 1941–1945* [hereafter cited as Axworthy, *Third Axis, Fourth Ally*] (London: Arms & Armour Press, 1995), p. 217.

55. D.D. Frolov, *Sovetsko-finsky plen. 1939–1944. Po obe storony koliuchei provoloki* [Soviet-Finnish captivity. 1939–1944. On both sides of the barbed wire, hereafter cited as Frolov, *Soviet-Finnish Captivity*] (St Petersburg: Aleteiia, 2009), pp. 132, 137.

56. Streit, *They Are Not Our Comrades*, p. 19.

57. M.A. Gareev, 'Srazheniia na voenno-istoricheskom fronte' [Battle on the military-historical front], *Sbornik statei: Ob aktual'nykh problemakh voennoi istorii* [Collection of articles: on topical military history issues] (Moscow: Insan, 2008), p. 496.

58. M.A. Gareev, *Nezavisimoe voennoe obozrenie* [Independent military review], 20 April–13 May 2010, no. 13 (613).

Chapter 4: Soviet armed forces' actual irrecoverable losses

 1. *Russia and the USSR in Wars of the 20th Century*, 2001, p. 7.
 2. http://www.soldat.ru/doc/directiva.html.
 3. Shabaev and Mikhalev, *The Tragedy of Opposition*, p. 41.
 4. S.A. Il'enkov, 'Pamiat' o millionakh pavshikh zashchitnikakh Otechestva nelz'ia predat' zabveniiu' [The memory of the millions of fallen defenders of the Fatherland cannot be consigned to oblivion, hereafter cited as Il'enkov], *Voenno-istorichesky arkhiv* 2001 (7), pp. 76–7, 78.
 5. *Russia and the USSR in Wars of the 20th Century*, 2001, p. 252, Table 134.
 6. Il'enkov, pp. 77, 78.
 7. *Russia and the USSR in Wars of the 20th Century*, pp. 431, 434, Table 167.
 8. Ibid., p. 200, Table 100.
 9. Ibid., p. 211, Table 110.
10. Ibid., p. 211, Table 109.
11. Ibid., p. 211.
12. Ibid., p. 237, Table 120; p. 247, Table 132; p. 461.
13. Ivlev, *Military Archaeology*, 2011 (4), pp. 9, 10.
14. TsAMO RF, f. 404, op. 9743, d. 12, ll. 61–2.

15. Ivlev, *Military Archaeology*, 2011 (5), p. 17.

16. *Russia and the USSR in Wars of the 20th Century*, 2001, p. 237, Table 120.

17. RGVA, f. 4, op. 12, d. 97, ll. 263–72, cited in *Russky arkhiv: Velikaia Otechestvennaia. Prikazy narodnogo komissara oborony SSSR. 1937–22 iiunia 1941 g.* [Russian archive: Great Patriotic War. Orders of People's Commissar for Defence. 1937–21 June 1941], Vol. 13 (2–1) (Moscow: TERRA, 1996), p. 258.

18. RGVA, f. 4, op. 12, d. 106-a, l. 512, cited in *Russky arkhiv: Velikaia Otechestvennaia. Prikazy narodnogo komissara oborony SSSR. 21 iiunia 1941 g.–1942 g.* [Russian archive: Great Patriotic War. Orders of People's Commissar for Defence. 21 June 1941–1942], Vol. 13 (2–2) (Moscow: TERRA, 1997), p. 358.

19. *Russia and the USSR in Wars of the 20th Century*, 2001, p. 7.

20. Ibid., p. 246, Table 131.

21. Ibid., p. 237, Table 120.

22. Ibid., p. 458.

23. *Otkroveniia i priznaniia. Natsistskaia verkhushka o voine 'tret'ego reikha' protiv SSSR. Sekretnye rechi. Dnevniki. Vospominaniia* [Revelations and admissions. The Nazi higher-ups about the war of the 'Third Reich' against the USSR. Secret speeches. Diaries. Recollections] (Moscow: TERRA, 1996), p. 120.

24. *Russia and the USSR in Wars of the 20th Century*, 2001, pp. 474, 475, Table 186.

25. At this same Reichstag meeting Hitler openly stated German casualties: in his words, by 1 December the German Army had lost 158,773 men dead, 563,082 wounded and 31,191 MIA on the Soviet-German Front. These figures coincide well with the summary information of German ten-day casualty reports (http://ww2stats.com/cas_ger_okh_dec41.html).

26. *Velikaia Otechestvennaia voina 1941–1945 gg.: Deistvuiushchaia armiia* [The Great Patriotic War, 1941–1945: Field forces] (Moscow: Kuchkovo pole, 2005), p. 541.

27. M. Kolomiets and I. Moshchansky, *Tanki lend-liza* [Lend-lease tanks] (Moscow: Eksprint, 2000), pp. 7, 12.

28. Streit, *They Are Not Our Comrades*, p. 135.

29. Schustereit, p. 73.

30. *Kriegstagebuch des Oberkommandos der Wehrmacht*, Vol. 1: 1 August 1940–31 December 1941, p. 1106.

31. *Germany and the Second World War*, Vol. IV. *The Attack on the Soviet Union* (New York, NY: Oxford University Press, 1999), pp. 1176–7.
32. Streit, *They Are Not Our Comrades*, p. 378.
33. K. Streit, 'Sovietskie voennoplennye v Germanii' [Soviet POWs in Germany], *Vtoraia mirovaia voina. Vzgliad iz Germanii* [The Second World War. The view from Germany] (Moscow: Iauza, Eksmo, 2005), p. 254.
34. Vsevolodov, *Go in Peace*, p. 63.
35. *Mir istorii*, 1999 (1).
36. *Russia and the USSR in Wars of the 20th Century*, 2001, p. 459.
37. Ivlev, *Military Archaeology*, 2011 (5), p. 17.
38. Ivlev, *Military Archaeology*, 2011 (5), p. 16.
39. Ibid.
40. Ivlev, *Military Archaeology*, 2011 (5), p. 17.
41. TsAMO RF, f. 73, op. 12109, d. 3919, ll. 36–8; d. 3928, l. 83.
42. Ibid., f. USUR GSh [General Staff Directorate for the Construction of Fortified Regions], op. 179381, d. 137, ll. 312–16.
43. *Velikaia Otechestvennaia voina 1941–1945 gg. Deistvuiushchaia armiia* [The Great Patriotic War, 1941–1945. Field forces] (Moscow: Kuchkovo pole, 2005), pp. 222–4.
44. Iu. A. Gor'kov, *Gosudarstvennyi Komitet Oborony postanovliaet (1941–1945). Tsifry, dokumenty* [The State Defence Committee resolves (1941–1945). Numbers, documents] (Moscow: OLMA-PRESS, 2002), p. 499.
45. Ibid., p. 497.
46. *Podvig rostokintsev. Istoriia formirovaniia i boevogo puti 13-i Rostokinskoi divizii narodnogo opolcheniia. Uprava raiona Rostokino* [Exploits of the inhabitants of Rostokino. History of the formation and combat path of 13th Rostokino People's Militia Division. Rostokino District Council] (Moscow: 2010).
47. *Russia and the USSR in Wars of the 20th Century*, 2001, pp. 457–8.
48. Ibid., p. 511.
49. P. Polian, *Ne po svoei vole ... Istoriia i geografiia prinuditel'nykh migratsy v SSSR* [Not of their own will ... History and geography of forced migration in the USSR] (Moscow: OGI – Memorial, 2001), p. 209.
50. Ibid., p. 211.
51. Ibid., pp. 210, 216.
52. Ibid., p. 216.
53. TsKhIDK, f. 1p, op. 5e, d. 2, ll. 111–111 back, cited in *POWs in the USSR*, pp. 207–8.

54. TsKhIDK, f. 1p, op. 01e, d. 15a, ll. 92–95, cited in *POWs in the USSR*, pp. 332–3.

55. GARF, f. P-9401, op. 12, d. 178, ll. 30–32, cited in *Spetsial'nye lageria NKVD/MVD SSSR v Germanii. 1945–1950 gg. Sbornik dokumentov i statei* [Special USSR NKVD/MVD camps in Germany, 1945–1950. Collection of documents and articles hereafter cited as *Spetsial'nye lageria NKVD/MVD SSSR v Germanii. 1945–1950 gg.*] (Moscow: ROSSPEN, 2001), p. 17.

56. GARF, f. P-9401, op. 1, d. 2410, ll. 335–336. Ibid. f. P-9409, op. 1, d. 213, ll. 3, 20. Ibid. d. 224, l. 7, cited in *Spetsial'nye lageria NKVD/MVD SSSR v Germanii. 1945–1950 gg.*, pp. 47, 52.

57. RGASPI, f. 17, op. 128, d. 782, ll. 126–134, cited in *Sovetsky faktor v Vostochnoi Evrope. 1944–1953 gg. V 2-kh tt. Dokumenty* [The Soviet factor in Eastern Europe, 1944–1953. In two volumes. Documents], Vol. 1, 1944–1948 (Moscow: ROSSPEN, 1999), p. 171.

58. RGVA, f. 1p, op. 06e, d. 8, ll. 38–46, cited in *Vengerskie voennoplennykh v SSSR. Dokumenty 1941–1953 godov* [Hungarian POWs in the USSR. Documents, 1941–1945, hereafter cited as *Hungarian POWs in the USSR*] (Moscow: ROSSPEN, 2005), pp. 391–2.

59. RGVA, f. 1p, op. 01e, d. 37, ll. 19–22, cited in *Hungarian POWs in the USSR*, p. 288.

60. TsKhIDK, f. 1p, op. 01e, d. 15a, ll. 92–95, cited in *POWs in the USSR*, pp. 331–3.

61. Vsevolodov, *Go in Peace*, pp. 79–80.

Chapter 5: Irrecoverable casualties of the German armed forces on the Soviet-German Front

1. *Russia and the USSR in Wars of the 20th Century*, 2001, p. 508, Table 196.

2. B. Müller-Hillebrand, *Sukhoputnaia armiia Germanii 1933–1945 gg.* [Germany's Ground Forces 1933–1945, hereafter cited as Müller-Hillebrand, *Germany's Ground Forces*] (Moskow: Izografus, 2002), pp. 76, 78.

3. *Germany and the Second World War*, Vol. V/I. *Wartime Administration, Economy, and Manpower Resources 1939–1941* (New York, NY: Oxford University Press, 2009), p. 959.

4. *Russia and the USSR in Wars of the 20th Century*, 2001, p. 507.

5. Müller-Hillebrand, *Germany's Ground Forces*, p. 77.

6. Ibid., p. 703.

7. P-011. *Statistics Systems*. By Generalmajor Burkhart Mueller-Hillebrand and seven others. Office of the Chief of Military History. Department of the Army. Washington 25, DC, 1949, p. 75.

8. M.L. Van Creveld, *Fighting Power. German and U.S. Army Performance, 1939–1945* (Westport, CT: Greenwood Press, 1982), p. 65.

9. F. Hahn, *Waffen und Geheimwaffen des deutschen Heeres 1933–1945* [Weapons and secret weapons of the German Army, 1933–1945], Vol. 2: *Panzer- und Sonderfahrzeuge, 'Wunderwaffen', Verbrauch und Verluste* [Armoured vehicles and special vehicles, 'superweapons', consumption and losses] (Eggolsheim: Dörfler Verlag, 2003), p. 303.

10. J. Ellis, *The World War II Databook* (London: Aurum Press Ltd, 1995), p. 253.

11. R. Overmans, *Deutsche militarische Verluste im Zweiten Weltkrieg* [German military casualties in the Second World War, hereafter cited as Overmans, *German Military Casualties in the Second World War*] (Munich: Oldenbourg Verlag, 2000), p. 257.

12. *Russia and the USSR in Wars of the 20th Century*, 2001, p. 514, Table 199.

13. Ibid.

14. Ibid., p. 512.

15. *Russia and the USSR in Wars of the 20th Century*, 2001, pp. 512, 514, Table 199. Overmans, *German Military Casualties in the Second World War*, p. 269.

16. *Russia and the USSR in Wars of the 20th Century*, 2001, p. 514.

17. Ibid., p. 512, Table 198.

18. *Russky arkhiv: Velikaia Otechestvennaia. Nemetskie voennoplennye v SSSR. Dokumenty i materialy 1941–1955 gg.* [Russian archive: Great Patriotic War. German prisoners of war in the USSR. Documents and materials, 1941–1955], Vol. 24 (13–2) (Moscow: TERRA, 1999), p. 9.

19. *Russia and the USSR in Wars of the 20th Century*, 2001, p. 515, Table 202.

20. *POWs in the USSR*, p. 1041.

21. *Russia and the USSR in Wars of the 20th Century*, 2001, p. 512, Table 198.

22. Overmans, *German Military Losses in the Second World War*, p. 335.

23. Ibid., p. 336.

24. Ibid., pp. 239, 279.

25. *POWs in the USSR*, p. 1041.

26. Ibid., p. 34.

27. GARF, f. 9401, op. 1, d. 2227, ll. 250–2, cited in *POWs in the USSR*, p. 235.
28. TsKhIDK, f. 1p, op. 01e, d. 15a, ll. 69–73, cited in *POWs in the USSR*, p. 217.
29. L.W.G. Neihorster, *The Royal Hungarian Army, 1920–1945* (Bayside, NY: Axis Europa Books, 1998), p. 157.
30. Vsevolodov, *Go in Peace*, pp. 104, 106.
31. Ibid., p. 106; TsKhIDK, f. 1p, op. 01e, d. 15a, ll. 92–5, cited in *POWs in the USSR*, p. 333.
32. *Russia and the USSR in Wars of the 20th Century*, 2001, p. 510.
33. Ibid., p. 515, Table 201.
34. RGASPI, f. 644, op. 2, d. 502, ll. 7–16, cited in *Hungarian POWs in the USSR*, pp. 161, 165.
35. GARF, f. 9401, op. 1, d. 726, ll. 21–2, cited in *POWs in the USSR,*, pp. 610, 611.
36. GARF, f. 9401, op. 2, d. 98, ll. 135–7, cited in *POWs in the USSR*, pp. 54, 800.
37. GARF, f. 9401, op. 1, d. 728, ll. 121–5, cited in *POWs in the USSR*, pp. 801, 802.
38. RGVA, f. 1p, op. 12e, d. 20, ll. 2–3, cited in *Hungarian POWs in the USSR*, p. 321.
39. GARF, f. 9401, op. 1, d. 2227, ll. 250–2, cited in *POWs in the USSR*, pp. 234–5.
40. *Russia and the USSR in Wars of the 20th Century*, 2001, p. 512, Table 198; p. 515, Table 201.
41. RGVA, f. 1p, op. 2z, d. 3, ll. 139–143. Ibid. op. 12e, d. 20, ll. 2–3, cited in *Hungarian POWs in the USSR*, pp. 312, 321.
42. GARF, f. 9401, op. 1, d. 2226, ll. 400–1, cited in *POWs in the USSR*, p. 206.
43. *Russia and the USSR in Wars of the 20th Century*, 2001, p. 511.
44. TsKhIDK, f. 1p, op. 01e, d. 15a, ll. 92–5, cited in *POWs in the USSR*, pp. 331–3.
45. GARF, f. P-9401, op. 12, d. 178, ll. 9–9k, cited in *Spetsial'nye lageria NKVD/MVD SSSR v Germanii. 1945–1950 gg.*, pp. 19–20.
46. GARF, f. P-9401, op. 12, d. 178, ll. 30–2, cited in *Spetsial'nye lageria NKVD/MVD SSSR v Germanii. 1945–1950 gg.*, p. 17.
47. *Russia and the USSR in Wars of the 20th Century*, 2001, p. 515, Tables 201, 202.
48. Ibid., p. 512, Table 198.
49. Ibid.

Chapter 6: Irrecoverable casualties of German and Soviet allies on the Soviet-German Front

1. Ibid., p. 515, Table 201.
2. *The Seal of Secrecy Has Been Removed*, p. 392, Table 104.
3. *Russia and the USSR in Wars of the 20th Century*, 2001, p. 515, Table 201.
4. B.R. Mitchell, *International Historical Statistics: Africa, Asia & Oceania, 1750–1993* (London, UK: Macmillan Reference Ltd, 1998), pp. 7–11; B.R. Mitchell, *International Historical Statistics: Europe, 1750–1993* (London, UK: Macmillan Reference Ltd, 1998), pp. 3–8; B.R. Mitchell, *International Historical Statistics: The Americas, 1750–1993* (London, UK: Macmillan Reference Ltd, 1998), pp. 3, 6.
5. Lopukhovsky and Kavalerchik, pp. 702–5.
6. Frolov, *Soviet-Finnish Captivity*, pp. 292–3.
7. *Russia and the USSR in Wars of the 20th Century*, 2001, p. 514, Table 200.
8. In Finland these events are known as the Lapland War.
9. Yu. Pekkarinen and Yu. Pokhonen, *Poshchady ne budet. Peredacha voennoplennykh i bezhentsev iz Finlandii v SSSR* [No mercy. The transfer of prisoners of war and refugees from Finland to the USSR] (Moscow: ROSSPEN, 2010), p. 27.
10. *Russia and the USSR in Wars of the 20th Century*, 2001, p. 450, Table 173.

Chapter 7: Overall ratio of irrecoverable losses of the opposing sides in the Great Patriotic War

1. Ibid., p. 518.
2. K.M. Simonov, *Istorii tiazhelaia voda* [The heavy water of history] (Moscow: Vagrius, 2005), p. 98.
3. E. Kulikov, M. Miagkov and O. Rzheshevsky, *Voina 1941–1945* [The war, 1941–1945] (Moscow: OLMA-PRESS, 2005), pp. 419–22.
4. *Russia and the USSR in Wars of the 20th Century. Book of Casualties*, 2010, pp. 545–6.
5. Ibid., p. 546, Table 208.
6. Overmans, p. 255.
7. *Russia and the USSR in Wars of the 20th Century. Book of Casualties*, 2010, p. 546, Table 208.
8. Overmans, p. 285.
9. *Russia and the USSR in Wars of the 20th Century. Book of Casualties*, 2010, p. 546, Table 208.

Chapter 8: Conclusion

1. *Russia and the USSR in Wars of the 20th Century*, 2001, p. 451.
2. Das Deutsche Reich und der Zweite Weltkrieg. Band 8. Die Ostfront 1943/1944. Der Krieg im Osten und an den Nebenfronten. München: Deutsche Verlags-Anstalt, 2011. S. 153.

Appendix A

1. TsAMO RF, f. 14, op. 3028, d. 8, ll. 1–2, cited in Shabaev and Mikhalev, *The Tragedy of Opposition*, p. 214.

Appendix B

1. TsAMO RF, f. 14, op. 113, d. 1, ll. 228–38, cited in Shabaev and Mikhalev, *The Tragedy of Opposition*, p. 215–16.
2. This should be read as 126,000 of them were sent as field replacements for *fronts* and 2,330,000 contributed to the creation of new formations and units.

Appendix C

1. TsAMO RF, f. 14, op. 113, d. 1, ll. 187–97, cited in Shabaev and Mikhalev, *The Tragedy of Opposition*, pp. 217–23. The document is cited in an abbreviated form.
2. In accordance with State Defence Committee Resolution no. 2100, dated 26 July 1942, urgent measures were taken to strengthen the Red Army in connection with the acute difficulties regarding the strategic situation on the Soviet-German Front.
3. Labour columns were created out of those persons who were temporarily or permanently not subject to conscription into the army but who were fit to work in industry, as well as conscripts not sent to the army for socio-political or nationality reasons (members of families of repressed persons and persons liable for military service of nationalities of countries fighting against the USSR).
4. This refers to wounded recovering in army and *front* hospitals.
5. E.A. Shchadenko (1885–1951), General-Colonel; in 1941–1943 he was Chief of the Main Organization and Recruitment Directorate of the Red Army (Glavupraform).
6. Table 2 was omitted.
7. Regarding Table 3: the total of human contingents used by 1 September 1942 (minus those who were reused) is 12,069,000. The deficit (18,069,000 − 12,069,000 = 6,000,000 expresses the overall number of casualties by this time (including killed, died of wounds, MIA and

captured, or released as being unfit for military service). According to information from paragraph 10 of the Report, the overall number of the indicated casualty categories as of 1 September was 6,247,300.

Appendix D
1. Schustereit, p. 73.
2. Included are those who died, were released or escaped.
3. On 20 December 1941 the overall number of POWs was substantially corrected to a lower number.
4. Reports on those captured in the Kiev encirclement are only partially cited.

Selective Bibliography

Axworthy M.W.A. *Axis Slovakia: Hitler's Slavic Wedge, 1938–1945.* Bayside, NY: Axis Europa Books, 2002

Axworthy M., Scafes C. and Craciunoiu C. *Third Axis Fourth Ally. Romanian Armed Forces in the European War, 1941–1945.* London: Arms & Armour Press, 1995

Bitva pod Moskvoi. Khronika, fakty, liudi. Book 1 [The Battle of Moscow. Chronicle, Facts, Men]. Moscow: OLMA-PRESS, 2001

Bock, Fedor von. *The War Diary. 1939–1945.* Atglen, PA: Schiffer Military History, 1996

Ellis J. *The World War II Databook.* London: Aurum Press Ltd, 1995

Frolov D.D. *Sovetsko-finsky plen. 1939–1944. Po obe storony koliuchei provoloki* [Soviet-Finnish captivity. 1939–1944. On both sides of the barbed wire]. St Petersburg: Aleteiia, 2009

Gareev M.A. *Srazheniia na voenno-istoricheskom fronte* [Battle on the military-historical front], *Sbornik statei: Ob aktual'nykh problemakh voennoi istorii* [Collection of articles: on topical military history issues]. Moscow: Insan, 2008

Germany and the Second World War, Vol. IV. *The Attack on the Soviet Union.* New York, NY: Oxford University Press, 1999

Germany and the Second World War. Vol. V/I. *Wartime Administration, Economy, and Manpower Resources 1939–1941.* New York: Oxford University Press, 2009

Gor'kov Iu. A. *Gosudarstvennyi Komitet Oborony postanovliaet (1941–1945). Tsifry, dokumenty* [The State Defence Committee resolves (1941–1945). Numbers, documents]. Moscow: OLMA-PRESS, 2002

Grif sekretnosti sniat. Poteri vooruzhennykh sil SSR v voinakh, boevykh deistviiakh i voennykh konfliktakh. Statisticheskoe issledovanie [The seal of secrecy has been removed. USSR armed forces casualties in wars, combat operations and military conflicts. Statistical research], under the general editorship of General-Colonel G.F. Krivosheev. Moscow: Voenizdat, 1993

Hahn F. *Waffen und Geheimwaffen des deutschen Heeres 1933–1945*
[Weapons and secret weapons of the German Army, 1933–1945], Vol. 2:
Panzer- und Sonderfahrzeuge, 'Wunderwaffen', Verbrauch und Verluste
[Armoured vehicles and special vehicles, 'superweapons', consumption
and losses]. Eggolsheim: Dörfler Verlag, 2003
Isaev A.V. *'Kotly' 1941-go. Istoriia VOV, kotoruiu my ne znali* [The
encirclements of 1941. The History of the GPW that we did not know].
Moscow: Iauza, Eksmo, 2005
Kolomiets M. and Moshchansky I. *Tanki lend-liza* [Lend-lease tanks].
Moscow: Eksprint, 2000
Kriegstagebuch des Oberkommandos der Wehrmacht [War Diary of the Armed
Forces Supreme Command]. Vol. 1: August 1940–31 December 1941.
Frankfurt am Main: Bernard & Graefe Verlag, 1965
Krivosheev G.F., Andronikov V.M., Burikov P.D. et al. *Rossiia i SSSR v
voinakh XX veka. Kniga poter'* [*Russia and the USSR in Wars of the
20th Century. Book of Casualties*]. Moscow: Veche, 2010
Kulikov E., Miagkov M. and Rzheshevsky O. *Voina 1941–1945* [The war,
1941–1945]. Moscow: OLMA-PRESS, 2005
Lopukhovsky L.N. *Prokhorovka. Bez grifa sekretnosti* [Prokhorovka. Without
the seal of secrecy]. Moscow: Iauza-Eksmo, 2008
Lopukhovsky L.N. *Vyazemskaia katastrofa* [The Viaz'ma catastrophe].
Moscow: Iauza-Eksmo, 2008
Lopukhovsky, Lev. *The Viaz'ma Catastrophe, 1941: The Red Army's Disastrous
Stand against Operation Typhoon*. West Midlands, England: Helion &
Company, 2013
Lopukhovsky L.N. and Kavalerchik B.K. *Iiun' 1941. Zaprogrammirovannoe
porazhenie* [June 1941. Preprogrammed defeat]. Moscow: Iauza-Eksmo,
2010
Manstein E. *Uteriannye pobedy* [Lost victories]. Moscow: ACT, 1999
Mikhalev S.N. *Liudskie poteri v Velikoi Otechestvennoi voine 1941–1945
(Statisticheskoe issledovanie)* [Human casualties in the Great Patriotic War,
1941–1945 (Statistical study)]. Krasnoyarsk: RIO KGPU, 2000
Mitchell B.R. *International Historical Statistics: Africa, Asia & Oceania,
1750–1993*. London, UK: Macmillan Reference Ltd, 1998
Mitchell B.R. *International Historical Statistics: Europe, 1750–1993*. London,
UK: Macmillan Reference Ltd, 1998
B.R. Mitchell, *International Historical Statistics: The Americas, 1750–1993*.
London, UK: Macmillan Reference Ltd, 1998
Müller-Hillebrand B. *Sukhoputnaia armiia Germanii 1933–1945 gg.*
[Germany's Ground Forces 1933–1945]. Moskow: Izografus, 2002

Neihorster L.W.G. *The Royal Hungarian Army, 1920–1945.* Bayside, NY: Axis Europa Books, 1998

Nevzorov B.I. *Moskovskaia bitva: fenomen Vtoroi mirovoi* [The Battle of Moscow: phenomenon of the Second World War]. Moscow: SiDiPress, 2001

Nevzorov B.I. *Moskovskaia bitva 1941–1942* [The Battle of Moscow 1941–1942]. Moscow: Patriot: 2006

Otkroveniia i priznaniia. Natsistskaia verkhushka o voine 'tret'ego reikha' protiv SSSR. Sekretnye rechi. Dnevniki. Vospominaniia [Revelations and admissions. The Nazi higher-ups about the war of the 'Third Reich' against the USSR. Secret speeches. Diaries. Recollections]. Moscow: TERRA, 1996

Overmans R. *Deutsche militarische Verluste im Zweiten Weltkrieg* [German military casualties in the Second World War]. Munich: Oldenbourg Verlag, 2000

Pekkarinen Yu. and Pokhonen Yu. *Poshchady ne budet. Peredacha voennoplennykh i bezhentsev iz Finlandii v SSSR* [No mercy. The transfer of prisoners of war and refugees from Finland to the USSR]. Moscow: ROSSPEN, 2010

Polian P. *Ne po svoei vole … Istoriia i geografiia prinuditel'nykh migratsy v SSSR* [Not of their own will … History and geography of forced migration in the USSR]. Moscow: OGI – Memorial, 2001

Reinhardt K. *Povorot pod Moskvoi* [The turning point at Moscow]. Moscow: Veche, 2010

Rossiia i SSSR v voinakh XX veka: Poteri vooruzhennykh sil. Statisticheskoe issledovanie [Russia and the USSR in wars of the 20th century: armed forces casualties. Statistical research], under the general editorship of General-Colonel G.F. Krivosheev. Moscow: OLMA-PRESS, 2001

Russky arkhiv: Velikaia Otechestvennaia. Kurskaia bitva. Dokumenty i materialy. 27 marta–23 avgusta 1943 g. [Russian archive: Great Patriotic War. Battle of Kursk. Documents and materials. 27 March–23 August 1943], Vol. 15 (4–4). Moscow: TERRA, 1997

Russky arkhiv: Velikaia Otechestvennaia. Nemetskie voennoplennye v SSSR. Dokumenty i materialy 1941–1955 gg. [Russian archive: Great Patriotic War. German prisoners of war in the USSR. Documents and materials, 1941–1955], Vol. 24 (13–2). Moscow: TERRA, 1999

Schustereit H. *Vabanque. Hitlers Angriff auf die Sowjetunion 1941 als Versuch, durch den Sieg im Osten den Westen zu bezwingen* [Vabanque. Hitler's attack on the Soviet Union in 1941 as an attempt to defeat the West by victory in the East]. Herford: Mittler & Sohn, 1988

Shabaev A.A. and Mikhalev S.N. *Tragediia protivostoianiia. Poteri vooruzhennykh sil SSSR i Germanii v Velikoi Otechestvennoi voine 1941–1945 gg. (Istoriko-statisticheskoe issledovanie)* [The tragedy of opposition. Casualties for the armed forces of the USSR and Germany in the Great Patriotic War, 1941–1945 (historical and statistical research)]. Moscow: Moskovsky gorodskoi fond 'Veteran Moskvy', 2006

Shneer A. *Plen. Sovetskie voennoeplennye v Germanii. 1941–1945* [Captivity. Soviet prisoners of war in Germany 1941–1945]. Moscow, Jerusalem: Mosty kul'tury, 2005

Simonov K.M. *Istorii tiazhelaia voda* [The heavy water of history]. Moscow: Vagrius, 2005

Sovetskaia voennaia entsiklopediia [Soviet military encyclopedia], Vol. 1. Moscow: Voenizdat, 1976

Sovetsky faktor v Vostochnoi Evrope. 1944–1953 gg. V 2-kh tt. Dokumenty [The Soviet factor in Eastern Europe, 1944–1953. In two volumes. Documents], Vol. 1, 1944–1948. Moscow: ROSSPEN, 1999

Spetsial'nye lageria NKVD/MVD SSSR v Germanii. 1945–1950 gg. Sbornik dokumentov i statei [Special USSR NKVD/MVD camps in Germany, 1945–1950. Collection of documents and articles]. Moscow: ROSSPEN, 2001

Stark T. *Hungary's Human Losses in World War II.* Uppsala: Reprocentralen, HSC, 1995

Streit K. *'Oni nam ne tovarishchi . . .' Vermakht i sovetskie voennoplennye v 1941–1945 gg.* ['They Are Not Our Comrades . . .' Wehrmacht and Soviet POWs in 1941–1945]. Moscow: Russkaia panorama, 2009

Van Creveld M.L. *Fighting Power. German and U.S. Army Performance, 1939–1945.* Westport, CT: Greenwood Press, 1982

Velikaia Otechestvennaia voina 1941–1945: sobytiia, liudi, dokumenty (kratky istorichesky spravochnik) [The Great Patriotic War: Events, Men, Documents (short historical reference handbook)]. Moscow: Politizdat, 1990

Velikaia Otechestvennaia voina 1941–1945. Voenno-istoricheskie ocherki v 4 kn. [The Great Patriotic War, 1941–1945. Military-historical essays in four books]. Kn. 1, *Surovye ispytaniia* [Book 1, *Severe Trials*]. Moscow: Nauka, 1998

Velikaia Otechestvennaia voina 1941–1945 gg. Strategicheskie operatsii i srazheniia. Statistichesky analiz [The Great Patriotic War, 1941–1945. Strategic operations and battles. Statistical analysis]. Book 1. Moscow: Institut voennoi istorii, 2004

Velikaia Otechestvennaia voina 1941–1945 gg. Deistvuiushchaia armiia [The Great Patriotic War, 1941–1945. Field forces]. Moscow: Kuchkovo pole, 2005

Vengerskie voennoplennye v SSSR. Dokumenty 1941–1953 godov [Hungarian POWs in the USSR. Documents 1941–1945]. Moscow: ROSSPEN, 2005

Voennoplennye v SSSR. 1939–1956. Dokumenty i materialy [Prisoners of war in the USSR. 1939–1956. Documents and materials]. Moscow: Logos, 2000

Vsevolodov V.A. *'Stupaite s mirom': k istorii repatriatsii nemetskikh voennoplennykh iz SSSR (1945–1958 gg.)* ['Go in peace': on the history of the repatriation of German prisoners of war from the USSR (1945–1958)]. Moscow: MID, 2010

Vtoraia mirovaia voina. Vzgliad iz Germanii [The Second World War. The view from Germany]. Moscow: Iauza, Eksmo, 2005

Zakharov M.V. *General'nyi shtab v predvoennye gody* [The General Staff in the prewar years]. Moscow: ACT, 2005

Zviagintsev V.E. *Voina na vesakh Femidy. Voina 1941–1945 gg. v materialakh sledstvenno-sudebnykh del* [War on the scales of Themis. The 1941–1945 war in materials of investigative and trial cases]. Moscow: TERRA, 2006

Index